GOOD
SNAKEKEEPING

Philip Purser

tfh

Good Snakekeeping
Philip Purser

Project Team
Editor: Tom Mazorlig
Copy Editor: Stephanie Fornino
Indexer: Dianne L. Schneider
Designer: Angela Stanford

T.F.H. Publications
President/CEO: Glen S. Axelrod
Executive Vice President: Mark E. Johnson
Publisher: Christopher T. Reggio
Production Manager: Kathy Bontz

T.F.H. Publications, Inc.
One TFH Plaza
Third and Union Avenues
Neptune City, NJ 07753
Copyright © 2010 by T.F.H. Publications, Inc.

Library of Congress Cataloging-in-Publication Data
Purser, Philip.
  Good snakekeeping : a comprehensive guide to all things serpentine / Philip Purser.
    p. cm.
  Includes index.
  ISBN 978-0-7938-0642-3 (alk. paper)
  1. Snakes as pets. I. Title.
  SF459.S5P875 2010
  639.3'96--dc22
                          2009040367

This book has been published with the intent to provide accurate and authoritative information in regard to the subject matter within. While every reasonable precaution has been taken in preparation of this book, the author and publisher expressly disclaim responsibility for any errors, omissions, or adverse effects arising from the use or application of the information contained herein. The techniques and suggestions are used at the reader's discretion and are not to be considered a substitute for veterinary care. If you suspect a medical problem consult your veterinarian.

The Leader In Responsible Animal Care For Over 50 Years!®
www.tfh.com

TABLE OF CONTENTS

Brazilian rainbow boa

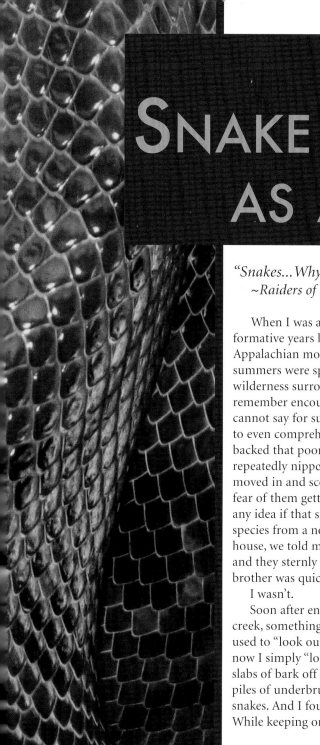

SNAKE KEEPING AS A HOBBY

"Snakes...Why did it have to be snakes?"
~Raiders of the Lost Ark

When I was a child, I had the luxury of spending my formative years living in the hardwood foothills of the Appalachian mountains of northwest Georgia. Thus, my summers were spent roaming the few thousand acres of wilderness surrounding my home. The first snake I can remember encountering in those woods was a black snake. I cannot say for sure what species it was because I was too young to even comprehend what the word "species" meant. Our dogs backed that poor snake against a rock face near the creek and repeatedly nipped and barked at it until my older brother, Virgil, moved in and scooped up the dogs, one under each arm, for fear of them getting bitten. At that time, neither he nor I had any idea if that snake was venomous or how to tell a venomous species from a nonvenomous species. When we got back to the house, we told my mom and dad about what had happened, and they sternly warned us to always stay away from snakes. My brother was quick to heed this advice.

I wasn't.

Soon after encountering that angry black snake beside the creek, something changed in my mind about snakes. Where I used to "look out" for snakes during my escapades in the forest, now I simply "looked" for them. I flipped over logs, peeled slabs of bark off dead trees, hefted up flat rocks, poked through piles of underbrush, and generally beat the bushes looking for snakes. And I found a lot of them—and brought them home. While keeping one here and there in a box for the afternoon

The same snake may be called different names in different regions. The black rat snake is also called black snake, pilot snake, pilot black snake, chicken snake, and several other names.

and then letting it go in the morning worked for a while, I soon found myself keeping my captured compatriots for longer and longer spans of time. I saved my allowance for a few weeks and bought my first terrarium. By the end of that summer, I had housed more than a dozen species in it, capturing a specimen and keeping it only until my daily snake hunts could turn up a more interesting or desirable species.

Over the years, my collection grew and grew. My mom and dad watched with mixed feelings of fear, apprehension, and reserved parental tolerance as their son's obsession reached new levels. They both came to tolerate and (possibly) actually like snakes due to my constant engagement with my scaly friends. They allowed me to keep my pets because they believed in education, and nothing on earth got me into the library or book store more than snakes. My love for my captive snakes taught me the natural sciences, they taught me a keen sense of responsibility and cleanliness (cage cleaning day was always a big ordeal in my collection), and they taught me a general love for nature and the sacred value of living things. For these reasons, my parents suffered me my legless pets.

These reasons are no less valuable today than they were some 30 years ago. Children, until they are taught otherwise, show a natural fascination with snakes. Walk through your local pet shop and observe the kids and teens prowling the reptile and amphibian section. Visit your local zoo and listen to the gasps and sighs of wonderment of the children as they tour through the reptile house. Children are universally fascinated by snakes, and as they develop and mature into adolescents and young adults, they frequently want to keep one or more snakes as a pet. And insofar as some of us never truly "grow up," that child-like fascination for the scaly friends of our youth never truly goes away.

Why Keep Snakes?

Although the reasons for keeping snakes as pets certainly vary from individual to individual, the upward trend in keeping snakes and the inherent value present in these animals are unquestionably present. In recent decades, the exotic pet industry has experienced a massive boom in its inventory, its accessories, and its affordability. As a result, more snake species are available now than ever before. Moreover, the knowledge base for keeping these species has grown accordingly. In the 1980s, when few hobbyists kept certain species, new findings, information, tips, etc., were slow to surface. With the advent of the Internet age and the growth of the herp hobby, however, the exponentially higher number of reptile enthusiasts can now spread the word of their triumphs and failures with unprecedented speed to untold numbers of people. Because so many private and professional breeders have captive-bred, healthy livestock for sale, the price of many of the most sought-after species has dropped to such levels that virtually all hobbyists can afford their pets.

Like many hobbies and pastimes in the world today, the keeping of snakes has become much more democratic than it once was. Science classrooms all over the world boast snakes as class pets meant to inspire and teach. Naturalists and their slithering friends go on tour and televise specials to spread awareness of conservation and the natural value of snakes to the ecosystem as a whole. The children who fall in love with these cryptic and mysterious yet surprisingly compelling animals may indulge their passion for snakes in unprecedented ways.

What's a Herp?

One word that snake (and other reptile) keepers should learn is the word "herp." Herp refers to reptiles and amphibians collectively and derives from herpetology, the study of reptiles and amphibians. Herpetology comes from the Greek language and roughly means "the study of crawling things." Someone who keeps reptiles and/ or amphibians as a hobby is often called a herp hobbyist or herper.

Some Useful Terms

As is true of any hobby, the snake-keeping hobby has some terminology that hobbyists use. Many of these are scientific terms that have come into common usage among snake keepers and other herp hobbyists.

caudal: relating to or near the tail

clutch: a group of eggs laid by the same female at the same time

diurnal: active during the day

dorsal: relating to the top or back region of an animal

ectotherm: an animal that depends on the temperature of its surroundings to regulate its body temperature; all reptiles are ectotherms

gravid: the condition in which an animal is carrying developing eggs; i.e., pregnant with eggs

hatchling: a young reptile that has hatched out of its egg recently; it is usually applied to individuals less than six months old, but it is not an exact term

Jacobson's organ: a sensory organ in the roof of a snake's mouth that detects scents brought to it by the forked tongue

juvenile: a young herp that has not reached sexual maturity

labial: relating to or near the lips; the scales on a snake's upper lip are the supralabials, while those of the lower lip are the infralabials

labial pits: shallow depressions in the lips of boas and pythons that allow them to sense differences in temperatures and therefore detect and catch warm-blooded prey even if they can't see it

musk: a malodorous secretion that many species of snakes release from the vent when molested

nocturnal: active at night

spectacle: the clear scale covering a snake's eye; also called a brille or eye cap

thermoregulation: altering body temperature to the preferred temperature, usually by moving to warmer or cooler areas of the herp's environment

vent: the opening where waste products are expelled from the body

ventral: the underside, or belly

Conservation awareness, personal responsibility, love and respect for nature, and a general willingness to participate in a global community of ecologically minded people—all of these things and more stem from the growth of snake care and husbandry. Thanks to the keeping of snakes in personal terrariums, zoological institutions, and scientific laboratories, more people are better educated about snakes and their role in the world's ecosystem today than ever before in the earth's history.

On a more practical note, many snakes are not difficult to keep. Most species don't require a lot of space and may eat only once a week. Although they often can be handled and handling them is an enjoyable activity, snakes don't need to be handled, nor do they need training. Snakes do not trigger allergies or asthma, and they may be perfect pets for kids of all ages (within reason).

About This Book

And it is for those "kids of all ages" that I write this book. Deeper understanding, keener insight, and broader scope of knowledge are all critical to an enjoyable and successful snake-keeping endeavor. Thus, this book is for all of the snake enthusiasts and nature lovers out there. Open it, read it, and dog-ear the corner of a page or two. Use it. Store it beside your snake's terrarium so that you'll always know where it is. Ultimately, I want you to keep it open and keep it handy. When your snake gets ill, check out the health care chapter so that you'll better know what to tell the vet when he is examining your pet. When you are thinking about building a more elaborate terrarium for your snake, read about the natural habitat in which your pet naturally occurs so that your new naturalistic terrarium can be as true to its needs as possible. And when you are considering adding a new specimen to your snake collection, read the species profile on that animal *before* making a purchase so that you'll know for certain that your time, resources, and experience level are going to be enough to support and maintain that particular animal.

Bumblebee morph ball python

Chapter One

ACQUIRING A HEALTHY, HAPPY SNAKE

"Be ye, therefore, as wise as serpents, and as harmless as doves."
~**Matthew 10:16**

In all my years of keeping and breeding reptiles and amphibians, there is one question hobbyists have asked me more than any other: "How do I select a healthy snake?" This really is a good question. After all, if your initial purchase goes badly, you've truly hit the wall: Your hopes of a long and positive serpentine-pet endeavor are dashed, the snake itself may have died in your care, and your monetary and emotional investments are lost. I hope to prevent as many broken hearts and lost herps as I possibly can with this first chapter. Within the next few pages, we'll cover the purchase of a healthy animal. You'll learn what you should look for and what you should look out for in a potential snake purchase. You'll learn all the hallmarks of a healthy, stalwart snake that is likely disease-free and ready to be a rewarding reptilian companion.

Point of Purchase

Before we go into the specifics of what to look for in the snakes themselves, we need to address the matter of just where you're going to get your snake. Today, snake enthusiasts can take their business to one of three major points of purchase: the local pet shop, the weekend reptile expo, and an online venue. Hundreds of

The first step in selecting a pet snake is to research the species and decide which one is right for you. Rosy boas make excellent pets for keepers of any experience level.

dealers, importers, and wholesalers offer their slithering wares via the Internet, and hundreds more flock to herp expos to sell snakes of all kinds. And of course, the local pet shops—both the "Mom and Pop" operations as well as nationwide corporate retailers—are still a source of snakes and their necessary supplies. Each of these three sellers has a wide array of advantages and drawbacks associated with it. And each of these pros and cons bears consideration before you decide which avenue to take in purchasing your snake.

LOCAL PET SHOPS

The local pet shop is a standard and often very reliably stocked depot for all of your pet snake needs. Local pet shops have some advantages over either of the other two potential venues, but they may also have a few critical failings that can leave a snake enthusiast wanting more.

First, the pros. Local pet shops are businesses that depend on the local clientele for their livelihoods. Thus, they are quick to accommodate the needs of their customers by, for example, making a special order if you have need of a product or item that isn't currently in stock. Likewise, local pet shops typically have a wide variety of items and products, so if the exact item you need is not in stock, the shop can likely recommend another product or brand that will work

A Rose by any Other Name...

Throughout this book, you will see snake species referred to by two different names. The English name is the common name, and the Latin is the scientific name. This system, developed by Carl Linnaeus in his 1735 booklet *Systema Naturae*, exists to eliminate the problem of local name variation, pseudonyms, and other linguistic problems that crop up around certain species. The best example I can think of is the black rat snake. Within the homeland of my youth, this snake was called pilot snake, pilot black snake, black snake, chicken snake, rat snake, and black rat racer. You can imagine the confusion that arises when one species goes by so many colloquial monikers. Despite this litany of local names, the black rat snake will always and unvaryingly be known as *Pantherophis obsoletus obsoletus*. Of course, Latin nomenclature is also subject to change; until recently, this snake was called *Elaphe obsoleta obsoleta*. The difference here is that while local names may change without notice or acceptance, Latin nomenclature is a universally accepted change.

You'll also notice that only the first word in the name is capitalized. This is the genus name. A genus (plural: genera) is a group of closely related specises. The second names is the species name, which is never capitalized. The third name indicates the subspecies. Also, some snakes do not have the third name because not all species have subspecies. It would be acceptable, therefore, to refer to the black rat snake as *Pantherophis obsoletus* when no other closely related rat snake species are in question. Yet *Pantherophis obsoletus obsoletus* goes even further in eliminating species-based confusion—the reader knows that the black rat snake is being discussed and not the closely related Everglades rat snake (*Pantherophis obsoletus rossalleni*).

Once a scientific name is used once in a publication, it may be abbreviated later on. Only the genus is generally abbreviated, although the species name may also be abbreviated when the subspecies is indicated. So we could now call our two example snakes *P. o. obsoletus* and *P. o. rossalleni*.

just as well. Pet shops also have fixed hours and a concrete location, and believe me when I say that this can be *extremely* useful when an emergency arises. When you need an item quickly, waiting on a product to ship to your door can be problematic. When a heat apparatus fails, for example, your tropical boa is simply not going to wait for the postal service to deliver its next heat lamp. This is where the local pet shop really shines: Simply hop in the car, drive down to the pet store, drop your cash on the counter, and you're back home before you know it, giving your snake the product or food it needs to survive. To take advantage of this speed and convenience, I highly recommend getting to know the pet shops in your local area. Even if you don't buy your snake from one, it's always best to know where these shops are and their hours of operation.

One of the biggest advantages of the local pet shop is the ability to walk into it and personally inspect the snakes in stock. You can evaluate each specimen's state of health. You can ask the shopkeeper to let you handle each snake so that you can get a feel for that individual's disposition.

Ask to see the snake you want to purchase eat. (Snake feeding often does not occur during business hours because of the sensitivity of some customers.) Watching your potential pet snake eat can be a definite turning point in the likelihood of your purchase; if the snake has a hearty appetite and eats well in the shop,

Most pet stores will allow you to physically examine the snake that interests you. Healthy ball pythons are excellent pet snakes.

14

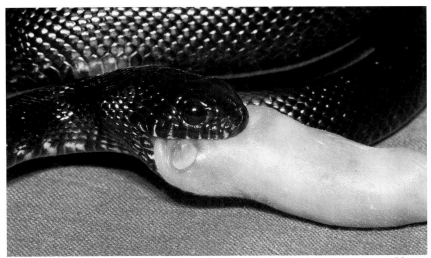

It is best to see a snake feed before you buy it. Refusing food is a common problem with snakes, but this Mexican black kingsnake has no such issues.

chances are high that it will dine with the same vigor in your home terrarium. If, however, it refuses to feed or must be force-fed, you should not purchase it. Something is wrong. The snake may not be adapting to captivity or may have parasites or some other issue. My best advice is, unless you are very skilled in snake husbandry and can pinpoint the exact reason why the snake is not feeding, you should never buy a snake that will not feed in captivity. Sometimes the local pet shop may not allow you to witness that specimen feed. In this case, simply ask for its feeding record. If the snake has been in the shop for several weeks and looks healthy, with good muscle tone and a flat belly (not concave or sunken in), then it has been eating during its time in the pet shop's terrarium and will likely eat under your care as well.

The local pet shop is not without its drawbacks, however. One of the greatest failings of local pet shops is the lack of expert knowledge on staff. I do not mean to criticize all pet shop employees; many resident experts do know quite a bit about the reptiles the shop sells because they themselves are passionate about herps. So when you're going out in search of a solid pet shop with which to do business, make sure that it has a true snake expert on staff. Get to know this person, and maybe ask about his interest in snakes. This local snake expert can be an infinitely valuable source of information to you over the course of your new pet's life.

Local pet shops may also be poorly managed, and their animal care may leave a lot to be desired. They may be run by merchants who are interested only

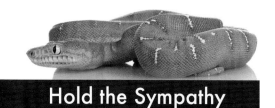

Hold the Sympathy

Never buy your pet from a subpar pet shop. Cold, cramped quarters in pet shops are breeding grounds for disease. Mites, ticks, starvation, and a host of internal parasites and bacteria run rampant in such establishments. By buying a snake from such a shop, you are setting yourself up for failure, as your snake will likely be ill and you'll engage in a long and costly (monetarily and emotionally) battle to nurse it back to health. More often than not, the snake will die despite your best efforts, and you'll be left with a dead snake and an empty wallet.

in money or by those who are inexperienced with and uneducated about animals. If you find a pet shop that meets these terrible criteria, do not do business with them; don't support an establishment in which the comfort, health, and lives of the animals are overlooked or outright abused. Typically smelly, dirty, cold, and/or disorganized, these shops are black eyes to the responsible shopkeepers in the pet industry. As consumers and animal lovers, our duty is clear: Buy consumable goods and living reptiles from responsible, clean shops in which the lives and health of the animals are given high priority.

ONLINE SNAKE SELLERS

The next potential venue for your snake is the online retailer. These are people and companies that advertise and sell their livestock over the Internet. There are numerous types of online retailers, each with its own advantages and disadvantages.

SPECIALIZED BREEDERS

First on the list is what I call the "specialized breeder." These are people who breed and cultivate certain species of snakes specifically for the pet trade. Typically, they have devoted a large portion of their lives to the animals they breed and are profoundly knowledgeable about their chosen species. A specialized breeder might, for example, breed Brazilian rainbow boas. This person will know essentially all there is to know about rainbow boas: care, habits, breeding habits, longevity, disposition, specialized needs, and basically any other nuance there is to keeping the rainbow boa in captivity. And the best part about it is that these people are typically willing to share that knowledge with their customers.

A second benefit to purchasing from a specialized breeder is the amount of information you'll get about your chosen animal. A reputable breeder will be able to provide you with genealogical information (especially important if you are purchasing a genetic morph—a snake bearing an inherited difference in color or pattern, such as an albino or hypomelanistic snake), hatch date, growth rate, body weight, number of sheds, number and type of meals taken, and a host of other information that is unique to your chosen animal. Once a purchase is initiated with a specialized breeder, the customer and breeder typically develop a healthy relationship based around the snake being purchased. If any problem or concern ever arises, the purchaser and specialized seller can usually solve the issue together in a short time. These experts really do a lot to foster a wonderful sense of community between all snake lovers and reptile enthusiasts. You simply can't go wrong in purchasing from one of these dedicated and knowledgeable people.

The only real drawback to purchasing from a specialized dealer is the price tag that accompanies such personalized care. Specialized breeders typically put great amounts of effort into breeding, incubating, conditioning, feeding, rearing, and housing their livestock (and keeping records accordingly), and all that time and effort equates to a higher purchase price. But most hobbyists will agree that the peace of mind

Online vendors may be your best option if you want a specific color or pattern morph of a snake, such as this albino red-tailed boa.

and quality of snake that you get from a specialized breeder is worth the extra up-front expense. Some snake enthusiasts might also think that not being able to physically inspect the animal they're buying could be problematic, but remember, these snakes are the livestock of some of the most experienced and caring professional breeders in the world and typically come with a health guarantee. Buying from a reputable professional breeder is almost always a positive experience.

IMPORTERS/ONLINE PET DISTRIBUTORS

The next form of online snake seller is the importer or online pet distributor. Think of this seller as a local pet shop that simply sells its livestock over the Internet. All of the same problems (sanitation, overcrowding, diseased specimens, etc.) that you might encounter in a local pet shop potentially exist. But the major advantages are the wide range of serpents available and the typically lower price of these snakes. Hard-to-find species can easily be bought from these sellers (because they import specimens from all over the world), and many hobbyists (and professional or educational institutions, such as zoos or nature centers) use online importers as a source for their reptiles with good results.

Breeders—especially those producing high-end animals, such as emerald tree boas—often feature photos of individual snakes on their websites, allowing buyers to pick the exact one they want.

However, there are a few things to keep in mind when dealing with a general online reptile distributor. Do your homework. Research the seller and check up on his reliability and track record. Are there forums or blogs out there that praise or decry this seller? How long has he been in the business? What kind of guarantee does he offer? The industry standard guarantee is live arrival plus one to two weeks on most reptile species. If the seller in question doesn't offer any kind of live arrival guarantee, then you should look for another seller. You'll also want to check out his sources. Where does he get his livestock? Is it freshly imported, or has it been in captivity for some time? You're really taking a chance with recently imported specimens, as they are likely to be loaded with internal and external parasites. What you might save in initial purchase price, you could lose again in veterinary bills and medicines just to bring your snake back to a good state of health. Is the seller's livestock collected legally? Although this last question may sound

Captive Bred Is Better

Whenever possible, hobbyists should purchase captive-bred snakes. Snakes bred in captivity usually are healthier—and often less aggressive—than those taken from the wild. Additionally, buying captive-bred snakes does not contribute to the depletion of wild populations.

a little odd, illegal collection of wildlife continues to be a serious problem. I spent several years as a state ranger for the Georgia Department of Natural Resources (DNR). During that time, I was part of an anti-poaching taskforce. My job was to hunt down people who illegally collected wildlife for sale on the pet, leather, and exotic food and medicine trades. A staggering and truly sad amount of wild species were being collected, and during my tenure with the force, I personally assisted in the arrest of numerous poachers and stopped thousands of animals from being shipped out of their native environment. It is the ethical duty of all responsible snake enthusiasts to check up on their sources and make sure that their chosen importer is within all international, national, and regional laws.

Always ask if the snake you are interested in is captive bred or wild caught. Wild-caught specimens tend to have diseases and may never fully tame to life in the home terrarium. I highly recommend buying captive-bred animals whenever possible. You'll also want to ask for a feeding and shedding record for your chosen animal. If any such records exist, your snake seller should send them to you. You may also want to ask to see a picture of the *exact* animal you will be purchasing. Many online sellers (especially breeders) post specimen-specific photographs on their retail websites, and if your chosen seller does not, it is not unreasonable to ask for one. If you are thinking of spending a considerable amount of money with a seller and he refuses to e-mail you any pictures of the specimen you'll be receiving, look for another seller. Considering how minor this request is, how much more hesitant is that seller going to be when and if

Good Snakekeeping

Breeders at herp expos will normally have a number of snakes of the same species from which to choose. Young blood pythons are shown here.

a greater problem arises? A minor problem may only be minor, but it may be indicative of that seller's disposition and general lack of customer service.

Bear in mind also that many online snake sellers have minimum purchase orders, and you'll have to pay overnight freight on shipping, so buying an inexpensive snake might not be practical.

SWAP-EXCHANGES

The third and final type of online snake-selling site is what I call the swap-exchange. Sort of like an online flea market, the exchange site is a great place to find snakes and meet snake experts and fellow snake enthusiasts. It's also a great place to get buffaloed out of your hard-earned cash. As is true of both the specialized breeder and the importer, you must do your homework before making a purchase through an online swap-exchange website.

Structured like the classified ads in a newspaper, these websites allow users to register and then post the animals they have for sale or trade. You can find all kinds of interesting species available through such sites, and sometimes you can even find awesome deals: moving sales, divorce sales, and similar sales can really save you some cash! Simply find the forum that lists the species you desire, and scope out the individual ads from there.

The main drawback to this avenue of purchase is that you have next to no knowledge about the seller. How well did he care for his snakes? How honest is this person? Is he selling you what he is advertising? I have personally been burned twice on such websites. Once I inquired about an ad for a 10-inch-long (25.4-cm) Kenyan sand boa (*Eryx colubrinus*). What I received—after paying a hefty price—was a malnourished Kenyan sand boa that was roughly 5 inches (12.7 cm) long. Of course, in anticipation of receiving my 10-inch (25.4-cm) snake, I had already purchased mice suitable for its size; now I had a snake that needed meals that were less than half that size! After a few days, the minuscule sand boa expired, and I lost a load of cash.

While such horror stories do exist, there are far more positive stories to be told. I have purchased and sold dozens of snakes on such sites, and I have nothing but good things to say about those transactions. Many swap-exchange sites monitor and control the sellers and buyers; anyone who is proven disreputable or who abuses the policies of these sites is subject to banishment, which is good for

Importation Time Line

Remember when I said that it's best to buy a snake that's been in a pet shop's care for a while because it's more likely to be healthier than a recently imported specimen? There's a caveat to that: Some experts recommend buying only those animals that have been freshly imported, especially when dealing with highly specialized or delicate species. The theory is that these snakes will spend the minimum time in the inadequate conditions and severe overcrowding that are frequently found at all of the steps along the way to the pet store—the collector, exporter, importer, and wholesaler. They are less likely to have contracted some manner of disease or parasite related to poor care. The basic idea is that the sooner these animals get into a proper habitat, the better.

This is, of course, a variable for which there is no hard and fast rule. If the animal is being imported into a herp-specific shop that employs knowledgeable staff and that cares for its animals above and beyond the average shop, then you might wait a little while longer—the snake in question is already in good hands. If, however, the snake is in a shop that is not as herp specific, you might want to go ahead and buy the snake to get it out of the unhealthy conditions. Again, this is a personal decision that depends on your skill as a keeper and the shop's reputation and housing standards.

Good Snakekeeping

Savings in Numbers

To save some money when buying snakes that have to be shipped to you, order with a friend or two. By combining your individual orders into one order, you each will save money on the shipping and handling charges.

the honest among us. You'll also likely need to set up an electronic payment account, as many sellers prefer payment made through these media. As is true of most online auction or swap sites, cash sales or sales outside the venue are often risky.

Another potential downside to the swap-exchange site is your limited access to the animal in question. To counteract this, I usually contact the seller directly and ask for e-mailed images of the snake, as well as health, feeding, weight, shed, and any other records that the seller may have on that particular snake. Most sellers will not hesitate to send this information. A final consideration of the swap-exchange website is the matter of returns. Unless both parties are willing to determine something in the way of a guarantee or return policy in advance of the purchase, all sales are pretty well final. The bottom line is that the swap-exchange website is simply a venue through which snake enthusiasts can get together (virtually) and buy, sell, and trade some snakes.

REPTILE EXPOS

Now we come to my all-time favorite way of buying a snake: the weekend reptile expo (also called a herp expo or reptile show). Imagine a lecture hall, conference center, or even a small stadium filled to the brim with rows upon rows of tables. At each of these tables, a vendor has put up for sale all of his reptilian, amphibian, and/or arachnid livestock, and throngs of reptile and amphibian enthusiasts swarm the aisles, bartering, buying, and generally getting their fill of the cold-blooded animals they love so much. Imagine all of these things and you'll have a good idea of what the weekend reptile expo is all about. These shows occur every month at various cities all around the nation and globe, and they bring in the most amazing selection of snakes imaginable—from the mundane and everyday snakes to the rare, exotic, and even freakish or aberrant: Two-headed snakes put in appearances more often than you might think (but are seldom for sale, of course).

There are two primary things you must remember if you are considering buying a snake from a reptile expo: Bring cash and all sales are final. The dealers at herp expos seldom make any kind of guarantee, and they less frequently offer any kind of money-back policy should something go wrong with your purchase. They typically don't take personal checks, and they are seldom set up for credit purchases—although this is becoming more common. It's a cash-and-carry

Choose a snake that fits your space, budget, and experience level. Corn snakes are excellent choices for beginners.

world in the reptile expo, so make absolutely sure that you really want the species and specimen you are considering *before* buying it.

That being said, it is possible to get a guarantee on your snake purchase usually by buying from one of the larger, well-established vendors. Vendors who offer such guarantees are, of course, concerned with customer service and satisfaction, and they are willing to go that extra mile to ensure that both you and the snake you purchase are guaranteed against disaster. Again, this is rare, so ask any questions about your potential pet snake purchase before committing yourself.

Perhaps the best thing about the reptile expo is the sheer volume of snakes and snake enthusiasts you'll find there. The range of species is usually vast, and you can really have a great time just prowling the aisles in search of your perfect pet snake. You'll see juvenile snakes, adult snakes, and everything in between. You can hold and handle as many snakes as you like. (I recommend cleaning your hands between specimens to prevent spreading disease; many vendors will insist on this and have hand sanitizer available at their table.). You can also closely inspect your potential snake for any defects or problems before making a purchase. In addition, you can ask any snake-related question of virtually anyone in the room and come away with some solid information about that species. If you are a total newcomer to the hobby and know little about snakes, the reptile expo can be a great place to get started, as everyone there is enthusiastic about snakes and will happily help you learn all you need to know about your potential purchase.

Guard against purchasing illegally collected wildlife, however. Some unscrupulous sellers will sell anything, whether it is legal or not. These sellers used to be detected based on the small amount of inventory they have and the fact that each animal is in a different tank or container. (Most professional sellers have their snakes in uniform containers—appropriately sized deli cups, for example.) However, many illegal vendors now set up large, elaborate, and commercially intricate displays and booths, so spotting a herp poacher is much more difficult than it used to be. Such sellers are likely to have species native to the general area in which the show is being held. These people seldom drive far to sell their ill-gotten reptiles, so if you see a local species being sold, the chances are good it was harvested illegally, as most states have laws against trade in native or indigenous species. This is not universally true, but it is a good guideline to go by. If you suspect a poacher or illegal salesman present at a show, alert one of the show officials or a law enforcement officer (almost always present at large expos), and they'll handle it from there. Legally collected and lawfully sold snakes are paramount in keeping the hobby alive and well. Legislation on trade in reptile life (even in captive-bred specimens) has tightened in recent years, and laws will only become more restrictive as abuse and illegal trade continue. Stop illegal trade at its source by reporting any suspicious seller. The law-abiding snake enthusiasts among us are quick to defend our hobby, and we realize that a few bad apples can spoil the entire industry.

In addition to all of the snakes present, a huge variety of new and used husbandry items can also be found at these shows: tanks, heaters, lighting equipment, water dishes and bowls, and natural and naturalistic fixtures, such as hollow logs, caves, rocks, and other hides. Most of these items can be bought at expos at a hefty discount from retail prices, and a wider selection may be available at the expo as well. Some vendors also sell frozen and live feeder animals.

In the end, the reptile expo is something that I wholeheartedly believe each and every potential snake hobbyist should attend. It will truly open your eyes to the wide variety and unique diversity of snake species available for purchase.

Selecting the Right Snake

Now that you have a solid handle on the potential sources from which you might acquire your snake, let's talk a little more about how to select the snake itself. If you see 40 corn snakes for sale at a table at a reptile expo, or if your local pet shop has five in stock, how do you decide which one is right for you? What do you look for? How do you tell if a snake is truly healthy or not? Are there things you can look for to determine whether one specimen is in a better state of health than all of the other individual snakes in the store? The answer is a resounding yes. There certainly are a number of physical, behavioral, and mental or psychological factors that can help you determine the exact snake you should buy. While most beginning hobbyists are governed primarily by aesthetics (i.e., the external appearance, color, or pattern of an individual snake), when selecting a snake, it is important to keep a wide variety of factors in mind. Knowing exactly what to look for when selecting a snake from a pet shop or from a vendor's table at a reptile expo can mean the difference between long-lived success and short-lived failure in this crucial phase of your pet snake endeavor. The important thing to remember is that there are a lot of "perfect" pet snakes out there.

PHYSICAL INSPECTION

Begin your search for the perfect pet snake with a general physical inspection. Obviously, the first part of this is aesthetics: What does the snake look like (in terms of color or pattern) and what do you like? You'll want a snake whose coloration and pattern are pleasing to you and that you find interesting or somehow striking.

EYES

Once you've found a few specimens that fit the bill color- and pattern-wise, start inspecting the candidates closely. Remove the snake from its enclosure and take a good long look at its body. Inspect its eyes. Are they clear and free of debris, or are they smoky? Smoky blue or hazy eyes occur naturally in all

Before buying a snake, look carefully at its head for signs of retained shed, mouth rot, and other issues. This Taiwan beauty snake looks to be in perfect health.

snakes just a few days prior to a shed, but a smoky eye can also be indicative of a retained ocular cap from a previous shed. When a snake sheds its skin, it sheds every part of its skin, including the coverings over its eyes. Sometimes a shed can run afoul and tear away before the ocular scale can pull free. This retained scale can inhibit vision in the short term, and if left untreated, can permanently damage the eye. (See Chapter 5.) Smoky eyes can also be indicative of infections within the eye, and a snake with infected eyes should not be purchased.

Nostrils, Mouth, and Vent

Now look at the nostrils, mouth, and vent. The nostrils of all snakes should be dry, scaly holes just above the mouth on the snout. There should be no crust, pus, mucus, exudate, or any other substance around or coming from the nostrils. If your chosen snake has small bubbles of mucus that swell and detract (or pop) as it inhales and exhales, it has a serious lung infection and must not be purchased.

The outside of the mouth should likewise be free of any crust, dried mucus, etc. The scales surrounding the mouth (called the upper and lower labials) should meet smoothly and evenly; no swollen or uneven edges or raised corners (which expose the gums) should be present. Such deformities are symptomatic of mouth rot (also known as infectious stomatitis), a bacterial (and sometimes fungal) infection in the mouth that, if left untreated, can lead to a slow and

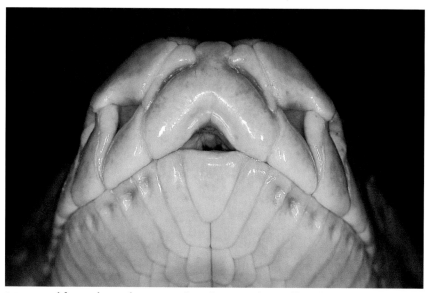

It is normal for snakes to have a notch in the upper lip to allow the tongue to emerge without opening the mouth.

The scales of your potential pet should look normal for the species. Many snakes, such as red-sided garter snakes, have keeled scales—scales that have a ridge down the center.

painful death. Even if the outside of the snake's mouth looks fine, you should take a look inside its mouth, as the early stages of mouth rot are undetectable with the mouth closed. While holding the snake firmly but gently, carefully insert the edge of a credit card (a cardboard business card will work for small specimens) in the front of its mouth. Do not force it into the snake's mouth, and do not wriggle it back and forth or up and down, as this can damage the teeth and gums. Once the edge of the card goes into the mouth, the snake should open up wide and wriggle its head from side to side in an attempt to dispel the card from its mouth. This is what you want.

When the mouth is open wide, take a good, quick look around in there. The inside of the mouth should be pinkish purple around the teeth with veins of purple in the roof and down the throat. A clear layer of saliva will likely be covering most of the inside of the mouth. Chunks of white to yellowish "cheese" between the teeth or in the gums is a sure sign of mouth rot, and blackened or reddened patches that are swollen are also a bad sign. Because an infection of the mouth can easily turn fatal, especially in the case of a very young snake, you shouldn't purchase a snake with any sort of ailment about the mouth. Be aware that tropical species suffer from mouth infections more frequently than temperate species due to the poor housing conditions (excessively low

More on Scales

Most snakes seen for sale in the pet trade are smooth; they are covered in an even coat of smooth but not slimy scales that may appear more or less iridescent, depending on the species and the angle of the light striking the scales. Brazilian rainbow boas, for example, are highly iridescent. A few species, however, do display variation in body scales; i.e., the scales on some parts of the body vary in size and texture from the scales elsewhere on the body. The Kenyan sand boa is a good example of this—the scales over most of its body are small, round, and flat, while those on its tail are granular and raised. As a general rule, however, a patch of discolored or alternately textured scales on a snake's body are a sign of a topical infection. Although scars or old wounds may also appear to be breaks in the continuity of scalation, they are seldom indicative of an unhealthy snake. I see nothing wrong in buying a snake with small, old scars marring its appearance.

temperatures for prolonged periods) under which they are so frequently kept during import or in transit from the pet distributor to the pet shop.

The final matter to attend to for now is the vent, or the cloacal opening. This is the opening through which the snake does all its business: excretes wastes, mates, and lays eggs or births young. The opening varies slightly based on the species in question, but in general it is a folding overlay of scales that is situated between the end of the body and the beginning of the tail. Like the mouth and nostrils, this area should be free of any buildup or exudate. Crust, liquid, or any other such residue left clinging to or oozing out of the cloaca is never a good sign. Bear in mind, however, that a scared snake may open its cloaca upon being scooped up out of its terrarium; such an opening is an act antecedent to musking (some species produce a pungent secretion as a defense) or pooping on you. So a nervous or startled snake's cloaca may appear very different than a calm snake's. Allow the animal to calm down in your grasp before inspecting its cloaca.

SCALES

Let's move on and look for some more physical features that may indicate the overall health of your chosen snake. What do the scales look like? Are they colorful and even, or are they washed out or cankered looking? Patches of discolored scales—typically yellowish to tan or even milky gray—usually indicate that the snake has been kept in exceedingly moist conditions and has contracted a fungal or bacterial infection. While not fatal if treated immediately, such a condition is not something I'd want to see in a specimen that I was considering purchasing. Such cankering, if present, most often occurs on the snake's belly, or ventral surface.

Do the snake's scales snugly and uniformly hug the body, or are their ends curled up? If the ends of the scales are curled up and pulled away from the body,

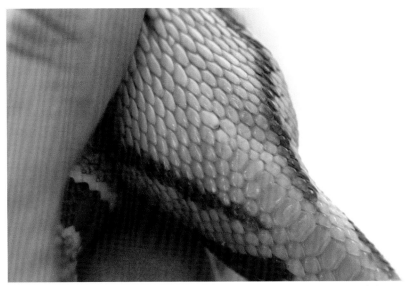

Look closely for mites, which tend to hide under the jaw, in the corners of the mouth, around the eyes, and near the vent.

the snake is dehydrated and its scales are excessively dried out. It's worth noting that in some species, particularly some of the African tree vipers (genus *Atheris*), such curling scales are natural and are not indicative of poor health. Good body scales will hug the body all over and will have a definite uniform shape and texture.

MITES AND TICKS

Next, check for mites and ticks, which hide under the scales. These insidious little vermin will be discussed in much more detail in Chapter 5, but I want to touch on them here because they can present an unsuspecting snake buyer with a *very* big problem once they enter the home terrarium. Ticks are reddish to gray or black in color and appear as lumps or flaps attached to the skin. Ticks are particularly common on wild-caught or newly imported snakes. To determine if ticks are present, inspect the snake's head (around the eyes) and snout very closely, as well as the cloaca.

The second—and far more insidious—skin-dwelling pest that might plague your chosen snake is the mite. Like a very small tick, these bloodsucking arthropods multiply rapidly and can kill an otherwise healthy snake in a surprisingly short amount of time. It is critical that you inspect a snake for mites before you buy it. To do so, moisten a plain white paper towel and rub it repeatedly down the length of the snake's body, remembering to massage the scales under the lower jaw (as this is an area where mites often congregate). After stroking the snake's body a dozen or so times, inspect the paper towel. Are there any small black or reddish dots moving about the paper towel? If you see them, the snake is infested with mites and you should neither buy that snake nor any other snake from that pet shop or vendor. If mites are present on one snake in a pet shop, they are likely to be present on all snakes and you should not purchase from that shop! Mites are highly invasive; they spread readily from one terrarium to the next and can hitchhike on any specimen. Usually, by the time you notice the mites, they have already reproduced to plague-like proportions.

OTHER ISSUES

A final thing to look for when physically inspecting your potential pet snake is anything and everything that I did not list here: bumps, lesions, open sores, wounds, infected areas, and any other topical malady. Because the initial

Top 10: Temperamental Serpents

Although I discuss a great many aspects of a snake's disposition in this chapter and I tell you that most snakes, even if they seem a little temperamental when young, can be tamed or made more mellow with age and by regular, gentle handling, I must now confess that some snake species simply have bad dispositions, with few exceptions. The following list contains ten of the most classically ill-tempered serpents. Of course, this is not to say that these snakes cannot make beautiful and captivating "pets." It's all a matter of what you as a hobbyist are looking for. If you want one of these species, know what you're getting yourself into. But if you want a pet that you can readily and easily handle, avoid members of these particular species.

Top 10: Notoriously Temperamental Species
1. African rock python (*Python sebae*)
2. Amazon tree boa (*Corallus hortulanus*)
3. Argentine boa constrictor (*Boa constrictor occidentalis*)
4. black racer (*Coluber constrictor*)
5. Cuban boa (*Epicrates angulifer*)
6. eastern coachwhip (*Masticophis f. flagellum*)
7. reticulated python (*Python reticulatus*)
8. Texas rat snake (*Pantherophis obsoletus lindheimeri*)
9. water snakes (*Nerodia spp.*)
10. yellow anaconda (*Eunectes notaeus*)

purchase is so critical to a successful pet snake endeavor, there is absolutely no reason at all why you should have to settle for an inferior specimen. It's just bad practice to settle when buying a pet snake, especially if you are buying a hatchling or juvenile snake, which will be much more sensitive to health problems and which could more easily succumb to ill health than an older, more mature specimen.

Once you've found a snake that passes this rigorous physical exam, you can move on to an inspection of its movements, its mood, and its general serpentine behaviors. For more in-depth information on any of the physical maladies we briefly discussed here, see Chapter 5: Health Care.

BEHAVIORAL INSPECTION

By behavioral, I do not mean the snake's disposition or demeanor. That matter is covered in the next section. For our purposes here, "behavioral inspection" is another tool for determining the general health of your snake. While the last section covered things you could see wrong on the outside of the body, this bit centers on things that could be potentially wrong on the *inside* of the snake in question.

A healthy snake will not lie limply in your hands. It will move around and flick its tongue, as this Burmese python is doing.

Begin your behavioral inspection before you even take the snake out of its enclosure or container. Just looking through the glass, what do you see it doing? According to normal wild snake behavior, it should be doing one of three things: attempting to hide under something, or (if there is nothing to hide under) lying quietly coiled in a corner or beside/behind some bit of structure (a water dish, for example) within the terrarium, or nosing around the edges of its enclosure. This last activity is a little trickier to read than the other two, as a highly stressed and mentally uncomfortable snake will continually nose about looking for escape, even to the point of rubbing away the scales on its nose and head. By nature, all species of snakes are secretive animals, and when they are not actively hunting for food, water, a more desirable temperature, or a mate, they coil up and hide. Snakes absolutely *love* to hide in tight-fitting spots, and a generally healthy snake will spend almost all of its time doing just that. So when you approach the pet shop's terrarium, your potential snake should be either hidden in some way or looking for somewhere to hide.

Something your potential snake should not be doing is lying stretched out and exposed in the open. Instinct is very powerful in reptiles, and Mother Nature programs her snakes to never lie stretched out, motionless, and exposed. In such a position in the wild, that snake would be highly vulnerable to a predatory attack from above (from a hawk, for example). A snake that is healthy will seldom do this. Typically, when a snake lies about in such an exposed and unnatural position, something is seriously wrong and you should not consider purchasing that specimen.

There are two instances in which an exposed snake may not be truly ill. In an overcrowded tank (when all of the hides and corners in the terrarium are filled with other snakes), an individual may have no choice but to slither along in the open. The other is when a snake is purposefully slithering, such as going toward food or when trying to start a shed.

Fool's Gold

Many hobbyists believe that, in much the same way that virtually all members of some snake species are intolerant to any measure of handling, that virtually all members of other species will *always* be tolerant of handling. This is not true! Although many species can generally be classified as gentle, easygoing, or mild mannered, there will always be exceptions to this rule. I share two personal experiences here and could relate several more. A friend once had a corn snake, which is widely acclaimed as the best possible snake you could ever keep because of its gentle disposition. One afternoon, as he was pulling his newly bought corn snake from its terrarium, the reptile struck out at him and bit his lower lip. To make matters worse, it hung on! It took more than 20 agonizing minutes for he and I to gently free the snake's recurved teeth from his bleeding lip. As my second example, I once bought a large rough green snake with a decidedly foul disposition. It would vibrate its tail, hiss, hold its mouth agape, and even lunge at me when I came too close.

I offer these anecdotes simply as proof that a sort of fool's gold exists within the pet snake hobby. Just because a certain species is known for its mild disposition doesn't mean that every specimen within that species will exhibit those benign tendencies. You must make sure that you are actually getting a mild-mannered snake. Don't purchase a benign species and assume that the uninspected snake will be as benevolent as you expect. Even the most docile species can produce some aggressive specimens—not all that glitters is gold.

If you want a snake you can handle, check its disposition before you buy it. This red-tailed boa looks ready to strike.

The key to discerning a healthy exposed snake from an ill one is the matter of movement. If a snake is lying stretched out with its head down and it's not flickering its tongue, then it is likely in poor health and not exposed for a reason. Bear in mind also that very large snakes may also keep themselves exposed without being sick or injured. Large boas, pythons, and very large rat snakes or some pine snakes may lounge about in the open because they are simply too large to fit in any hide within their terrarium, and owing to their large size or the amount of time they've been in captivity, their instinctual drive to hide is not nearly as pronounced as when they were juveniles.

So let's assume that you've found a snake that seems to be exhibiting all of the natural behaviors you'd expect from a healthy snake. Now take it out and inspect it further. When you grasp the snake, it should do something: strike, hiss, flicker its tongue, try to get away—something. A big mistake that beginning hobbyists make surprisingly often is to purchase a snake that is listless when handled. If you pick up a snake, which may *appear* perfectly healthy on the outside, and it moves awkwardly or seems pained to have to move at all or simply refuses to move, then something is wrong, and its behavior may be the only key that can clue you in to this fact. Any and every healthy snake will look around and flicker its tongue when picked up or handled. If your chosen specimen does not react normally to handling, take

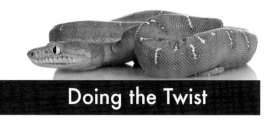

Doing the Twist

It has been my personal experience that of all of the high-stress behaviors that a snake can exhibit, the only one that is guaranteed not to really go away is thrashing or twisting wildly when held. Snakes such as the racers, coachwhips, and many types of water snakes (genus *Coluber, Masticophis,* and *Nerodia,* respectively) will often perform these gyrating feats even to the point of seriously injuring themselves in trying to escape from a handler's grasp. Such animals virtually never settle into life in the captive environment.

that specimen out of your pool of potential snakes. Remember, the general behavior of a snake in its terrarium and in your grasp can tell you a lot about the overall health of that animal: listlessness, pained or stilted movements, lying exposed, not flickering its tongue, not looking around, and not holding its head up are all behavioral cues that something is seriously amiss. Healthy snakes will be alert, active, curious, or even semi-aggressive when initially handled.

MENTAL INSPECTION

This section addresses the social disposition of your chosen snake. Of course, snakes are not social animals in the same sense that dogs or cats are, but you might be surprised at how the mental state of a snake can alter its suitability as a pet. Before taking the disposition of your chosen snake into account, think about why you are purchasing it and in what manner you intend to keep it. If you are buying a snake strictly for its beauty and don't intend to take it out of its cage or terrarium often, then a snake with a "bitey" disposition, or one that does not like to be handled, could be the one for you. An excellent example of this is the emerald tree boa (*Corallus caninus*). Renowned by hobbyists the world over for its stunning beauty, this snake commands an exceedingly high price among advanced enthusiasts but is handled only rarely. Emerald tree boas can be aggressive, and because their dentition is so formidable—their sharp, inward-curving, very long teeth are specially designed for hanging on to mammalian and avian prey when hunting in the jungle canopy—few hobbyists ever really hold these animals in the same way that a ball python or California kingsnake can be handled and played with for hours on end. So if you find yourself wishing to own species with a reputation for aggression, the mental disposition of your chosen specimen is of minimal concern, as you are not going to be handling it unnecessarily anyway.

If, however, you desire a snake that you can handle, you'll want to make sure that the specimen you select is likely to take to gentle handling. Begin your inspection by gently removing the snake from its enclosure or container. Lift it from the bottom or allow it to slither into your hand. Obviously, smaller or younger snakes will require a more delicate touch than will larger, more robust

Some snake species are almost always too aggressive to handle, such as the garden boa.

specimens. Never grab the snake by the head or the tail, as this will send even the most benign of specimens into a defensive posture. Once you have removed the snake from its enclosure, watch its behaviors. Does it vibrate its tail rapidly? Does it hold its mouth agape and hiss? Does it thrash and twist wildly in your grasp? Has it emptied its cloacal contents on you? (This is an industry euphemism for "Did it poop all over you?") Has it or is it still biting you repeatedly? If any of these behaviors occurs and does not stop shortly thereafter, chances are this snake has an edgy or aggressive disposition. If startled, scared, upset, or otherwise highly stressed, any snake may react to you in any of these ways. A snake that is mild mannered will soon calm down and may even begin to slither about in your grasp. One that is truly high strung and that may not be as desirable as a pet you intend to handle will continue to display these behaviors.

Another major consideration is the age of the snake in question. Juvenile or newly hatched snakes are very small and are easily frightened by the massive size of a human keeper. As a result, they often exhibit aggressive behaviors out of sheer terror and survival instinct. With regular handling, most of these snakes will calm down as they mature and may be very handle-friendly specimens indeed. If, however, you are considering purchasing an adult snake and it vehemently exhibits these behaviors, chances are less in your favor that the snake will tame to your touch. The simple fact of the matter is that adult snakes are set in their ways in a way that juvenile snakes are not; for that reason, an ill-mannered adult snake is not likely a wise purchase for the hobbyist wishing to have a handle-friendly snake.

Ball pythons normally are quite docile and tolerant of handling.

But to return to our original scenario. You've taken the snake out of its enclosure, and either it struck or vibrated its tail or gave some other indication of instinctual self-defense. If the snake bites you, don't jerk away or make any sudden moves. If the snake is a juvenile, its teeth are very small and its jaws very weak—it cannot really hurt you. Of course, this rule depends on the size of the snake; baby Burmese pythons and baby reticulated pythons can pack quite a wallop! Just hold the snake gently; support the bulk of its body but don't squeeze it. Allow its head to move about freely and do not pinch its tail. After a moment of hissing or posturing, most juvenile snakes will begin to calm. It will start by flickering its tongue and getting used to your scent. In another moment, it should relax its coils and begin to slither curiously about your hands. Don't drop it, but don't be afraid to allow it to slither about, either, as it's only natural for a small snake to explore its surroundings.

It's always smart to handle a small or juvenile snake over a countertop or above a table so that if the animal does slip out of your grasp, it will not be injured by a long fall all the way to the floor. I also recommend that you keep a pet shop employee or expo vendor handy when handling a snake you are considering purchasing. Before you make a cash transaction, the snake is still the property of the seller, and it's just good etiquette to stay close at hand. Likewise, if you are unskilled at handling a small snake or if you are buying the snake as a first pet for a child, then it's a good idea to have an expert standing by to lend a hand if necessary.

So now, after you've been handling your potential pet snake for a few minutes, you should once again take inventory of its behaviors. What is it doing? Slithering slowly and seemingly comfortably about, flickering its tongue? Is it trying to slither up your arm or into your hair, or maybe up your sleeve, or under the palm of your hand? All of these behaviors are natural, and they are indicative of a snake that is comfortable. Congratulations, you've found a specimen that will not likely suffer from any undue stress or mental unease as a pet! If, however, the snake continues to display aggressive or defensive behaviors after several minutes of handling, you might want to put that animal away and take out another specimen for inspection. Such a high-strung animal will likely present numerous problems in the home terrarium: quick to bite or poop on you should you take it out of the terrarium, refusal to feed in captivity, frequent escape attempts, or it may rub its nose bloody raw against the glass or screen lid of its enclosure. Always, *always* select a snake that exhibits a calm, comfortable, and unstressed mental disposition.

Snakes and the Law

Like most things in life, snake ownership, import, export, and interstate trade are regulated by local, state, and national laws. It is the personal responsibility of the hobbyist to know those laws. Some species of snakes cannot be owned in certain areas. Venomous species, for example, are frequently regulated by both state and local laws, and in many states, like my neighboring state of Florida, permits and licenses are required to legally house and maintain any type of venomous species. Likewise, indigenous species may be protected in an area by a total ban on trade for that species in that area. Corn snakes, for example, are native to my home state of Georgia; thus, they are illegal to own, capture, or sell within Georgia. Other species have even tighter levels of regulation. Rare or endangered animals may also be federally protected. It is the duty and ethical responsibility of all snake owners and hobbyists to know and abide by local, state, and federal laws as relating to the herp hobby. Failure to abide by these laws—depending on the laws in question—can incur some steep penalties on the keeper, including confiscation of your pets, financial fines, and even imprisonment in extreme cases. Don't take any chances with your pets and yourself. Know the law.

Blue-striped garter snake.

Chapter Two

HOME AND HABITAT

"There are no snakes to be met with throughout the whole island."
    ~Horrebow, *Natural History of Iceland*

Housing your snake is both fun and challenging, and the outcome can be extremely rewarding. By working with natural and/or artificial plants, sticks, rocks, and other such decor, you get a chance to express yourself and indulge in your creativity, while your pet snake gets an attractive, properly constructed, and environment-appropriate (i.e., desert conditions for a desert-dwelling species, jungle-conditions for a jungle-dwelling snake, etc.) habitat that it can call home. It's win-win! Conversely, you can also build a spartan home for many species of snakes. If time, money, or living space is a concern for you—as it is for many young hobbyists, apartment dwellers, and professional breeders—you can establish a habitat for your snake that meets its necessary requirements for temperature, space, lighting, hides, etc., but that makes a minimal impact on your wallet and living space.

Selecting an Enclosure

All good snake endeavors begin with a good terrarium or tank. What type of tank you select will largely depend on what type of snake you will be housing. Because this enclosure will be its home, the snake's needs for space (height versus width), lighting, heat, air circulation, etc., will take precedence. After these conditions have been satisfied, some secondary concerns may come into play, such as your available time, space, money, aesthetic tastes, etc.

Glass aquaria work well as housing for small to medium snakes, such as this snow corn snake.

Obviously, if there is a big conflict between the two (e.g., you want to buy a very large python but you don't have nearly enough room in which to house it), you'll need to seriously reconsider the matter and perhaps go with a different species of snake.

Ultimately there are numerous pros and cons to each type of terrarium you might wish to use. Find out all that you can about the snake you intend to buy and its environmental and spatial needs before purchasing its enclosure. Also keep in mind your limitations in terms of space, money, time, aesthetic desires, and skill level.

GLASS AQUARIA

Within my own snake endeavors, I have always favored the all-glass aquarium. Originally designed as a fish tank, this type of enclosure has four sides and a floor made from glass. This makes the tank a little more fragile than other types, and I have broken more than a couple over the course of my lifetime. However, an all-glass tank makes for an aesthetically pleasing terrarium. Visibility is high (both for people looking in and for the occupants looking out) with aquaria and will likely stay that way, as glass is scratch resistant unless sandy or very rocky substrate is used. Aside from being potentially fragile, a glass aquarium, depending on its size, can also be *very* heavy. A glass tank large enough to accommodate a large colubrid or medium-sized python or boa, for example, can weigh more than 100 pounds (45.4 kg). This is certainly something to consider before deciding which type of terrarium to use. However, a glass tank can also be much less expensive than an acrylic tank, and the used market (newspaper want ads, yard sales, flea markets, etc.) also has a copious supply of good, used glass terraria from which to choose. Often, you can get these items at a fraction of their retail cost.

ACRYLIC ENCLOSURES

The second type of cage is the acrylic enclosure, sometimes called a molded plastic cage. Made from plastics and specifically designed for use with reptiles, these lightweight tanks come in a wide variety of styles. Tall habitats—made especially for arboreal occupants—are an option with acrylic styles, as are long, broad terraria, which are designed for housing larger snakes, such as the boas and pythons.

Acrylic enclosures have numerous advantages over glass tanks in that they are more durable and much tougher to break; they are much lighter weight; and they are molded in shapes, styles, and forms that are seldom seen in glass tanks. Many acrylic cages open in the front instead of the top. This has pros and cons. It makes them easier to clean, but it can make it easier for snakes to escape.

There are also some disadvantages to acrylic enclosures to consider. Acrylic cages tend to scratch up more easily than glass tanks (although they can be resurfaced or polished through some painstaking efforts). This happens especially quickly in terraria that house abrasive substrates, such as sands, rocks, or gravel. Many acrylic cages are opaque with glass doors, making scratches less of a concen. Another disadvantage to acrylic cages is algae, which becomes evident in swamp-type or jungle-type terraria that have a high level of humidity or standing pools of water. Acrylic tanks are, on the microscopic level, highly porous. The tiny pores in the surface of the acrylic can trap humidity in the form of water droplets. When light hits these droplets, algae can grow in them. When the algae

Build It First

Although it may seem obvious, it bears mentioning that you must always have your home terrarium established, warm, and waiting to receive your snake before bringing it home. If you will be using a quarantine tank (and it is important to do so if you already have a collection of reptiles and amphibians), it must be clean, warm, and ready to receive its new occupant prior to bringing it home. If you do not have a tank set up and ready, your snake will have to wait while you establish the tank. This is terrible, as it will be in the container in which the pet shop packaged it, and it will be cramped, cold, and stressed for the duration of the time it takes you to build its home. Also, setting up the tank in advance will allow you to discover problems with it before your snake is inside. Remember the golden rule of snake acquisition: Have your terrarium set up, warm, and fully outfitted (substrate, climbs, hides, water dish, etc.) *before* bringing home your new pet snake.

Acrylic cages are more durable and lightweight than glass aquaria. Some are big enough to hold sizable snakes, such as this pair of red-tailed boas.

dies or is scrubbed away, these pores retain micro amounts of algae, giving the tank a permanently green "stained" appearance. Over time, this staining effect can cloud the walls of the terrarium badly, thereby reducing visibility and ruining the beauty of the terrarium. The only way to effectively clean the stains off is through bleaching or polishing, or by resurfacing the inside of the tank.

WOODEN ENCLOSURES

A third type of terrarium that can work well for a snake is a wooden or homemade enclosure. By pulling blueprints off the Internet, buying your materials at a local hardware store, and giving the project a weekend's worth of effort, you can build your own snake enclosure. Although this process can be rewarding and enjoyable, like the other two terrarium types, the homemade terrarium has some pros and cons that go along with it. One advantage is that you can customize the tank to suit you and your snake's exact needs; the tank may be of any dimensions you can afford and maintain. Another advantage is the replaceable nature of the glass or Plexiglas portions of the tank. My father and I built a wooden tank for my large black rat snake when I was 12. The terrarium was screwed together and had sides and a front of glass and a back made of Peg-

Board for air circulation. The heavy screen lid was hinged and locked. Cleaning it one day, I broke one of the side panels. All my dad and I did was unscrew the wooden frame on that side, remove the broken bits of glass, insert a new pane, screw the frame back together, and voilà! The tank was as good as new. Try doing that with an all-glass or acrylic tank.

One drawback, however, is that the wooden tank is even more porous than the acrylic tank, and wood holds in moisture and odor. Custom wooden enclosures often have a permanent musty odor to them. Fungi, mold, and bacteria can be especially problematic in wooden tanks. Another drawback to the wooden or custom-made tank is the limitations placed on the environment types it can support. Although a wooden tank can house desert-going animals with no problems, a swamp-type habitat will not last long at all in a wooden tank. The humidity will cause the wood to warp and rot.

What's a Vivarium?

A vivarium is like a natural terrarium but with more living components. A natural terrarium may have sticks, leaves, and a potted plant inside it, while a vivarium may have composting leaf mulch and soil in which plants directly grow and flourish. A vivarium is more of a living system than just a terrarium, and in such a system, the plants, soil components, and other fixtures may be just as important as the animals.

RACK SYSTEMS

Another type of terrarium is the rack system of caging. This term is somewhat deceptive in that it does not always refer to a single type of terrarium but rather refers to a wide range of caging in which a tower or bookshelf-sized wooden, plastic, or acrylic frame supports numerous smaller terrariums within its framework. Although there are virtually endless variations on this type, the fundamental rack systems all work basically the same. Sweater boxes or opaque or clear plastic tubs are fitted into a larger framework, and the gap between each shelf in the larger structure is just barely wide enough for the tub to fit snugly into the gap. The end result is a tank in which the "lid" of the terrarium is merely the bottom of the shelf above that terrarium. (In some cases, there is more of a gap, and each terrarium has its own lid.) A standard rack system might consist of four, five, or six shelves with as many or more small tubs going across. So a rack of six shelf gaps with five tubs across could hold 30 tubs, each of which might contain a single snake specimen. As with all terrarium types, the rack system may be more or less elaborate; some rack systems have built-in lights, strips of heat tape (like a strip of undertank heating pad) beneath the tubs, ventilation fans, and UV lighting apparatuses. Obviously, a rack system is especially designed for advanced hobbyists, professional breeders, and zoological experts who find it necessary to house a high number of specimens in a minimal area.

OTHER TERRARIUM CONSIDERATIONS

STYLE

Once you have decided on a type of terrarium, find a style that suits both your needs and those of your snake. As I alluded to earlier, there is a plethora of terrarium styles available. Tall or vertically oriented cages are necessary for housing arboreal species, such as the tree boas, rough green snakes, and some species of tree-going rat snakes. Conversely, horizontally oriented tanks are useful for housing heavy-bodied and fully terrestrial species, such as blood pythons or sand boas.

SIZE

There is a general rule of thumb regarding snake enclosure size that most hobbyists swear by: The length of your snake's terrarium must be at least 1.5 times the length of the snake itself. This allows for plenty of room for the snake to fully stretch itself out. Thus, a 4-foot-long (1.2-m) snake should be housed in a terrarium that is 6 feet long (1.8 m) (4 x 1.5 = 6). This rule is not always

Snakes are escape artists that require totally secure cages. This mountain kingsnake's cage is secured with a lock.

The Desert Habitat

There are basically six major types of naturalistic terrariums, each on a graduated scale based on the level of moisture present. Beginning at the driest end of that scale is the desert. The desert habitat is a dry place with relative humidity seldom rising above about 50 percent. Desert habitats have a sandy substrate that tends to be liberally strewn with rocks and some dry branches of wood. Keep the water dish small, and make sure that the tank gets plenty of air circulation. Daily temperatures in the desert environment may top out in the upper 80s F (about 30.5° to 31.5°C) with a warmer basking spot for most snake species, with nightly drops of at least 10° to 15°F (5.6° to 8.3°C). Some excellent species to house in the desert environment include the Kenyan sand boa, the rosy boa, the gopher snake, and the gray-banded kingsnake.

applicable, however, and does not apply to some of the strictly arboreal snakes, such as the members of the genus *Corallus*, which spend all of their time coiled in tight loops high in the branches of their terrarium.

You'll also want to consider the heating and lighting needs of your snake when purchasing a tank and how the size relates to those needs. For most snakes, you'll want a cage that can get warm at one end but that stays cooler at the other end so that the snake can regulate its own temperature. This temperature variation (called a thermal gradient) can be difficult to set up in a small enclosure.

SECURITY

Another critical aspect of the home terrarium is the matter of security. In fact, *the most critical element of your snake's terrarium is security!* All species of snakes are masterful escape artists, and their housing must be as secure as possible. When shopping around for a terrarium, consult the reptile and amphibian expert at your local pet shop or some other trusted source. Tell him what type of snake you're going to purchase, and ask his advice as to what style or manufacture of cage is the most secure for that species. For example, a locking lid with a screen that is of heavy enough gauge to prevent an adult boa constrictor from breaking through it probably has holes in it large enough for a ribbon snake or small rat snake to slither right through. Conversely, a tank with a fine-mesh screen lid meant to hold in a small colubrid might just be so fragile that a powerful boid could burst right through it and escape. So making sure that your terrarium is escape-proof is only half the battle—you must make sure that it is escape-proof for your chosen species of snake.

Locks, not Rocks

When I was a kid, I used to lay boards across my terrarium's lid and place dumbbells on top of them. This made the lid heavy enough that my eastern kingsnake couldn't raise it up and slither out. This was a stupid idea. Suppose my kingsnake had managed to push up the edge of the lid and the dumbbell shifted and fell through the screen, crushing and potentially killing my beloved "Kingy"?

I've heard of other hobbyists using rocks, trophies, heavy books, or other items to weigh down their enclosure lids. These are disasters—either escapes or crushed snakes—waiting to happen. Be smart and use locks to keep your prized pet in its habitat.

It is also critical that you find a terrarium with a snug-fitting and *locking* lid (or door if the terrarium opens in the front or side). Always look for terrariums that come with or that can be fitted with a lid that snaps or lock in place. Although this style of lid may be slightly more expensive initially, bear in mind that the cost of replacing your snake, should it escape, will far outweigh the purchase price of a locking lid—to say nothing of the emotional expense of losing your pet. Most glass aquaria have a plastic lining with a lip around the top. Many woodworking outfits make counter-sinking wooden and screen lids that can be fitted into this lipped plastic frame. These counter-sinking, locking lids are, in my opinion, the best you can ever buy. Other lid styles have pins that lock into place around the outside of this plastic frame, and other terrariums come with locking lids already attached.

One good thing about an acrylic enclosure is that many of them come with locking lids, or sometimes doors, already built into them, so matching a cage with an appropriate lid is a nonissue. Bear in mind also that any lines or cords running out of the tank (such as those powering water pumps or heating apparatuses) can create a gap through which your snake could easily escape. A good rule of thumb for evaluating whether your snake can escape through a hole in or around the lid is this: Is the hole as wide or tall as the width of your snake's head? If the answer is yes, then it can probably escape through it. Owing to the girth at the middle of a snake's body, a perfectly circular hole is considerably more difficult for a snake to escape through than is a crack or gap, as a snake can flatten itself and easily slide through a tight gap or crack.

Substrates

If you spend any time hanging around pet shops or talking about reptiles with anyone, you'll hear the word "substrate" come up pretty often. "Substrate" simply refers to the materials placed atop the bottom layer of the terrarium. So a tank that is filled with sand and meant to accommodate a rosy boa has a sandy substrate, and a simpler terrarium with a rectangle of newspaper atop which

Corn snakes, as well as many other species, do well when housed on a substrate of dried leaves.

a small ball python lives has a paper substrate. Obviously, there are numerous types of substrates, and not every type is appropriate for every species of snake.

NATURAL SUBSTRATES

The natural substrates are my personal favorites to use. They are aesthetically pleasing, can be used for long stretches of time, and many (such as stones and pebbles) can be used and cleaned and reused again.

LEAVES

The first type of natural substrate is the most versatile and useful in the naturalistic terrarium: leaves. Leaves of most tree species can be placed in the terrarium in as thick a layer as you care to establish. If you are opting for a living vivarium, leaves will be absolutely integral. Mix a layer of composting leaves in with the orchid bark, coconut husk, or topsoil, which composes the lion's share of the tank's living substrate.

If you are using leaves as ground cover, simply place a thin layer of dried leaves over whatever the rest of the substrate is. The good news is that snakes all over the world, and most of the species described in this book, will naturally

Good Snakekeeping

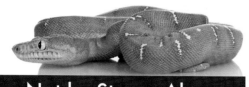

Not by Stones Alone

Many hobbyists use stones as substrates in their terrariums. Stones—usually in the form of aquarium pebbles—are inexpensive, come in a variety of colors and sizes, and can be washed and reused several times. There is a major drawback to using aquarium pebbles, though: They are not really an appropriate substrate type for most snake species. Few snakes in the wild make their dwellings strictly atop rocks. If you must use rocks, use paint- and dye-free pebbles or round river rocks. These stones are smooth and can be washed and cleaned easily. But because rocks are cold, hard, and abrasive and because so few snakes naturally live on rocks alone, I recommend mixing rocks or pebbles with some other type of substrate to create a more naturalistic substrate compound within your terrarium.

utilize leaves as hides. If you notice your snake suffering from stress or it seems to be adapting poorly to life in your home terrarium, try adding about a 1-inch-thick (2.5-cm) layer of leaves to the tank. You might be surprised how readily your snake's stress level drops simply by adding this one natural substrate to the tank.

PINE STRAW

Another natural substrate that I find useful when housing colubrid species (I don't ever use it with boids, as it tends to irritate their heat-sensitive facial pits) is pine straw (fallen pine needles). Many North American colubrids naturally live in and around pine straw, and by adding some to the terrarium, you will provide your snake with some welcome and natural ground cover. If you get good, fresh, clean pine straw—freshly fallen and taken from the uppermost layers of the forest floor—there is no need to sterilize it before adding it to the tank.

The only potential drawback to using pine straw is that it tends to dry out or dehydrate the snake if it is used exclusively or if the humidity in the terrarium is not maintained. Employ a large water dish or light mistings with a spray bottle to prevent the pine straw from staying overly dry. Green or freshly fallen pine needles remain much moister than do red or brown needles, which must be lightly misted more frequently. Hay or yellow straw is not a good substrate/ground cover choice because it holds moisture and grows fungus colonies readily. Pine straw, on the other hand, is dry, light, airy, and provides excellent hiding places and ground cover. I recommend that pine straw only be employed with those snake species indigenous to piney woods; avoid mixing pine straw with jungle species and boids.

SOIL MIXTURES

Soil can be an excellent substrate for snakes—after all, most species spend a lot of their time on the ground. However, do not just use soil from outdoors. It tends to clump up like concrete or become a fetid, swampy mess, depending on how wet you keep it. Instead, purchase organic topsoil or create your own mixture fit to the habitat you are creating.

When buying soil, I recommend getting a mixture with some coconut husk and/or bark chips already included in it; this prevents the soil from clumping too tightly and allows your snake to burrow easily. And you'll definitely want to avoid getting a prefertilized mixture or any variety that is chemically treated. (Many topsoils come pretreated with herbicides, insecticides, or fungicides.) Avoid buying potting soil, as this will clump or dry out quickly in the home terrarium. Additionally, potting soil almost always has fertilizers or perlite in it. Sphagnum moss and orchid bark make excellent choices to mix in with your topsoil as well, as these items loosen the soil and help the terrarium retain moisture.

A soil and pebble mixture works well for many species. Mix pebbles and topsoil in a 50-50 mixture (by volume), or better yet, make a mixture of half stones and half soil, then mix that (again, 50-50) with coir, or shredded coconut husk. (See section "Coconut Husk.") The end result of this mixture will comprised one part gravel/pebbles, one part topsoil, and two parts coir. This mixture is soft enough that your snake can lie on it and burrow in it comfortably and is rich enough in nutrients that you could successfully anchor living plants in it.

The soil-mixing process that I just described in the previous paragraphs is a fun and effective way to build a terrarium with natural substrate, but if you do not like getting your hands dirty, your local pet shop may sell materials that take

The Savanna Habitat

Although not quite as dry as the desert habitat, the savanna is a warm, semi-arid habitat that may play host to a wide range of snake species. Daily temperatures in the savanna are slightly lower than those of the desert: mid-80s F (about 29° to 30°C) with nightly drops to the low 70s F (about 22° to 23°C). Humidity levels are also somewhat higher at a bit above 55 percent. Broad, wide conditions allow for plenty of room to slither, while extensive hideaways allow all of the plains-dwelling species to retreat whenever they desire. Outfit the savanna terrarium with plenty of hides, a water dish, and not too much ground cover. A low climbing branch will be appreciated, as will some large, flat rocks for basking. Some excellent choices for the savanna habitat include the California kingsnake, the bullsnake, the Baird's and Great Plains rat snakes, the ball and carpet pythons, the prairie kingsnake, and the western hognose snake.

Sand is a good substrate for housing most desert species, such as the Kenyan sand boa.

all the work and guesswork out of the matter. Prepackaged naturalistic soils and substrates of all types are sold in the reptile section of the pet shop. "Jungle-mix" style substrates combine a variety of soils, barks, mosses, and other wood and bark by-products to create a light, moisture-retaining substrate that is good for both jungle herps and living plants. Sandier packaged mixtures are also available that combine sands with some bark types to produce a substrate suitable for snakes that need dry, arid conditions.

BARKS AND WOODS

Another substrate type that you might encounter is the barks and woods. Typically sold in the reptile section of the local pet shop (and also in larger bulk quantities in the outdoor and yard section of hardware and department stores), some types of barks and wood shavings make great substrate. Loose, lightweight shredded woods will not scratch up the surface of a glass tank in the way that sand will. Mulches and wood shavings also tend to absorb odors better than inorganic substrates, so you get a little more "mileage" out of each changing of the substrate. Obviously, this aromatic advantage is no substitute for regular, timely changes of your snake's bedding. Change any manner of bedding once it becomes soiled.

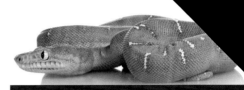
Many hobbyists swear by shredded aspen, which unlike cedar and pine, is not very aromatic or resinous. These lightweight shavings allow for burrowing and some spot cleaning. Aspen is not recommended for species requiring high humidity because it tends to get soggy.

Cypress mulch also works for many snake types, as this lightweight substrate allows burrowing species to tunnel easily through their home environment without you having to deal with the hassle of sand. (Deep sand in a large tank is oftentimes heavy enough to crack the base glass.) Cypress also holds humidity quite well while resisting rot. Orchid bark has similar properties to cypress mulch, but the bedding tends to be in bigger pieces.

Care must be taken, however, against using certain wooden substrate types with some snake species because not all species thrive on all wood-bedding types. Very aromatic wood shavings (or those that feel slightly "sticky" or resinous to the touch) should never be used because they contain oils that can irritate your snake's olfactory organs. See section "Substrates to Avoid" for more on this topic.

Avoiding Impaction

If you use sand, soil, or some other substrate composed of fine particles, you may want to feed your snake in a separate container or put its food on a plate or flat rock so the snake doesn't ingest the substrate. Swallowing these substrates can cause a life-threatening gut impaction.

COCONUT HUSK

Sold in blocks or bricks, finely shredded coconut husk is an inexpensive and organically sound form of substrate. Simply cut the brick out of its package,

The Forest Habitat

A bit cooler and moister than the savanna habitat, the forest is defined by thick vegetative cover, moist understory, and plenty of climbing branches. The forest is the perfect habitat for the corn snake, the black rat snake, the eastern kingsnake, the twin-spotted rat snake, the rough green snake, and the pine snake. Maintain warm temperatures (upper 70s to low 80s F [about 25° to 29°C]) by day with mild drops by night. Keep relative humidity higher than the savanna—60 to 65 percent—but not too high. A large water dish with plenty of large, flat stones around it will mimic a forest pool. The forest terrarium does well with full-spectrum lighting and plenty of living plants, such as pothos or philodendron. Include plenty of hides in the forest habitat, and the substrate should be liberally covered with leaf litter.

Habitat

Snake and Bake

ver been walking outside and spotted a twisted stick or tall rock ught would look fantastic in your snake's terrarium? If you are e me you have, and maybe you even dropped the item into your snake's tank. In the weeks that followed, did anything odd happen—did ticks or mites appear, or did your snake get some skin ailment? Sometimes when we introduce a wild item to the controlled environment of the home terrarium, we also unwittingly introduce numerous types of parasites, molds, bacteria, and other biological gremlins. Thus, it becomes necessary to sterilize anything you might find outdoors that you want to use in your snake's terrarium. Fortunately, I have a foolproof method for sterilizing anything you might want to add to your tank.

Begin by washing all dirt, mold, and debris off the item in question. Then let it dry (in the sun, if possible). Once the item is completely dry, wrap it in a thick layer of aluminum foil and place it in your oven. Once the item is fully wrapped in foil and inside the oven, turn it on for an hour at 300°F (148.9°C). This process will bake to death any parasites, worms, mites, ticks, fungi, molds, bacteria, and any other unwanted microbial life forms that may be living in or on your natural item. After an hour has passed, turn off the oven and let the item cool down for 24 hours before placing it inside your snake's terrarium. This process is known as heat-treating, and thousands of hobbyists around the world use it to sterilize the sticks, logs, and porous stones they want to use in their terrariums. Do not heat-treat at temperatures any higher than 300°F (148.9°C), as this may cause wood to ignite into flames in your oven. It is also not possible to heat-treat any living items, such as plants or mosses.

soak it in a 5-gallon (18.9-l) bucket filled with the appropriate amount of hot water (volume will vary, so read the instructions on each brand's package), and watch the dehydrated, tightly compressed brick swell into a copious amount of bedding. Let it cool to room temperature before your snake comes into contact with it. Ever since these coir bricks hit the market, I have used them within my own snake endeavors and sung their praises to all of my friends, colleagues, and readers. Soft, airy, and moist enough to maintain an appropriate humidity level within the terrarium, shredded coconut husk is an excellent substrate for virtually any type of snake described in this book, with the exception of the desert species.

SAND

There are a number of different sands available, and each one has its pros and cons. Natural sands are sold in smaller bags in pet shops and in larger bags (for a fraction of the cost) at garden shops and hardware stores. Sold as playground sand or sandbox sand, they are typically light in color, smooth in texture, and may be dusty straight out of the package. Such fine-grained sands are great choices for devout burrowers, such as the Indian and Kenyan sand boas or most other desert species. Some North American desert snakes, however, such as the Western hognose snake and some of the gopher snakes, prefer harder, rockier soils over loose, sandy soils.

Another type of sand is the manufactured calcium sand. This sand-like substance is made primarily from calcium and carbon. Because of its organic composition, it passes through the digestive tract of any reptile that consumes some of it. Inorganic sands and pebbles can get lodged in a snake's intestinal tract, thereby causing a condition known as impaction or an impacted gut. Although it is much more common in lizards (who take broad, sweeping bites at their prey), an impacted gut is excruciatingly painful, and if left unchecked, eventually proves fatal. Highly digestible calcium-carbonate sand will pass through your snake's system with minimal threat of becoming impacted

This Arizona mountain kingsnake is housed on recycled paper bedding, one of the safest substrates for most snakes.

The Swamp Habitat

The wettest of all of the snake habitats, the swamp or wetland environment is the perfect place for water snakes (*Nerodia*), garter and ribbon snakes (*Thamnophis*), and some species of boids (such as the yellow and green anacondas and rainbow boas). Construct a swamp terrarium by employing either several large water dishes or by establishing a large pool of water within the terrarium. Some companies sell half-and-half conversion kits that allow you to construct a terrarium that is part water and part dry land. Equipped with filters and a trough for a flowing waterway, these kits are fun and make for an interesting and aesthetically attractive swamp/wetland terrarium. Although water is important within this terrarium style, dry land is even more important, as all species of snakes must be supplied with dry places; a perpetually wet snake will not live long. Haul-outs (sticks, logs, rocks, etc.) allowing the snake to get out of the water are also critical, as it may quickly tire and drown if it cannot escape a pool of even shallow water.

(although ingesting large amounts can cause an impaction, but this is not likely with snakes). As you might imagine, these chemically manufactured sands are expensive, but they come in a wide variety of colors to suit the tastes of any hobbyist.

RECYCLED SUBSTRATE

Recycled substrates are a great way to get extra mileage out of some household materials that would otherwise simply go straight to the landfill. Sales circulars and newspapers can make a great substrate for many snake species. Just don't use glossy paper because it won't absorb waste and may not be safe for your snake. Some hobbyists place a heavy layer of newspapers or sales circulars flat in the bottom of their terrarium. This works well for many colubrid and nonspecialized boa and python species. Using such papers in the hospital or quarantine tank can also allow for easy observation of newly acquired or ailing specimens, as well as of their droppings. Although smaller snakes can disappear between the layers of newspaper, larger pythons and boas typically sleep on top of all layers of paper.

I do not recommend using newspaper for specialized snakes, however, such as the sand boas, rosy boas, rainbow boas, and tree boas. If flat newspaper isn't to your liking, get a document shredder and shred these items, then place them in the bottom of your snake's terrarium. This makes for a much looser substrate into which any snake can readily burrow and hide. Newspaper substrate can quickly dehydrate many species of snakes, so always provide a large dish of clean water in any terrarium utilizing shredded or flat newspaper substrate.

RECYCLED PAPER BEDDING

Another type of recycled newspaper substrate is, in my opinion, the best manufactured substrate going: literally, recycled newspaper. Appearing as lightweight, gray puffs of ground-up newsprint, recycled newspaper is soft, light, easily burrowed in, and much gentler to the touch than is shredded or flat newspaper. When your snake poops in its terrarium, recycled newspaper also has a habit of clumping together; thus, the spoiled bits may be removed quickly and easily. Recycled newspaper substrate is also quite inexpensive. The only real drawback to this substrate medium is that it holds moisture (wetness dries slowly in recycled newspaper) and odors well. So a messy trip to the bathroom for your snake can leave the rest of the substrate smelling foul for some time to come. If spot cleaned and kept dry, however, recycled newspaper is one of the best artificial substrate types I've ever encountered.

BEDDING-STYLE SUBSTRATES

What I here call bedding-style substrates are the pelletized forms of bedding that are commercially manufactured and sold in pet shops. They are sold under various names and are lightweight, inexpensive, and disposable. Manufactured from alfalfa, hay, straw, or any number of other grasses, many of these substrates are also edible; if a lizard or snake gets a little bit in its mouth when feeding, it will either digest the bit or pass it without a problem. I personally do not use these pelletized beddings for aesthetic reasons, but I have had friends and colleagues use them for years with nothing but positive results. Most hobbyists who employ such substrates do so on a small scale; a 10-gallon (37.9-l) terrarium with a small garter snake can easily be filled with a bag of pelletized bedding, while the task of filling a 100-gallon (378.5-l) terrarium housing a small rock python can be much more daunting and fiscally taxing. Expense can be a limiting factor when it comes to outfitting large terrariums.

Other types of bedding-style substrate are chipped or ground materials, such as corncobs or ground walnut

Avoid a Stuck Snake

A word of caution is in order because many acrylic, clay, and ceramic decorations meant for use in the fish aquarium are hollow inside. Although fish can easily swim into and out of such hollow fixtures, some snakes can get into but cannot get back out of hollow fixtures. One quick remedy for this problem is to take a hammer and a nail or chisel and make a small, controlled break in the back of your chosen fixture. By making certain that the aperture is big enough and accessible enough that your snake can escape, you can ensure that it never gets trapped inside any item of decor within its terrarium. The good thing about such items is that an item purchased as a climbing stone or simple bit of decor can now double as a hideaway for your pet.

Although there are exceptions, most snakes will use climbing branches if provided with them.

shells. These ground beddings are typically designed for use with rodents, and I recommend that things stay that way. These substrates are dusty and fibrous, and they tend to either get lodged in or irritate the nostrils, eyes, mouth, and heat-sensitive pits in the faces of many boid species. Like recycled newspaper, these ground or chipped beddings tend to dehydrate a snake when dry and hold copious amounts of moisture—which spawn enormous fungal colonies—when wet. A spilled water dish in a terrarium filled with ground corncob bedding is like spilling a bowl of milk inside a box of cereal: The end result is a sloppy, soggy mess that is entirely useless and must be disposed of at once. Additionally, these substrates commonly cause gut impactions.

CARPET

Tiles or rectangles of reptile carpet have long been popular in the pet trade. Made of acrylic fibers and tightly woven to resist degrading over time, these substrates are, in my opinion, useless for all but the largest snakes. Think about all that we've said about snakes thus far: They like tight-fitting enclosures, they like to burrow and hide beneath things, and they like the feeling of safety and security that they glean from their leaf and vegetative cover. So why would we hobbyists think that our smaller snakes would be happy lying quietly coiled on a square of carpet? On the other hand, the large boas and pythons are protected from predators and do not always feel the same desire for protective cover that smaller snakes do. Thus, while a larger snake might not mind an exposed slab of carpet, few smaller snakes will do anything other than perpetually hide beneath the carpet, desperately searching for denser cover. Additionally, the liquid wastes that snakes produce pool beneath the carpet, creating an unhealthy environment.

SUBSTRATES TO AVOID

Although some substrates are excellent and easily maintained, others are a bane to both the keeper and the kept. Chipped or shredded cedar, redwood, and many types of pine wood (not bark) are rich with aromatic oils that can be extremely irritating to your snake's scales, skin, and olfactory organs. When these oil-rich, scented wood chips are present in the terrarium, the snake is bombarded with a powerfully irritating scent. These oils become irritating to the olfactory system, causing severe stress and the corresponding decreased appetite and weakened immune system that accompany spikes in stress. These wood chips have also been anecdotally linked to liver problems. Thus, cedar, pine, redwood, and other such resin-rich wood products are in no way acceptable substrate choices for captive snakes. Coconut husks, cork bark, orchid bark, and pine bark (only the outermost bark layers), however, are acceptable wood product choices.

Other unacceptable substrate types include random items that you might run across in your local pet shop that serve as substrate for other animals. These include crushed coral—used in marine aquaria—and lava rock gravel. Although

Rocks can serve as basking sites, climbing areas, and rough surfaces to aid shedding. They add a natural touch to the terrarium of a desert-dwelling snake, like this rosy boa.

Even large snakes should have some type of hide box. This adult red-tailed boa has curled up inside a hollow piece of cork bark.

a hunk or two of lava rock can be placed in a terrarium for both aesthetic effect and as a shedding aid or hide for your snake, a substrate of crushed or pebble-sized lava rock is too abrasive on which to house any species of snake.

Furnishings and Decor

When it comes to outfitting your terrarium with furnishings and decor, you really have a lot to choose from: artificial plants, climbing branches, acrylic vines, living plants, sand-blasted grapevine, ceramic hides, plastic and acrylic caves, artificial logs, slabs of cork bark, natural logs, flat rocks, clay pot halves, and a zillion other oddities. These items can function within your terrarium as potential hideaways, basking spots, climbs, etc., for your pet snake. Remember that as long as your snake's biological needs are being met, anything you choose to include within your terrarium is fair game. And when you go to the pet shop, don't feel compelled to stay strictly within the reptile and amphibian section—look around the fish and aquarium section too. You may be surprised at how many aquarium decorations (slabs of stone, gnarled spirals of driftwood, ceramic caves, etc.) are entirely functional within the pet snake terrarium.

CLIMBING BRANCHES

With the exception of a few specialized snakes (namely the sand boas), all snakes utilize and enjoy climbing branches. Although they don't have to be anything elaborate, all climbing branches must be thick enough and sturdy enough to support your snake's weight and bodily movements, and they must be anchored securely enough that they won't shift, tilt, or fall while your snake is climbing on them. Most pet shops sell acrylic and bendable vines (which can be secured at the upper reaches of the tank with hooks or suction cups), lengths of driftwood, and gnarled knots of sand-blasted grapevine, which makes a superior climbing branch for virtually all types of small- to medium-sized snakes. I do not recommend bringing in logs or sticks from the yard to add to your snake's terrarium—you may inadvertently introduce a parasite infestation along with these items. Heat-treat any natural objects you introduce into the terrarium.

HIDES

One of the most critical aspects of the terrarium, hides are the safe havens into which your snake can retire when it feels the need to escape the light of day, digest a large meal, sleep, or simply get out of the open. Virtually all species of snakes hate being exposed out in the open (when not basking). Without any tight nooks or dark crevices in which to hide, all snakes will stress and may begin to suffer in the captive environment. In the wild, a perpetually exposed snake is basically a dead snake; birds, mammals, and other reptiles will make short

The Jungle Habitat

Best constructed in a tall terrarium to accentuate its towering trees and dense, lofty canopy, the jungle terrarium is just what the doctor ordered for the tree-top-dwelling species: Garden boas, green tree pythons, and emerald tree boas. Some terrestrial species also do well in a jungle habitat, including rainbow boas, sunbeam snakes, and others. Maintain warm temperatures (in the upper 70s to low 80s F [about 25° to 29°C]) and a high level of relative humidity (varies based on the species in question, but 70 percent is pretty standard). Lighting must be bright enough to support any living plants you have inside the tank; I recommend employing full-spectrum lighting. Using lots of decomposing leaves as part of your substrate is a great idea—mix these with orchid bark, sphagnum moss, and coconut husk to create your own "jungle-mix" bedding. Include plenty of sturdy, well-anchored climbing branches for your tank's arboreal inhabitants. Once you've mastered the basics, try spicing things up in your jungle habitat by adding mosses, ferns, and bromeliads (rootless species often sold as air plants in pet stores) to your jungle canopy. If done well and maintained properly, a jungle habitat terrarium can make for a truly beautiful conversation piece.

work of an exposed snake. In the home terrarium, a snake will feel vulnerable to predatory attack if it does not have one or more dark, snug hideaways into which it can completely withdraw. Bear in mind also that most snakes like tight-fitting hides—they love to feel tightly enclosed whenever they retire. Feeling something pressing up against all sides of their bodies, snakes are assured that no predator can sneak up on them while they sleep.

Size-appropriate hides occur in all types, and virtually anything will work, from artificial cattle skulls to a naturalistic artificial cave purchased from your local pet shop to a slab of bark or plywood left lying on its side in the tank. In other words, hides can be constructed from virtually anything. Two excellent choices for hides are broken clay pot halves (with any sharp edges sanded smooth) and lengths of PVC piping, both of which are inexpensive and can be bought at any hardware store. I cannot stress enough the value of a good hide to a pet snake, and I recommend outfitting every snake terrarium with two or three good hides.

LIVE PLANTS

Live plants can be added to your snake's terrarium in one of two ways: left in the pot and tucked away in the corner or planted directly in the terrarium's substrate. Unless you are skilled with managing and propagating a living, thriving vivarium habitat, I recommend leaving your plants in their pots and watering them as they need it. Obviously, different terrarium styles and different species of snakes will require different species of living plants. A large python, for example, will easily crush even the most robust plants and may do better without any manner of plant in
its enclosure,

Snakes must have access to clean, fresh water at all times. A striped albino corn snake is pictured.

while smaller or shy snakes may never be visible at all in a tank filled with growing plants. Of course, there are some plant types that are universally applicable to virtually all terrarium types. Such durable, viable plants include pothos and philodendron, both of which are vine-like plants that will thrive under the care of even the novice terrarium keeper. Avoid using thorny, resinous, or odorous plants in your terrarium because they can injure or irritate your snake. Cacti, sundew, and other such plants are not recommended for these reasons. If you include live plants, you will need supplemental lighting to keep them alive, whether the snake needs such lighting or not.

WATER DISHES

Water is just as important to snakes as it is to almost every other animal on earth, and supplying your snake with a continual source of fresh, clean water is paramount. Change the water in its terrarium as often as it is fouled or every couple of days, whichever comes

Avoid Direct Sunlight

While ambient lighting in a room is fine for most snake species, never put your snake's terrarium in front of an open window. Sunlight from a nearby window can superheat a terrarium within a short amount of time. Such intense heat can overheat and kill any species of snake. Never establish a terrarium such that natural sunlight can strike it directly.

first. As for the style of dish to provide, that will largely be determined by the species of snake you house. Arid-loving snakes may suffer health problems if they are in an overly humid environment, such as a terrarium in which a large water dish is being jostled into overflowing or which has enough water evaporating out of it to raise the relative humidity inside the tank to unacceptably high levels. Conversely, a jungle or wetland snake needs a large water dish—at least large enough that it can immerse itself in the bowl as needed. Buy a heavy water dish with gently sloping sides. The weight will ensure that your snake's movements will neither tip nor undermine the dish, thus spilling the water into the substrate, and the gently sloping sides will ensure that any snake that falls into the water can easily slither out again. Many sorrowful hobbyists have lost a small snake to an overly deep water dish. The little reptile will swim as long as it can, but if it cannot find a means of escape, it will eventually tire and drown.

Lighting

Lighting your snake's terrarium is largely a matter of your aesthetic tastes. Unless you are supplying your snake with UV (ultraviolet) radiation, any manner of lighting is adequate, as long as you ensure that the lighting does not overheat the terrarium. UV lighting, also known as full-spectrum lighting, is the product of specially coated and manufactured lightbulbs. In the old days of the herp hobby, UV lighting only existed in the incandescent form, but now UV tube

Heat lamps work well for heating arboreal snakes, such as the tiger rat snake (*Spilotes pullatus*), an uncommonly kept species.

bulbs, which fit into fluorescent fixtures, are made and have a much longer life than the old-school bulbs. By synthesizing natural sunlight, UV or full-spectrum bulbs give your snake ample exposure to the rays of light that stimulate the development of vitamin D3 and the metabolism of calcium in your snake's body. Vitamin D3 and calcium metabolism are critical to adequate growth and muscular/skeletal development.

Some species of snakes need more exposure to UV radiation and some need less; while some hobbyists argue that no species of snake needs exposure to UV radiation, the lion's share of experts agree that those species known for their basking tendencies should receive more exposure to UV radiation than nocturnal or subterranean species.

As you might imagine, there are varying types of UV bulbs, some of which are stronger or more UV intensive than others. Some are sold as "desert" bulbs and emit higher levels of ultraviolet radiation, while some "rainforest" bulbs emit lower levels, which simulate sunlight being filtered through a forest canopy. Which type of UV bulb you use will be determined by your snake's needs. All types of UV bulb degrade over time. As they age and are used more and more, their UV-producing qualities go drastically downhill—old UV bulbs no longer produce any measureable amount of UV radiation. I recommend replacing your UV or full-spectrum bulbs every six months to get maximum UV production out of them.

Other types of bulbs are simply used for lighting your snake's terrarium so that you can observe its movements and it may observe its surroundings. If you have chosen a diurnal snake, you'll want to have the light on from sunrise to sunset. If, however, you have chosen to keep a nocturnal species, which is active by night, you'll want to get a "night-cycle" or "moon-glow" bulb. This is a low-wattage incandescent bulb made of blue-, red-, or purple-colored glass. When turned on, the bulb emits a soft, gentle light that truly does look like moonlight shining through the trees. With such mild, lunar-like light shining into its

The Montane Habitat

The rarest of all snake dwellings, the montane habitat is identical to the forest or jungle but is kept at a considerably cooler temperature. Montane-dwelling species are uncommon in the hobby but include the Mandarin rat snake, the Chinese garter snake, and the red bamboo rat snake. Construct a montane habitat by following all of the guidelines for a forest or jungle habitat, but cut back on both the temperature and the relative humidity level. Most montane species like temperatures in the upper 60s to low 70s F (20° to 22°C), with drier air of around 60 percent relative humidity. A basking spot, if employed, should not exceed the upper 70s F. Establishing such a basking spot is quite difficult, so most advanced hobbyists who deal with the montane species don't establish one. Lighting should be supplied by way of fluorescent bulbs (which produce minimal heat), and superior air ventilation is a must. I recommend keeping a montane habitat near an air-conditioning vent so that it can be maintained at an appropriately cool temperature. Because they can be more difficult to maintain than other habitats, I do not recommend that montane environments, nor their corresponding species, be the first choice of the beginning hobbyist. Get some serious experience under your belt with maintaining naturalistic terrariums/vivariums before tackling this complex, unique, and challenging habitat style.

Buy Used...Carefully!

You can save a whole lot of cash by buying used tanks and terrariums at a yard sale, but you could also wind up losing it all in the end if you are not careful. Sometimes these tanks were not used for fish—they were used for snakes. And sometimes the person selling that tank is doing so for a very special reason: The tank's former occupant died from an infection of cryptosporidiosis, which is a disease that can infect any species of snake. Once established in a snake, cryptosporidiosis, also known as "crypto" among hobbyists, has a 100 percent mortality rate. The worst part about it is that once it infects a snake, everything the snake came into contact with must be destroyed; there is no certain way to cleanse fixtures or terrariums of the disease. Oftentimes, rather than simply trashing an old terrarium, the hobbyist whose pets have died of crypto will attempt to get some money back by selling off the old tank. I've had several friends and colleagues whose pets contracted crypto after they bought a tank off the used market. The moral of the story is to always make sure of what you are buying before you expose your snake to a potentially life-threatening situation. Cryptosporidiosis is highly communicable and fatal, so what are you really saving if you purchase an infected terrarium? I only buy a used tank if it has been used exclusively for the housing of fish or rodents, neither of which can carry crypto.

habitat, your nocturnal snake should not be troubled or interrupted in its nightly movements, and you will have enough light to casually observe its activity.

Heating

The final key ingredient in the well-outfitted snake terrarium is one or more types of heating apparatuses. As exothermic animals, snakes rely on their environs for heat; thus, in the captive environment, we hobbyists must maintain a constant and appropriate temperature for our pets. Within my own snake endeavors, I use primarily two types of heating apparatuses: the undertank heating pad (or heat tape), which adheres to the underside of the terrarium and gently radiates its heat upward through the glass and into the tank, and the heating lamp, or spot lamp, which like earth's sun, radiates heat downward into the tank. Bear in mind, however, that you never want to make the terrarium too hot, and a heating lamp can quickly overheat a terrarium. Excessively hot temperatures can kill any species of snake in a matter of minutes. Always allow for a thermocline, or a temperature gradient, to exist within the terrarium. That way, a colder snake can slither over to the warm end of the tank, while a warmer snake can cool down by slithering back into the cooler reaches of a hideaway located at the other end of the tank. That being said, I always like to give my snakes a choice of temperature gradient in their hides. Thus, I have hides at both the warm and cool ends of the terrarium. I also have terrarium thermometers anchored on the walls at both ends of the tank so that I am continually aware of the temperature at both the warm and cool ends of the tank. The best thermometers are digital; adhesive-strip thermometers are not accurate. Round, stick-on-the-glass gauge thermometers work well.

Ceramic Heat Emitters

Similar to heat lamps are ceramic heat emitters. However, these devices emit heat but no light, so they make perfect heat sources for nighttime heating or in situations where you do not want any supplemental light. They produce a lot of heat for their size, so only use one in a ceramic light fixture rated for high-heat use. Although expensive, these items usually last for several years.

HEAT LAMPS

Many hobbyists use lightbulbs as heat sources for their snakes. This can be a great idea as long as the snake has a cooler place within its terrarium in which it can escape the heat when necessary. You must also ensure that the lightbulb does not melt the plastic upper lining of a glass terrarium, melt the wall of an acrylic cage, or break the wall of a glass tank. Aquarium glass that gets too hot will shatter! Thus, it is imperative that you suspend your spot lamp or basking bulb a good distance away from anything fragile, flammable, or "meltable." Most hobbyists keep their heating lights no less than 12 inches (30.5 cm) away from any material items.

It is also imperative that the reflector dome in which you use your heating lamp be rated for safe, long-term use with your tank's bulb. Many clamp lamps or dome lamps sold in hardware stores have a plastic or cork coupling that insulates the rubberized socket from the neck of the bulb. When a 100-watt spot lamp is left on for ten hours a day, it will not take long for that rubberized or cork insulation to melt or scorch, creating a fire hazard. Fortunately, your local pet shop should have specially rated dome lamps that have a thick ceramic layer of insulation between the rubber fittings and the bulb's neck. This ceramic layer is highly heat tolerant and will adequately function long after a regular clamp lamp or dome lamp has melted down or caught fire. Remember, prevent a short circuit or fire by always using lighting apparatuses that are rated to handle the wattage bulb you are using.

UNDERTANK HEATERS

Undertank heating pads are electrical resistors that heat up when they are plugged into the wall outlet. Made to adhere to the bottom of the outside of the terrarium, these pads stick to the glass and radiate gentle heat upward

Tank Security: A Two-Way Street

Sometimes we do not secure our snake terrariums so much to keep our scaly friends *in* as we do to keep some unwelcome intruders *out*. A curious (and perhaps hungry) house cat, a ham-fisted friend, a younger sibling or cousin, and a nosy roommate are just a few of the animals and people that should never be able to enter the terrarium without your permission, without your supervision, or ever at all. Securing your pet snake ensures that no one who is unauthorized can pester, injure, taunt, or steal your pet. Not only do some areas have laws requiring that certain species of snakes be kept under lock and key, but lawsuits can also be a problem. A roommate of mine in college once tried to sue me because he was nearly bitten by my timber rattlesnake (*Crotalus horridus*). Never mind the fact that I was not at home and he tried to take the snake out of the terrarium to impress some of his friends. Ensuring the safety of our pets is part of being a responsible, ethical pet owner—we owe it to our snakes to keep them safe. And a locking terrarium (and perhaps a locking herp room in which all of your terrariums are kept) is a great measure in keeping your snake safe from the jaws of other pets and out of the hands of children and fools.

through the glass and into the tank. This heat is easily muffled or weakened by thick substrate, however, so you should spread your substrate very thinly directly above the heating pad. This way, your snake can get the full warming benefits of the pad. To make things even better, these pads come in a wide variety of shapes and sizes to accommodate the unique needs of each terrarium habitat. Discreetly tucked away beneath the terrarium and supplying gentle, even warmth up to the terrarium's occupant, the undertank heating pad is a magnificent invention and has made the matter of heating your reptile easy indeed. Thousands of hobbyists swear by these pads and I do too. Take care when using an undertank heating pad that nothing heat sensitive (such as electronics or finely finished wood furniture) be kept adjacent to or directly beneath the pad.

More on Natural Terrariums

If you are interested in transforming your current tank into a natural or semi-natural terrarium with living plants, waterfalls, pools, rocky outcroppings, or anything else you can envision, then the book I wrote on the subject, *Natural Terrariums*, might be just the thing for you.

INTERIOR HEATING APPARATUSES

There is a third option of heating apparatus that I seldom use: the interior heating apparatus. In the old days, we used to call these items hot rocks because they were heating coils dipped in concrete or some other resin and then molded into the shape of a rock. You just had to plug the cord into the wall, and the heating coil inside the rock warmed up and the rock became an instant basking place for a reptile. Of course, these rocks were problematic too. Thin spots in the cement or resin allowed the coil inside to get too close to the reptile's skin, and external burns were common. Likewise, electrical problems could ensue; many lizards and snakes were shocked to death due to faulty wiring. Fortunately, the herp industry's standards are much higher now than they were 25 years ago, so in-tank heating apparatuses are much nicer and of a much higher quality. And they've been stylized in whole new ways too. Hot rocks, hot logs, hot caves, hot grottos, hot trees, etc., make supplying warmth to your reptile all the more aesthetically pleasing.

I just said that I seldom use these items with my pet snakes. I make this decision not out of a fear of the hot rock itself (although I have lost baby snakes to the old-style deathtraps; a snake would slither under the hot rock, couldn't or wouldn't slither out, overheated there, and died) but out of the escape route that is created when I leave an electrical cord running out of my snake's terrarium. The gap left by that cord is often wide enough for a pet snake to slither out and escape into the house. If you do choose to use such heating apparatuses (I find that they work much better with terrestrial lizards than with snakes), make sure that your snake cannot get trapped inside or beneath the heating apparatus. Place a heating rock on an angle, perhaps propped on another stone, so that your snake cannot, as mine did, burrow directly beneath the rock and get trapped there. Also, make sure that the gap left at the lid where the cord runs out to the wall is not so wide that the snake can escape. In addition, don't use a heat rock or similar device as the only heat source in the terrarium—your snake will stay coiled around it for warmth and possibly become burned. Lastly, to prevent the heating device from becoming too hot, attach it to a thermostat.

Humidity

Humidity refers to the amount of water vapor in the air. It is generally expressed as a percentage. If the humidity is 100 percent, the air is saturated with water, and that water is precipitating out. Obviously, the humidity varies with the habitat, time of day, wind, and other factors. A rainforest is going to be more humid than a savannah or desert. What is not so obvious is that even habitats that we think of as humid or dry will have microhabitats that may have significantly higher or lower humidity. For example, deserts have very low humidity, but there is water deep beneath the soil. Desert animals (including many desert-dwelling snakes) take advantage of this by creating burrows (or using those of other animals) where the humidity is higher—and the temperature lower—than it is in the desert overall.

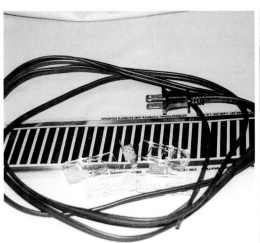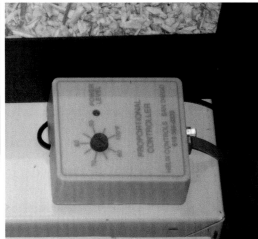

For most snakes, some type of undertank heating device will supply adequate warmth. One such device is heat tape (left). To prevent overheating and reduce the risk of fire, it is best to control the temperature of heat tape with a thermostat (right).

Going Underground

With the exception of fully arboreal snakes, virtually all snakes hide underground. Whether it is to escape the heat of day, hide from would-be predators, lay eggs, or simply to lie in the darkness and digest a large meal, almost all species of pet snakes require some type of cooler, more humid hide box into which they can retreat as needed. Construct a humid hideaway by situating a plastic, wooden, or clay/ceramic hide within the substrate of the terrarium. Most hobbyists find that a half-buried or nearly totally buried length of PVC pipe is an inexpensive and effective hide. Place the hide away from heat sources so that the temperature within is substantially cooler than the surrounding environs.

Finally, make sure that the relative humidity within this hide is higher than the rest of the terrarium. Placing a few damp paper towels in the hide may work (this is a good tactic for a smaller tank and with smaller colubrid species, such as the kingsnakes and rat snakes), while dripping some water into the substrate directly beneath the hide may also work well. You can also tuck some moistened sphagnum moss into the hide box to keep the humidity elevated. If you don't care about aesthetics, you can make a simple humidified hide box from an appropriately sized food storage container. In the lid or side of the container, cut a hole big enough for your snake to enter. (Smooth out any jagged edges.) Partially fill the container with damp paper towels, sphagnum moss, or coconut husk, leaving enough room for your snake to fit inside comfortably. Put the lid on it and place it in the cool end of the terrarium. Moisten it as needed.

The overall effect of this is to simulate as nearly as possible the natural conditions of the underground burrow. If your snake is fully arboreal, suspended hides (which can simulate humid knotholes or tree cavities) of similar construction can also work. Moistened hide boxes are excellent for species that require very high humidity (e.g., rainbow boas) and those that need high humidity but tend to get blisters when kept too moist (e.g., garter snakes).

Good Snakekeeping

Red-tailed green rat snake (*Gonyosoma oxycephala*) after being misted. Not only does this raise the humidity, but some arboreal snakes will lap up the water from their own scales.

Each species of snake is adapted to live in the humidity levels of its habitat. When you bring a snake into captivity, it's need for a given level of humidity doesn't change—a rainforest snake is not going to thrive in a bone-dry terrarium. You will need to make sure your snake's enclosure has the right level of humidity. For most species of snake, the exact level of humidity is not critical, but for others keeping tabs on the humidity is essential. Rainbow boas and emerald tree boas are two species that have exacting humidity requirements. For any species with specific humidity needs—either very high or very low humidity—purchase a good hygrometer, a device that measures relative humidity. Pet stores with good reptile departments should carry these and you can also find them online.

MAINTAINING HUMIDITY

There are various ways to maintain proper humidity within your snake's terrarium. For many species, just having a water bowl will provide enough humidity—the larger the bowl, the higher the humidity. For these snakes, you may want to raise the humidity when they are going into a shed cycle by lightly

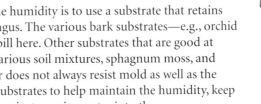

misting the enclosure. Use a plant mister reserved for this purpose and lightly spray the cage with lukewarm water once a day until your snake sheds. Species with high humidity requirements can be misted daily (or twice daily if necessary) to keep the humidity level high.

Another method for raising the humidity is to use a substrate that retains moisture but resists mold and fungus. The various bark substrates—e.g., orchid bark and cypress mulch—fit the bill here. Other substrates that are good at retaining moisture include coir, various soil mixtures, sphagnum moss, and recycled paper bedding. The latter does not always resist mold as well as the others. When using one of these substrates to help maintain the humidity, keep them from drying out by misting or just pouring water into the cage.

Snake Cage Maintenance Schedule

The following schedule will maintain healthy living conditions for you snake. A dirty cage is both inhumane and unhealthy, so keep up with these chores. These are general guidelines, and certain tasks may need to be done more or less frequently depending on the species you keep and other factors.

Every Day
- Check to see that the water bowl if clean; thoroughly clean and refill with fresh water as needed.
- Check the temperatures in the cage and adjust as needed.
- Check the humidity level in the cage and adjust as needed. If your snake has a humidified hide box, make sure it has not dried out.
- Check the substrate for feces or other soiling and clean it if necessary
- Remove any shed skin.

Every Week
- If using newspaper or paper towels as a substrate, replace them.
- Clean cage furnishings—branches, hide boxes, etc.
- Scrub and sanitize the water bowl.

Every Month
- Break down the cage completely and sanitize with a 10 percent bleach solution
- Discard old substrate and add new substrate to clean cage.

Hypomelanistic red-tailed boa

Chapter Three

SAFE HANDLING AND HYGIENE

"Do not despair, mighty Thór, Wielder of the Thunderbolt, for the beast with which you wrestled was Jörmungandr, the terrible World-Serpent, whose encircling coils can be moved neither by gods, nor by men."

~From the Icelandic *Edda*, 13th century A.D.

What is it that drives herp enthusiasts to buy a pet snake? For that matter, can we even consider a snake a pet in the truest sense of the word? The answer is absolutely! On some level, every snake hobbyist is attracted to the smooth, serpentine motions of his snake. Simply stated, snakes are attractive animals that just beg to be handled. Just as is true of dog and cat lovers, snake lovers deeply love their pets. While I tend toward the scientific end of snake husbandry, I do have one or two snakes around that are true pets. I take them out and let them slither all over the place. Handling is what makes a pet a pet, and it's what makes us as keepers so enthralled by our pets. But handling your pet snake is not all milk and honey—there are more than a few pitfalls in this paradise of human–snake interaction. Knowing and abiding by the rules of hygiene and sanitation, however, will help prevent any mishaps in your pet snake endeavors.

Some decade or so ago, an outbreak of salmonellosis (the illness caused by the *Salmonella* bacteria) made headlines across America, and it earned the pet reptile industry a lot of bad press. As the story goes, some careless pet shop owner had kept a number of baby green iguanas in a filthy terrarium environment, and when his customers and employees began getting sick with

Good Snakekeeping

To prevent injury and to keep your snake comfortable, support as much of its body as you can when handling it, as shown here with a red-sided garter snake.

the bacterial infection, a great medical mystery ensued. It was several weeks later before the source of the infection was found: a thick layer of iguana droppings left in the bottom of the terrarium was harboring the bacteria. The bacteria-rich poop became encrusted on the baby iguanas, and the keepers were getting sick after handling their new lizard pets or after getting scratched by their infected claws. The end result was a push among some lobbyists in Washington against the sale of green iguanas in America. Thankfully, the movement was abandoned when spokespeople for the herptile industry spread the word about general reptile sanitation: The salmonellosis was started by a careless and unethical shopkeeper, and the victims were made sick by their own poor attention to proper hygiene. The iguanas themselves were the hapless victims of multiple layers of human error. The outbreak was, thereafter, rightly attributed to human error and no longer wrongly attributed to some fundamental danger inherent in the reptiles themselves.

Every so often, the press picks up such stories and runs with them. Aquatic turtles are a favorite culprit of anti-reptile media, as are toads (anti-drug lobbyists like to demonize the secretions in the skin of some species of toads) and quite often the gigantic snakes, such as very large pythons (which escape or are released into the wilds of southern Florida and become a threat to indigenous species, domestic pets, and in some cases, humans). But the truth behind the matter is typically not what the sensationalist media would have you believe. Someone houses his pet reptile in a filthy terrarium (which is terribly cruel to the reptile) and then he or someone else handles the reptile and does not wash his hands afterward. The ensuing illness makes headlines, and parents everywhere panic and worry about the biohazard created by "that thing" living in their child's terrarium.

I mention all of this because handling your snake can be a lot like any other domestic duty. It's like cooking in the kitchen, bathing in the bathroom, or spreading fertilizer on the lawn—there are certain rules of hygiene and safety that must be followed to protect against injury and illness. You wouldn't go into the kitchen, crack an egg, mix it in a bowl, and then wait two days before scrambling it in the frying pan, would you? And certainly you wouldn't hop in the bathtub while your toaster oven is sitting on the edge of the tub, plugged in and toasting a slice of bread, would you? We know that all of these behaviors are extremely dangerous, and I list them here as examples simply because they sound so ridiculous that no one would ever think to do them. The same is true of handling your snake. There are certain rules that, once you learn them, will simply become second nature.

Hygiene and Your Health

Obviously, most people are concerned about their personal health and the health and well-being of their family. And while the headlines I mentioned earlier were sensationalized, they were loosely based on true events. Reptiles *can* harbor bacteria between their scales, and humans *can* get sick from these bacteria. But the ultimate responsibility of the matter always comes down to the actions taken and decisions made by the person both in terms of prevention and daily maintenance.

Separate Space

Many hobbyists place their snakes in separate spaces for various purposes, including feeding and handling. Placing a snake in a plastic tub, for example, for an hour or so and feeding it within the tub helps prevent it from associating its home terrarium cage with food. This may help prevent mild bites because many snakes fed inside their terrarium come to associate the opening of the tank's lid with feeding time and may bite their keeper in anticipation of a meal. Having a designated space for handling your snake is also a good idea, as some snakes become protective of their home and may feel threatened when petted or stroked inside their home terrarium. (Some species view this as an invasion of their territory.) For species like the sand boas, which may be aggressive or defensive against errant fingers probing through the sand of their home tank, it is especially important to remove the snake from the tank gently but quickly and move to an established handling area.

Cleaning your snake's cage regularly will help prevent illness in you and your pet.

KEEP THE CAGE CLEAN

Let's begin with the basics. Always house your snake in a clean, feces-free environment. This is simple to do. Keep the substrate clean. Unlike cats and dogs, which defecate often, snakes will defecate only once per feeding. One mouse in, one mouse out—just like clockwork. When your snake relieves itself, scoop out all visible feces (and the whitish or yellowish chalky substance, which is a semi-solid form of urine) and scoop out all of the substrate that was surrounding the poop, as it will certainly have soaked up some odor and fluids from the snake's wastes. If using paper or another type of substrate that doesn't allow for spot cleaning, you will have to replace the entire substrate and possibly clean the enclosure.

Scoop out these wastes as soon as you notice them. Waiting a day or two will only allow the bacterial or fungal colonies to begin growing on the poop and in the surrounding substrate, and that's where the trouble begins. Snakes that are allowed to slither through their own wastes can and will contract illnesses. Blister disease, for example, is a very real and painful skin infection that stems directly from exposure to wet filth in the home terrarium. And when you pick your snake up and take it out of its terrarium, you will be coming into direct contact with the bacteria and fungi that may have colonized the surface of its skin and scales.

CLEANING THE SNAKE

Under normal circumstances, snakes are very clean animals; it is only when they are forced to slither about in their own wastes that bacteria can colonize the interstitial skin between the scales. If your snake has slithered through its waste, change the substrate or bedding as described earlier, then bathe your snake in a tub of clean, lukewarm water. Allowing your snake to swim in the tub is highly advantageous: It may be induced to drink extra water upon entering the bath, it may release its bowels after being in the tub for a few minutes, it gets great exercise while swimming, and obviously, you can wash its body. If your snake is very small, I do not recommend washing it with any chemical substance. If, however, your snake is larger, you may want to bathe it with a washrag and some perfume-free, lye-free bar soap. Merely soap up the rag as if you were going into the tub yourself, and gently rub down the snake's body, paying particular attention to the belly and ventral surfaces, as these areas will almost certainly be the filthiest. I do not recommend lathering the snake's head or allowing its head to dip under the soapy water. Some experts recommend bathing filthy snakes with a 10-percent bleach solution, but I do not recommend this because even so dilute a solution can irritate a snake's eyes, nostrils, cloaca, and heat-sensitive facial pits. Always rinse your snake totally and thoroughly with clean, lukewarm water.

HYGIENIC HANDLING

All of the basic general health guidelines that accompany daily living can also be applied to handling your snake. In the same way that you don't crack open a half-dozen eggs, put them in a bowl on the counter, and then wait two days to scramble and eat them, you should never do certain things with your snake that are fundamentally unsanitary. Some common things to remember are as follows:

- Never rub your eyes during or immediately after handling your snake.
- Never kiss your snake or put any portion of its body inside your mouth. (Little children are prone to doing this, so always supervise.)
- Never eat or drink while handling your snake.

Wash your hands before and after each handling session to keep both you and your snake healthy.

- Never allow your snake to slither in areas where food is eaten or prepared.
- Never allow your snake to slither in areas that must remain hygienic (near infants, on kitchen countertops, etc.).
- Always wash your hands immediately after handling your snake.

Never get face to face with your snake. Although it is interesting to gaze so closely into the eyes of your reptilian companion, there is a twofold hazard that presents itself when you do this. Human beings have binocular vision; this means that both of our eyes are on the front of our head. Virtually all dominant land-going predators have binocular vision (wolves, bears, owls, cats, etc.), and as an evolutionary countermeasure to being eaten, most smaller animals have a fear binocular vision. Thus, a direct and up-close stare from an animal with huge eyes on the front of its head can be a scary thing for a smaller animal, as in the wild it would mean that a big predator sees it and it is seconds away from death! It is understandable, therefore, that when confronted with such massive eyes, a snake—even a seemingly tame specimen—might lash out in an attempt to defend itself. I once saw a man get bitten in the lip by an old, docile corn snake for just this reason. He put his face in his corn snake's face and the snake didn't like it. I said that this was a twofold hazard, and it is; it is hazardous to both you and your snake. While you might sustain a bloody bite, your snake could also be injured. If you are holding it and then drop it after it bites you, it could get hurt. Or if you suddenly pull away when the snake's teeth are in your skin or clothing, you could break its teeth out or injure its jaw. The teeth will grow back in a relatively short time, but the event is still needlessly painful and traumatic for your pet.

Chemical Alert!

The best general rule of thumb when it comes to cross contaminating your snake is this: If the chemical agent is unhealthy or unsafe to enter a human's mouth, eyes, nose, or bloodstream, it is all the more dangerous to a snake. Your snake's body is susceptible to all the same chemical agents as yours is, and owing to the fact that your snake is likely much smaller than you, it is far more sensitive to smaller amounts of those same chemicals. So wash your hands and make sure that you are chemical- and biohazard-free when handling your snake.

Hygiene and Your Snake's Health

Although it may sound strange at first, you are certainly not the only one at risk of infection or injury stemming from a handling session. Just as it is possible for you to catch something based on the cleanliness of your snake, your snake could also become ill based on any number of impurities in your own skin. Everyday items that you might

Children require adult supervision when handling snakes, no matter how docile the snake is.

never think about can cause some pretty serious health problems should your pet encounter them. Perfumes, dyes, lotions, cleaners, fuels, and other such household chemicals can pose potentially lethal risks to your snake's health should it come into direct contact with them. By following these safety tips, you can go a long way toward ensuring that no harm comes to your snake by way of any contaminants on you, your clothing, or your skin:

- Never douse yourself in perfume prior to handling your snake.
- Always wash your hands immediately prior to handling your snake.
- Don't wear lotion or cream on your hands prior to handling your snake.
- Avoid working in the yard or with wood immediately prior to handling your snake, as certain plant and wood oils and resins can be irritating to its sense of smell.
- Avoid handling your snake immediately after dealing with fertilizers and other agricultural chemicals.
- Never handle your snake after working with any petroleum-based chemicals (motor oils, grease, gasoline, etc.).

Good Snakekeeping

- Never handle one snake and then handle another in your collection without washing your hands. This may spread disease between specimens or highly stress the second snake by the scent of the first.
- Never handle a pet rodent, then handle your snake. (You'll likely get bitten because the snake will think that your fingers are food.)
- Don't handle your snake while you are sick with a cold, flu, or other contagion. There are few internal bacteria that can be transmitted from humans to reptiles, but there are some, and it's best not to risk the health and well-being of your pet.

If It's Furry, It's Food

I strongly recommend against wearing any manner of fur-based clothing while handling any mammal-eating species of snake. There was a news story some years ago about a man who was wearing rabbit-fur slippers around his house and went to sleep in them. He awoke an hour later to find that his 12-foot-long (3.7-m) pet python was swallowing his foot! The snake, which had free roam of the house (not a recommended practice), happened upon what it thought were two sleeping rabbits and began to devour the man's foot. The local fire and emergency officials got the snake off eventually, but not before it had chewed the man all the way up to his knee!

General Handling and Safety Tips

Aside from the ins and outs of the spread of illness or contamination by chemicals during handling, some other matters bear consideration. There are certain times during which you should never handle your snake. Likewise, there are certain ways and methods you should never employ when grasping or handling a pet snake. Third, not all snakes should be handled in the same fashion. A docile eastern kingsnake, for example, can safely be handled differently than can an overtly aggressive Texas rat snake. Similarly, a juvenile serpent must be handled with a considerably gentler touch than an old, strong, heavy-bodied adult snake. As is true of the cleanliness and sanitation issues discussed earlier, however, a little common sense is all that is necessary to understanding how to handle varying types of serpents. Here is a general list of handling tips (specifics follow later):

- When picking up your snake, always grasp it by the thickest portion of its body, lifting it carefully out of its tank.
- Support your snake's body carefully during handling; never let it dangle or hang by its neck, head, or tail.
- A handling session may consist mostly of your snake just slithering about. Most snakes do

not like to be petted or stroked in the same way that cats and dogs do.

- Never grasp a snake by its head or tail, and never attempt to pick up a snake thusly; this can injure, strain, or even break its neck or spine.
- Don't grab your snake suddenly or quickly. When opening the terrarium, place your hand inside, stroke your snake a couple of times to let it know you are there, and then gently pick it up. This is less stressful for even a tame snake and helps prevent sudden or frightened bites.

Another pointer to remember is that should you handle your snake high above a stone, tile, cement, or even hardwood floor, a fall from even a few feet (1 m) up could be traumatic to your snake. Broken bones, head injuries, and a host of other physical maladies—including death—can result from a bad fall onto a hard surface. When I was a kid, I dropped a common garter snake on the brick hearth of my living room. The fall was no more than about 4 feet (1.2 m), but the impact was enough to break its spine. After living paralyzed for a couple of days, the garter snake expired.

Prevent this scenario by establishing a standard of handling. Some hobbyists have a snake blanket that they spread out on the floor or bed. They sit atop this blanket with their pet snake and have a good, safe time. The snake

Your snake will be most comfortable if you restrain it as little as possible during handling sessions.

Good Snakekeeping

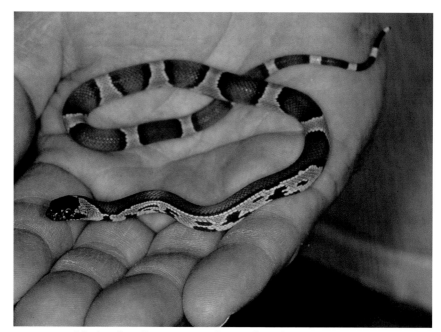

Be very careful when handling young snakes, such as this juvenile gray-banded kingsnake.

can slither about over the blanket (without fear of falling or contaminating sheets, quilts, or counter space), and if it wriggles loose from the keeper's grip, there's nowhere to fall. Everything that happens on the blanket is safe for all parties. And if the snake defecates (and many often do this—their bowels are stimulated by gentle handling and the exercise of slithering through your grasp) atop the blanket, a trip to the washer and dryer is all it takes to solve that problem.

Using a blanket is an excellent way to monitor young children when handling a snake as well. Not only does a brightly colored blanket serve as a safe backdrop, but it both illuminates the location of the snake (don't handle a black snake atop a black blanket—it'll disappear instantly) and helps train the child that there is always a certain time, place, manner, and procedure for safely and properly handling the family's pet serpent. This will help a child learn and appreciate the responsibility involved in preparing to handle the snake, handling it, and cleaning up after a handling session, and it will increase the importance that is placed on the snake within your household. A snake that needs prep work prior to and following a handling session is no knockabout pet; it is something to be respected and cared for. If young children (or teenagers or newcomers to the hobby or to animals in general) are involved in your pet snake endeavor, I highly recommend establishing a time, place, and methodology to your handling sessions.

SMALL AND YOUNG SNAKES

As is true of virtually every species of animal (including humans), the young members of that species are much more fragile than the adults and must be handled with great care. Young snakes are delicate in all ways, and their small, fragile bodies must be handled with this in mind. For starters, the skin and scales of a small snake are much more easily torn or injured, so a wriggling baby snake should never be gripped with the same strength that can be applied in holding an adult specimen. An injury of severely torn skin can prove so severe to a young snake that the animal must be euthanized. Second, the bones and spine of a small snake are fragile and easily broken. For this reason, small children, who may inadvertently squeeze too hard, should never be allowed to directly handle young snakes.

Because they can be so fragile, a young snake must be handled on different terms than adult specimens. Pick up a baby snake by placing one hand, palm up, in the terrarium. With the other, gently spur the baby snake into slithering into your open palm. Now gently but securely grasp the young snake and lift it out of the terrarium, supporting its body and head. During the rest of the handling session, it's best to simply allow the small serpent to slither through your fingers and open palms. This method allows the snake to have more control so that it is neither injured by an exceedingly firm grasp nor feels threatened. A young snake that feels frightened or threatened is much more likely to thrash or twist in your grip, thereby increasing the risk of injury. Some species (of the genus *Coluber* in particular) are prone to thrashing and injuring themselves in their keepers' hands. As discussed earlier, a fall onto a hard surface is also particularly dangerous to small or recently hatched snakes. When the handling session is over, gently return the hatchling back to its terrarium, being careful not to drop it too roughly back into its habitat. In the same way that human infants need tender, loving care, so do baby snakes.

Burn After Feeding (Calories, That Is)

Burning calories is an integral part of exercise, and exercise is important in most snake species in preventing or curing obesity. But how soon after feeding should you pull your snake out and begin handling it? In the same way that we should wait for a certain amount of time after eating before swimming, working too hard, or engaging in strenuous physical activities, snakes must also wait for some time after eating before engaging in physical exertion. Allow your snake at least 24 to 48 hours to begin digesting its meal before you take it out to handle it, let it swim, or give it general exercise. Wait 72 hours if the meal was large. Handling your snake too soon after it feeds can result in meal regurgitation, which is unhealthy for your snake and unpleasant for you.

If you must handle an aggressive snake, it is most important to control its head so that you don't get bitten.

Aggressive Individuals

As you might imagine, handling an aggressive snake is considerably more difficult than handling a docile animal. After all, a docile snake will simply enjoy the warmth of your hands and body, while an aggressive snake will violently try to defend itself against your touch. The difficulties of handling an aggressive or temperamental animal are twofold: You must ensure your own safety (after all, a bite from a reticulated python can be a bloody and painful experience), as well as the safety and well-being of the snake in question. Many species of snakes (particularly those of the genera *Coluber*, *Nerodia*, and *Drymarchon*) will also twist and thrash wildly in your grasp, even to such an extent that they inflict serious injury upon themselves; a very young specimen may rip its skin, while a stronger animal may break its ribs or spine.

For starters, there are two schools of thought on the matter. If you want to "tame" your snake, or get it used to human touch, you'll have to handle it regularly for quite some time before it will become accustomed to handling. On the other hand, some hobbyists believe it is unethical to "break" any animal's spirit or try to alter its behavior through handling. This is a personal choice.

Safe Handling and Hygiene

I have owned garden boas (*Corallus hortulanus*) that were so beautiful that I simply enjoyed them for their appearance, and I never even desired to handle them. However, I have owned Texas rat snakes that I never desired to handle for the simple reason that they were perpetually mean.

Before you even put yourself in a situation where an aggressive snake is involved, you'll have to ask yourself some hard questions: Do I want a pet snake that I'll never be able to handle? If I get a pet snake that is aggressive but can be made tame with lots of effort, am I willing to give my pet the time and effort it requires to become more docile? Am I considering purchasing a snake that could *really* hurt me every time it bites me (such as a large python, boa, rat snake, or bullsnake)? Is the snake I am considering purchasing an aggressive species that is not likely to ever become fully accustomed to human touch, such as a Texas rat snake or a species of *Coluber* or *Nerodia*?

Let's assume that you've responsibly answered the previous questions, and for whatever reason, you find yourself needing to pick up, hold, or transport an aggressive animal. If you are dealing with a large and powerful snake, such as any boa or python that is more than 6 or 7 feet long (about 2 m), you'll want to get help in handling it. When handling an aggressive snake, there are two things you must always maintain: head control and bodily support. Controlling the snake's head—grasping the animal behind the head firmly but not death-grip tightly—will prevent the snake from biting you, while supporting its body will prevent the animal from thrashing violently or placing all its weight on its neck. When you are holding the head in one stable position but the body is thrashing wildly, the neck is the fulcrum, and severely injured or broken vertebrae can easily result. Grasp the head in one hand, placing your index finger atop the head, your thumb on one side, and your remaining fingers on the other side—almost exactly the way you would grasp your computer's mouse. Support the body either by holding the coils firmly in your other hand, or in the case of a larger specimen, by gently but firmly squeezing its midsection under your arm and holding the remaining lower portions in your hand. As you can easily imagine, a considerably larger snake (again, greater than 7 feet [2 m] long) may require two or more handlers: one person using both hands to control the head and one or more people holding and supporting the weight of the body.

Hands Off!

Most snake species are sensitive around their head and tail. These areas are delicate and have a higher concentration of nerve endings than do other portions of the body. Any touch or stroke to this part of the body, therefore, will elicit a much more noticeable reaction from the snake. A snake that is grabbed by the head or tail will recoil, jerk quickly, and may even strike in self-defense. Always grasp a gentle snake by the mid portions of the body; allow its head and tail to remain free and unmolested. You may need to restrain the head of an aggressive or temperamental snake for safety purposes, however.

Good Snakekeeping

A snake hook is a useful tool for handling an aggressive snake, as shown here with a young Burmese python.

Obviously, it is best to avoid handling or transporting aggressive or high-strung snakes unnecessarily. If you must handle an aggressive individual, however, approach it slowly so as not to startle it needlessly. When you move for the head, do so quickly and confidently, but do not injure or strike the animal. Pin the head down with your hand, then grasp it as instructed earlier. Depending on the snake in question, you can more or less expect to be hissed at (bull and pine snakes), lashed with a tail (whipsnakes), pooped on (many species), sprayed with musk (rat snakes and kingsnakes), or a combination of all of these (water snakes). That's okay. Getting messy when handling an aggressive snake is simply par for the course. I've been bitten, musked on, and pooped on more times than I could ever count.

If you are handling the snake as part of a regular routine to tame it, what you do from here on in is basically up to you. Pet the animal, let it slither, let it swim in a tub of lukewarm water, etc.— whatever it takes to tame the snake is what you must do. Bear in mind, however, that relinquishing control of the snake's head will be necessary in taming it. A tame or gentle snake *must* feel comfortable and in control when being handled, or it will forever be aggressive or defensive. Let go of the head once in a while to see how your snake reacts. If it immediately turns on you and begins biting (as is often the case with garden boas), then it is not nearly tame and must be restrained; if it is merely jumpy or skittish and does not offer to bite, there is no longer any need to control the head.

I've seen many hobbyists who complain about their "aggressive" pet snakes. Then I see how they handle the snake: They are scared of it, they are rough with it, and they hold its head and neck in a death grip. I'd want to bite them too if I were that snake! Just as is true of dogs and some cats, half the taming process is change in the snake and half is change in the keeper—you must learn to read your snake's movements and understand the limits of its behaviors, and you must change your actions and behaviors accordingly. When it's time to let go of the snake's head, even though the animal may bite you, then it's simply time to let go, and you must be willing to do that if your snake is ever going to adapt to human touch. In time, a bitey snake will become a jumpy snake, and a jumpy snake will become a skittish snake, and a skittish snake will become a tame snake. Just give it time, patience, and lots of effort. You just might be surprised at how docile your formerly aggressive snake can become. Bear in mind also that younger and smaller snakes (owing to their fears of being eaten) tend to be much more skittish than older, larger adult snakes. Also, wild-caught specimens of almost all species are much more aggressive than captive-bred animals.

More Hands for Big Snakes

Never handle very large snakes by yourself. A good rule of thumb is to have two handlers for snakes over 7 feet (2.1 m) long, plus one more handler for each additional 7 feet (2.1 m) of length. So, a 15-foot (4.6 m) snake should not be handled by less than three people.

Venomous Species

Although venomous species are not covered in this book, it would be professionally negligent of me to not address the matter of handling them. Many hobbyists like to push the envelope of safety or display their bravado by handling or owning a venomous species of snake. I have this to say about handling a venomous species: *Don't do it! The risk you run to your health is much too great!* I have owned venomous snakes (or "hot" snakes as they are alternately known among hobbyists) in the past, and in October of 2002, I was bitten by a dusky pigmy rattlesnake (*Sistrurus miliarius barbouri*). My arm swelled to the point that the skin split, the flesh turned purple and green, I spent a week in the hospital (during which time it was feared I would lose the thumb on which the snake bit me), and it took another three months before my arm was totally back to normal. Now, seven years after the fact, my thumb aches constantly during the winter, and my doctors tell me the arthritis at the bite site will only worsen as I get older.

Good Snakekeeping

Depending on the virulence of the species in question, the risk of immediate death or long-term injury is simply too great when weighed against any benefits (being cool in front of your friends, the adrenaline rush you get from being so close to danger, or any spiritual sense of closeness to the animal) you feel you may glean from handling the venomous serpent. Certainly there is room for venomous reptiles in the pet trade, but it is a highly specialized niche that can only be occupied by the most advanced hobbyists and zoological professionals. And because I in no way wish to lighten the seriousness and graveness of dealing with hot snakes by addressing their needs in a cursory or tangential manner (after all, they are animals and their husbandry deserves in-depth discussion), the ins and outs of venomous handling and husbandry will not be discussed in this book. For our purposes here, I simply say this: Venomous species must only be kept and handled by professionals and highly experienced people, and I in no way endorse the keeping, handling, housing, etc., of any venomous species by a beginning, novice, careless, or unskilled hobbyist. Quite literally, handling a venomous snake is like taking your life in your hands. *Do not handle a venomous species!*

Transporting Your Snake

If and when you find it necessary to transport your snake long distances, an appropriate container will be necessary. Most field researchers and importers prefer using a pillowcase in conjunction with a hard-sided lockbox. Place the snake inside the pillowcase and knot the end tightly. Then place the pillowcase, as well as several other towels for added cushioning and stability, inside the lockbox. The softness of the towels and pillowcase will give the snake something against which to anchor its body while being carried, driven, etc., and the hard-sided lockbox will ensure that nothing heavy or sharp can fall against or injure the snake while in the pillowcase. Juvenile or very small snakes may be transported

That Bites!

What do you do if your snake bites you? The answer depends on the size of the snake and how badly you are bitten. In the overwhelming majority of cases, you will need simply to clean the wound, apply a little antibiotic ointment, and bandage it. Watch the area for signs of infection. Most bites do not require medical attention as long as they are kept clean and covered.

If you are bitten by a very large snake, the wounds are likely to be deep and bloody. You may need help getting the snake to let you go—never handle large snakes without assistance. Bites from these powerful serpents often require stitches and antibiotic/antiprotozoan treatment.

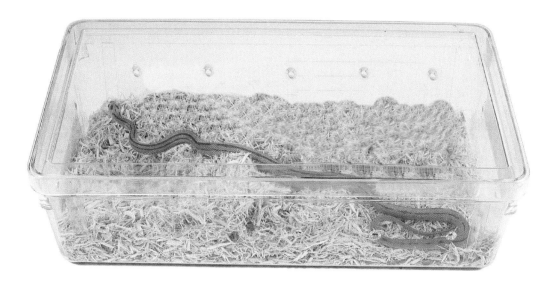

Plastic shoeboxes can serve as travel containers for small snakes.

in a deli cup or small plastic terrarium. (The kind sold along with hermit crabs at beach resorts work well.) Stuff several small cloths or paper towels in this container so that the small snake doesn't just slide around inside the box. Most experts suggest using a dark or opaque box, as blinding a snake to the lights and sights of the outside world does wonders to reduce the stress of transit.

In the end, we hobbyists handle our snakes because we enjoy them. We are mesmerized by their rhythmical, fluid movements. We are captivated by their legless grace and their lean, almost alien musculature. The ultimate goal of this physical relationship with our pets is pleasure. We receive aesthetic and physical joy from handling sessions with our snakes, and our snakes enjoy the even, gentle warmth emanating from our bodies. When joy and pleasure—for us and for our pets—do not issue from a handling session, then something is wrong. By making sure that we are careful and tender with our most delicate hatchlings, appropriate and smart with our adult specimens, and clean, sanitary, and safe in all that we do with our snakes, we can ensure that everyone involved benefits from a handling session.

Albino corn snake

Chapter Four

NUTRITION AND FEEDING

"Four snakes, gliding up and down a hollow for no purpose that I could see—not to eat, not for love, but only gliding."
~**Ralph Waldo Emerson,** *Journal* 1834

A snake's feeding and nutritional requirements can be simple. So simple, in fact, that they're a no-brainer. However, some snakes have very different nutritional needs than others, and some are considerably easier to feed and nourish in the captive environment than are others. Discussed throughout this chapter, therefore, are all of the ins and outs of feeding your pet snake.

General Nutrition Facts

All species of snakes are genetically and evolutionarily programmed to devour entire organisms. Unlike humans, cats, and dogs, which can thrive on eating bits and pieces of a whole host of organisms, snakes consume entire animals all at once: hair, teeth, bone, claw, muscle, organs, feathers, and scales. Depriving your snake of a whole meal, therefore, is a form of malnourishment and will not end well. I say this because many of my readers may have encountered the idea that it is okay to feed a snake pieces of larger animals: strips of catfish filet fed to large garter snakes, cubes of beef rubbed against a mouse and fed to large constrictors, and other such methods of feeding grocery store meats to snakes.

Although your snake may take these food items initially, a long-term dietary regimen of such fare will lead to the detriment of your pet. Such an imbalanced diet denies your snake the fats,

One thing all snakes have in common is feeding on whole animals. For most of the common snakes in the pet trade, this means rodents.

vitamins, calcium, and other minerals it gains from digesting the organs and bones of a whole-prey item. Bone disorders, accelerated or slowed growth rate, liver failure, and general malaise can quickly result from malnutrition. Many frugal herpers believe that he can save a few pennies by cutting corners at the dinner table with their snake. This is emphatically untrue; snakes draw their proteins, vitamins and minerals, fats, and all other necessary nutrients directly from whole-animal fare only. If you are uncomfortable with feeding whole organisms to your pet snake, then you need to look for some other type of pet. For millions of years, snakes have been thriving on whole-animal prey, and that is simply what they *must* have if they are to thrive under your care.

Vitamin and Mineral Supplements

For the common snakes that feed on rodents, vitamin and mineral supplements are usually unnecessary. However, sometimes it is necessary to supplement the whole animals you offer your snake with additional nutrients such as vitamins and minerals. Hatchling snakes, which need all of the nutrients they can get are one example; a female snake that you are planning to breed is another (she'll need plenty of extra calcium in her diet to produce eggs with thick, healthy shells); and an injured or sickly animal that is recovering in quarantine is a third example, as its immune system and other bodily systems may require additional nutrients to put it on the fast track to recovery. There are two basic ways to add vitamin supplements to your snake's diet.

METHODS

DUSTING

The first method is to dust pre-killed prey items. If you are feeding your snake frozen/thawed (hereafter referred to as "f/t") food items, you'll want to thaw them in a bowl of warm (not hot) water. Once the mouse is fully thawed, remove it from the water and dry it off with a paper towel. The mouse will still be damp. Sprinkle a light dusting of vitamin or mineral supplement along the mouse's back and hindquarters. Don't put any on the head—most snakes begin consuming their meals from the head, and because most vitamin supplements have a slightly bitter taste, a snake may not eat the mouse if its head and nose are dusted. But if the snake has already started consuming the mouse, it is not

Snakes often make yawning motions after feeding, probably to realign their flexible jaws.

Fishy Mice

I personally recommend feeding tropical fish flakes to mice prior to offering them to your snake. Fish flakes are protein rich and make a noticeable difference in the skin, scales, color, and overall health of a snake. Simply dust the meals that you feed your feeder items so that those additional vitamins and minerals are passed on to your snake.

likely to stop once it hits the vitamin-dusted hindquarters. After dusting down the back half of the f/t prey item, shake off any excess vitamin supplement and offer the fare to your snake. Liquid vitamin supplements may simply be measured out and injected into the f/t prey item prior to offering it to your snake, a method that tends to work better than dusting for fish and amphibian prey.

Gut Loading

A second type of vitamin and mineral supplementation is gut loading. Gut loading is the practice of feeding large amounts of highly nutritional foods to your snake's prey about 24 hours before offering that prey item to your snake. The logic is simple: The prey eats lots of vitamins and minerals, your snake eats the prey, and your snake consumes all those vitamins and minerals. This method, while more effective in my experience than dusting, is also more complex and takes up more space in your house, as you'll need to have room to feed and house the prey item for a day or so while it eats the supplemented food. You'll also have to make sure that the prey item consumes the highly nutritious or vitamin-laden foods.

Gut loading is an excellent way of ensuring that your snake is getting its proper nutrients as well. If there is any truth to the old saying "You are what you eat," then a diet of malnourished and protein-deficient mice will certainly lead to a malnourished and protein-deficient pet snake. I highly recommend gut loading any and all prey items you offer to your snake, especially feeder insects which are often deficient in calcium. Many hobbyists recommend employing both methods for optimum success: Gut load your snake's prey items and dust their pre-killed bodies prior to feeding. This will ensure that your snake gets the vitamins, minerals, and other nutrients it needs.

SUPPLEMENTATION SCHEDULE

Most hobbyists agree that you should establish a regular regimen of vitamin and mineral supplementation for your snakes (keeping in mind that your snake's vitamin and mineral needs may change based on its age and reproductive activity). Although hatchling and juvenile snakes should have every meal supplemented with calcium powder and every second meal supplemented with wide-spectrum vitamin powder, adult snakes should be given calcium and vitamin supplements less frequently. It is also important to know all that you can about your exact species of snake before you offer it any type of vitamin or mineral supplement because some species can have exacting requirements. Most kingsnakes and rat snakes, for example, thrive on wide-spectrum vitamin supplements, while insectivorous or piscivorous species may have more specialized requirements and need a varied supplement regimen. Consult your snakes veterinarian for a supplementation schedule that will work for your individual snake.

TYPES OF SUPPLEMENTS

What types of vitamin and mineral supplements are there, you ask? Good question. Powdered supplements come in a variety of concentrations and mixtures. Most of these are safe for general use, but others are not. Mixtures formulated for birds or mammals are not safe for reptilian use; never purchase these items, even if they are less expensive. Vitamin mixtures that are rich in vitamin A should not be used as often because vitamin A can build up in your snake's system and become toxic over time.

In a vitamin supplement, look for vitamin D3 mixed with plenty of calcium but not much phosphorous. Vitamin D3 allows the digestive tract to absorb calcium, and a calcium to phosphorous ratio should be at least 2:1 (preferably

Most baby snakes start out feeding on either pinkie (left) or fuzzy mice (right), although the young of some large pythons may be able to take larger fare.

95

Too Much of a Good Thing

When providing your snake vitamin and mineral supplements, precisely follow the manufacturer's or your veterinarian's instructions. It is very easy to oversupplement, causing the vitamins and minerals to build up to toxic levels in your snake's body.

3:1). Both calcium and vitamin D3 are essential to proper muscular and skeletal development.

Some manufacturers make liquid vitamin and mineral supplements, which are considerably more concentrated than dusts and can easily be given to overdose. Most liquid supplements are designed for veterinary application only. I do not recommend that a novice snake keeper utilize liquid vitamin supplements because giving a snake an overdose is all too easy. If you are buying a snake for the first time or if you are unskilled at measuring and administering nutritional supplements, leave the liquid vitamins alone.

Acquiring Food

As I said earlier, snakes are whole-food eaters, and getting these whole-food items can be a bit of a chore, especially if you are a newcomer to the hobby. Rodents may be purchased singly from neighborhood pet shops or in bulk from online retailers. Bulk mice are much cheaper than their single counterparts and give you the benefit of arriving conveniently at your door, shipped in a box of dry ice. Remove them at once from their packaging, and put them in the freezer immediately. Ordering in bulk can be a great thing if you live a long way from a town or your town does not have a local pet shop. Other prey items, such as feeder guppies, may be purchased in large numbers at a pet shop (and kept alive at home in a fish aquarium), or feeder minnows (chub, shad, or darters) may be purchased from local bait shops. Likewise, crickets and mealworms—prey for insectivorous species—may also be bought in bulk from local bait shops. Local bait shops can also be great sources for hard-to-find prey items, such as crayfish and salamanders (or "spring lizards," as they are known among bass fishermen and bait shop clientele), which can be extremely difficult to locate elsewhere.

This brings me to the next obvious point: Highly specialized fare can be considerably more difficult to obtain than common prey items. Eggs, birds, freshwater eels, locusts, and other such fare can be obtained through specialized online retailers or through the classifieds section in specialty reptile magazines. That being said, it's important to make sure that you have a reliable, long-term source of these specialized prey items *prior* to purchasing a snake, which thrives only on such hard-to-find items. Bear in mind also that the initial purchase price of the snake and its husbandry equipment (terrarium, substrates, hides, etc.) is but a fraction of the long-term cost of maintaining that snake. Your snake's long-term food cost, therefore, depending on how expensive those prey items are, as well as how frequently it must feed, can be exorbitant. Make sure that your feeding budget takes all of these fiscal commitments into account prior to obtaining the snake.

RODENT-EATING SPECIES

Easily composing the lion's share of snakes for sale in the pet trade today are rodent eaters. The rat snakes, kingsnakes, milk snakes and virtually all of the boids are primarily rodent-eating snakes and need rodents as a large part of their captive diet. Truth be told, these snakes compose the bulk of the pet shop species *because* they are rodent eaters: Sell snakes that eat mice, sell mice too! That governing economic philosophy is one reason why these species are so popular, but they are also hardy, stalwart animals, which greatly contributes to their popularity.

Rodent-eating snakes can thrive on a wide variety of rodents, and they should be offered a variety. Kingsnakes and rat snakes are seldom picky at the dinner table—mice, small rats, hamsters, and gerbils may all make up their diet, and most kingsnakes and rat snakes are not finicky about which of these

Most of the commonly available snakes kill their prey by constriction, as demonstrated by this Burmese python.

rodents turns up on the menu. Conversely, some other rodent-eating species are extremely finicky about the rodents they eat. The ball python is infamous for being picky about not only the exact species of rodent it consumes but also about its color. Many frustrated hobbyists have fed their ball python one white mouse after another for years, then fed it a black, tan, or gray mouse, only to find that the ball python thereafter refused to feed on a white mouse ever again. To make matters worse, the snake may now feed exclusively on the new colored mouse; thus, the hobbyist is now faced with the laborious task of seeking out only gray or black or tan mice on which to feed his overly finicky python. Although this scenario may sound outlandish, it has happened more times than you might imagine. Learn all that you can about your desired snake species to find out if it is similarly finicky. If so, find a color or species of rodent that your snake will eat, and do not deviate from that rodent type and color.

There are few specialized bird-feeding snakes in the pet trade, but most rodent eaters will eagerly consume birds if they are offered. Pictured is a wild gray rat snake feeding on a cardinal.

Larger rodent-eating snakes can be equally difficult to feed and may more appropriately be called mammal eaters. The boas and pythons (the so-called giant snakes) that grow to lengths of 10 feet (3 m) or more, such as the red-tail boa, the Burmese python, the reticulated python, and the African rock python, can present a whole new set of challenges at the dinner table. Where does one come up with a constant supply of rabbits? Many large snakes eat rabbits, so you'll need to supply them. Guinea pigs? Chickens? Same problem. Goats? It may sound far-fetched, but some of the biggest pythons need accordingly large fare, and small goats certainly fit the bill.

Fortunately, rabbits are farmed more frequently than you might think. Local breeders, online retailers, wholesalers, specialty shops, and ads in the back of herptile magazines can be great sources for some unorthodox menu items. Remember that the larger some of these prey items are, the more expensive they are likely to be. Keep all of this in mind when you are considering purchasing that oh-so-cute baby rock python; one day it will need enormous meals if it is to survive, and supplying those meals will be your responsibility. If there is a silver lining to this cloud, it's the fact that giant snakes feed much less frequently than do smaller snakes—a single goat or a half-dozen rabbits can feed a large python for months at a time, so the task and expense of these prey items may not be so daunting.

Of course, the opposite end of the spectrum also exists: Hatchling snakes and very small specimens also need to eat. As the pet snake industry has evolved, its food and husbandry items have evolved accordingly, and the widespread availability of tiny meals is no exception. Online retailers, local pet shops, and even nationwide chain pet shops have freezer sections in which you can purchase single or bulk frozen mice of all sizes. The smallest is the pinkie, a pink, hairless mouse that was frozen shortly after being born. If you need something a little bit bigger, you can get a fuzzy, which is a few days older than a pinkie. It takes its name from the slight layer of hair (i.e., fuzz) that has begun to grow on it. A little bigger still is the hopper, which still has its eyes closed in some cases but has hair and has begun to hop about in the nest. Next is the subadult, then the adult mouse. To further supply the hobbyist's need for size variety, rats also come in these graduated sizes, so if a pinkie mouse is too small, a pinkie rat may be just what the doctor ordered for feeding your hatchling snake—baby pythons often start on pinkie rats.

Going Native

The snake that may be most famous for being difficult to feed is the ball python. Many hobbyists have bought a ball python only to find out the hard way that these snakes can be finicky eaters. Many experts suggest feeding African soft-furred rats (*Praomys natalensis*) as a remedy to this culinary conundrum. The African soft-furred rat (also called the Natal rat) is one of the ball python's natural prey items in the wild, and most ball pythons readily accept it in captivity. Ball pythons that had consistently refused other prey items fed readily on the soft-furred rats. A moderately sized rodent, this rat is about twice the size of an adult mouse and makes a nice-sized meal for a ball python. African soft-furred rats are highly nutritious, and because they are not as aggressive or powerful as most rats often fed to larger ball pythons, they seldom present the same threat level to a snake as a large Norway rat can.

BIRD-EATING SPECIES

Some of the most problematic snakes to feed on a regular basis are the bird-eating species. Although few snakes in the hobby are specialist bird feeders, many species do feed on birds—sometimes heavily—in the wild. These include

Rough green snakes are the only common insectivorous species in the hobby. Feed them a varied diet of crickets, mealworms, silkworms, and other insects.

red-tailed green racers (*Gonyosoma oxycephala)* and several species of North American and Asian rat snakes. Although these animals can be fed a captive diet that is rich in rodent life, keep in mind that they are naturally evolved for dining on a varied fare of mammals *and* birds, and to deny them such prey is shortsighted and unnatural.

Fortunately, there are numerous sources for avian prey. Specialty shops, online retailers, and magazine ads can provide for your needs in the form of finches, chicks, quail, doves, and other species. Arriving individually frozen, these birds can be thawed and offered to your snake just like you would offer f/t mice. Local farms can also be great sources for a constant supply of baby chickens, turkeys, and ducklings (and adult fowl for hobbyists with larger pythons or boas). You might be surprised just how close a bird farm is to your home. Because chicks and small birds have not been alive long and because they will not have eaten many meals or developed much before your avian-eating snake consumes them, vitamin and mineral supplements are often necessary additions to these meals.

INSECTIVOROUS SPECIES

Insect-eating snakes are not common on the pet trade but are easily fed. Bait shops sell crickets by the tube, pet shops sell them individually or in bulk, and online retailers ship millions of the six-legged buggers annually around the country. Insectivorous species, like the rough and smooth green snakes, can be fed for their entire lives on pet shop or bait store crickets and a few other invertebrates. Other species, such as the garter snakes, can be fed wax worms, mealworms, and earthworms, all of which are available in both pet shops and bait stores. Many other insect species—silkworms, tropical roaches, tomato hornworms, and others—are available through pet stores and online sources. In most cases, bait store and pet shop crickets, which have been fed a poor diet of low-quality grains and chaff, will seldom provide your insectivorous snake with all of the nutrients it needs to thrive. Gut loading your crickets for 24 to 48 hours prior to offering them to your snake is highly recommended, as is dusting them with a vitamin and mineral supplement. In my experience, a high-quality fish flake is an excellent food for gut loading crickets prior to feeding them to your snake. Add a few slices of sweet potato, carrot, or oranges to give the crickets some moisture and extra nutrients.

PISCIVOROUS SPECIES

Feeding the piscivorous species—the fish eaters—is not difficult. As is true of the insect-eating snakes, the fish eaters can easily be satisfied through either a local

When feeding fish to your snake, feed whole fish rather than pieces of fillet (being fed to a northwestern garter snake here). Whole fish are much more nutritious.

Baird's rat snake consuming a swift. Many snakes feed on lizards in nature, and it can be difficult to switch them over to eating rodents.

pet shop or a local bait store. Feeder guppies, minnows (often sold as "tuffies" in pet stores), and shad are highly nutritious and inexpensive.

To save time and gasoline, many hobbyists will establish a small fish tank in their home, buy several dozen feeder fish at once, and feed and house them until the time comes to net some out and feed them to their snake. This also allows you to feed the fish a high-quality and nutritious flake food for several days or weeks prior to giving them to your snake. This is an excellent form of gut loading. The great thing (or the drawback, depending on your sensibilities) about fish eaters is that they almost always take their fare alive. Simply drop a couple of fish in your snake's water dish; it will smell and see the fish, dive headlong into the water dish, and come out with a struggling meal in its jaws! Change the water in the dish soon after feeding is over.

OPHIOPHAGUS (SNAKE-EATING) SPECIES

I have purposefully not discussed any species of true snake eaters in this book because most of them are venomous, and this book is not a venue for the discussion of venomous animals. But the fact remains that many species of snakes (some kingsnakes, for example) are snake eaters. Cobras and coral snakes are infamous ophiophages, as are a number of African colubrids and North and South American vipers within the genus *Agkistrodon*. If you ever find yourself housing an ophiophage during the course of your herpetological endeavors, you have your work cut out for you in supplying it with food. Specialty outfits that breed and sell water snakes (*Nerodia* ssp.) or common garter snakes (*Thamnophis* ssp.) supply such fare, but the meals do not come cheap. The feeder snakes themselves can be quite expensive, as is the freight for shipping them to your door. Do your homework before acquiring an ophiophage; make sure that you have both a constant and affordable source of serpentine prey for your snake before making a purchase.

OTHER COLD-BLOODED CUISINE

A number of snakes dine on other cold-blooded fare: nontoxic frogs, feeder lizards, and some types of salamanders find themselves on the menu of some types of snakes. If you have such an animal or you simply wish to supplement the diet of your snake and you know that in the wild it would accept such fare, then a local pet shop or bait store might be the best answer. Green tree frogs (genus *Hyla*) are inexpensive feeders, as are green and brown anoles (genus *Anolis*) and squirrel tree frogs (also genus *Hyla*). House geckos (genus *Hemidactylus*), when ordered frozen or in bulk, are another excellent and inexpensive source of reptilian fare for your pet snake. Although some types of prey can be offered live, I only offer cold-blooded fare to my snakes as frozen/thawed meals. This is because any internal parasites that feeder item may be carrying can, if fed alive to my snake, come to infect its internal systems. By freezing, storing, and then thawing such prey items, I've gone a long way in killing any internal parasites inside the prey item.

EGG-EATING SPECIES

Few snakes you might ever encounter on the pet trade are egg eaters. These snakes may be reared on chicken eggs from the grocery store (obviously only after they have warmed throughout to room temperature) or on quail eggs purchased from a farm or specialty retailer. Some of the egg eaters are so small that they require finch or parakeet eggs. Remember, the same farm that can supply chicks or small birds can usually supply fresh eggs too. It has been my experience that brown eggs are a better chicken egg choice for feeding to

Leave Them to the Experts

The snake species that have specialized diets are best left for expert keepers. These include egg-eating snakes (*Dasypeltis* spp.), snakes that feed primarily on salamanders (ring-necked snakes and others), and basically any snake that feeds on prey that is not likely to be found at your local pet or bait shop. Because there are so many beautiful and interesting snakes that feed on rodents, insects, and other easily found items, there's really no need for most keepers to acquire species that are difficult to feed.

Earthworms make an excellent food for garter snakes, such as this baby common garter snake.

snakes because they tend to have a much thinner shell than do white chicken eggs. Most snakes can more easily break (internally) and digest these thinner-shelled eggs. Don't be fooled, however, into thinking that eggs are exclusively reserved for only those few rare snakes that eat only eggs. Eggs are a great addition to the diet of rat, bull, pine, and gopher snakes too. Large kingsnakes are also known to accept the occasional chicken egg.

SNAKE SAUSAGES AND PROCESSED FOODS

Over the years, there have been many changes within the herp hobby, and the progress made in the nutritional "shelf foods" is one of them. What I call "shelf foods" here are the prey items that are manufactured, processed, and/or preserved for later consumption by reptiles. Canned crickets, bottled mealworms, freeze-dried fruit flies, and snake sausages are all different types of shelf foods. A snake sausage is a tube of food that is packaged much like the link or Italian sausages meant for human consumption, but they are packed with radically different ingredients. Early snake sausages were packed with chicken, beef, pork, and other by-products of the human agricultural industry and frequently led to obese snakes. (These sausages were loaded with fats and cholesterol.) Modern snake sausages, however, are typically made from ground-up mice, chicks, and other such nutritious fare. Snakes that feed on these sausages now are healthy and happy, and hobbyists who feed such fare to their snakes never have to smell the stink of living mice, never have to pre-kill a single rat, and never have to worry about whether the rat will chew on their pet python if they step out of the room for a minute to answer the phone. If you do choose to offer your snake some manner of manufactured fare, always look for the phrase "whole organism" on the package, as some makers of snake sausages still use strictly muscle meat or other agricultural by-products in their foods.

That being said, I also do not recommend feeding your snake—any species of snake—a diet that consists entirely of manufactured foods. Offering as much variety as your snake will accept is a great thing because some foods have more

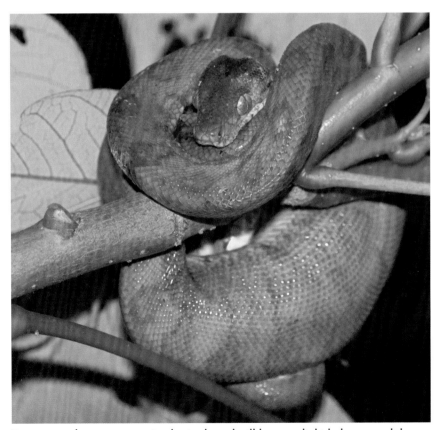

For most snakes, an appropriately sized meal will leave a slight bulge around the middle of the body, shown here on a wild garden boa.

The skin of a snake's neck stretches considerably to allow the animal to eat a large meal.

vitamins and minerals than others, and it is important that your snake get that variety. Many hobbyists report great success with using snake sausages as a supplemental fare—maybe offer such manufactured foods once a month in addition to other live or pre-killed whole organisms.

Although some other processed foods may technically be made of the same ingredients that some snakes will eat (canned crickets, for example, should appeal to insectivorous snakes), I have found that this is seldom the case. Aside from snake sausages, there are few processed foods that will appeal to snakes in the home terrarium. Whether they find them too hard to swallow because they are so dry or the lack of movement and life in the prey make them undesirable, most snakes simply turn their noses up at canned or otherwise preserved insect fare.

Size-Appropriate Meals

Now that you know a little more about the types of food that your potential pet snake may have to consume, let's talk about the size of those prey items. Ask a hundred different herp hobbyists how large or small a meal you should feed your snake, and you'll likely get a hundred different answers.

The best advice is to feed items that are not larger around than the average circumference of the snake's body halfway between its neck (the smallest circumference in question) and the midpoint of the body (the largest circumference point on the snake). A meal thusly sized will still stretch the neck of the snake somewhat in swallowing but will not sit so heavily on its belly that the snake cannot move well or is uncomfortable. Bear in mind that it is natural for snakes to swallow large prey items, and doing so—within limitations—will not harm them. But excessively large meals can become problematic. An extreme example of this problem appeared in newspapers nationwide and on the newsfeeds on the Internet some years ago. It seems that a wild Burmese python living in the Florida Everglades (yes, there is a breeding population of Burmese pythons living in the Florida Everglades and elsewhere in the United States) killed and consumed an American alligator. Although the snake seemed to be victorious at first, it was the gator that had the last laugh, as the photo showed the python lying dead in the glades, its sides split open and the alligator's body spilling out—the size of the meal literally burst the snake's gut and sides. Again, this is an extreme example, but overly large meals can inflict discomfort, pain, or even internal injury to your snake.

Remember that an excessively large meal to a snake is like a trick-or-treat bag to a little child on Halloween: The parent *must* limit how much candy the child eats, or the child will eat too much and get sick. The same is true of your snake—if it can wrap its jaws around a meal, it *will* swallow it, regardless of the internal damage the meal could inflict.

Of course, the converse of this rule is also true. Some meals can be too small for a snake. A very small mouse presented to a very large snake could be like a human adult eating a hot wing; it might take a lot of those little meals to satisfy the nutritional needs of that snake. And do you have all day to offer small mouse after small mouse to your adult boa constrictor? Every year, many hobbyists make the mistake of offering excessively small fare to their snake only to have the snake disregard the prey item altogether. If the mouse is too small to be regarded as food, the snake will ignore it. If you are feeding f/t mice purchased in bulk, you're also out the money you spent buying a bulk quantity of individually frozen rodents too small for your snake's attention or appetite.

Finally, size-appropriate meals are more efficient for your snake to consume metabolically. Prey that is too small affords your snake too little nutrients, while excessively large meals may rot in the stomach before they can fully digest, and the snake will have to regurgitate them and lose precious nutrients. Appropriately sized meals, therefore, are the best of both worlds: The snake gets full from the mouse or frog or lizard or chick and can digest it in good order, leaving it hungry and ready for more when the next feeding comes around.

Feeding Frequency

Another question most new hobbyists ask is "How often should I feed my snake?" Again, if you ask a hundred experts you will likely get a hundred different answers. As is true of the size of the meal you should offer, the frequency at which you should offer food depends on your snake's age, health status (in shed, obese, breeding, etc.), species, and, the temperature at which you house it.

AGE

Younger snakes grow fast, and they need to eat more often. I feed my juvenile rat snakes once every four days, then once every five days in rotation so that two meals occur every nine days. Some hobbyists feed their young more often, some less. I find that this rotating schedule works well, however. Once the snakes get

Scenting

Some snakes may refuse some types of food while eagerly accepting others. This can be problematic when the rejected food item is a rodent and the only accepted food item is a lizard or bird, which can be much harder to acquire on a regular (and inexpensive) basis. The task you are faced with, therefore, is weaning your pet snake away from the rarer food and toward the cheaper, more readily available fare. This can be done through a process known as scenting. Scenting is done by simply rubbing the desired prey item (e.g., the rodent) against the nondesired prey item (e.g., the bird, lizard, or whatever), transferring the scent of the prey the snake eats to the prey you want the snake to eat. Now offer the scented prey item to the snake. It should smell its favorite meal and attack its prey with gusto. Over time, the snake will come to identify the rodent as a food source, and the problem will be solved. Although a number of attempts may be necessary to successfully wean your snake onto the new food item, this tactic does, in the long term, meet with a high rate of success.

Because scenting is often necessary, many herp hobby manufacturers have created sprays and liquids that can be misted onto one prey item to make it smell like another so that you don't even need the desired prey item to scent the other. I've heard reports of these sprays working well for some hobbyists and not at all for others. Some of the most commonly kept snakes that often require that its prey be scented are Mexican kingsnakes (such as gray-banded and Ruthven's kingsnakes), milk snakes, rosy boas, and Baird's rat snake.

Adult boas and pythons need an appriopriately sized meal every week to two weeks.

a little older (about 12 months old), I feed once every five days. At 24 months, I feed once every six days. For the rest of that snake's normal adult life, it can expect a juicy mouse to show up every seventh day. If I were to keep feeding that snake every four days, it would become obese because it would no longer need so much food now that its metabolism and growth rate had slowed down. Although snakes continue to grow throughout their lives, adults grow much slower than juveniles and need less food.

HEALTH STATUS

The state of my snake is the second factor concerning how often it should eat. Is it well and hearty? If so, it should have a regular schedule, and that's that. But perhaps my snake is gravid (with eggs) or pregnant, in which case she's now eating for 12 or 20 or 101, and she needs to eat more for the developing young inside her. Some species of gravid or pregnant snakes will not eat at all during their actual pregnancy, so it will be important for you to feed them copious

Signs of Obesity

Recognizing an obese snake is not difficult if you know what warning signs to look for. Here's a short list to help you determine if your snake needs to lose some weight:

1. A rounded bodily form. Most snakes are lean, sleek, and relatively shaped like a loaf of bread: very flat ventral surface, slightly vertical and muscular sides, and a rounded back. When this general form changes into an overall roundish form, your snake is obese. The loss of the snake's visible neck or slender regions immediately behind the jaws may also be a key indicator of obesity.

2. Sluggishness. Although many species of snakes spend long periods inactively resting under shelter, all species will become active during certain times and under certain conditions. If you feel that your snake should be active but isn't (or its movements have changed drastically), obesity could be the culprit. A snake that lies about in the open when it used to seek the shelter of a nearby hide may be obese.

3. Space between the scales. In most species of snakes and in most areas of their bodies, the scales are close together and little of the skin in between them is visible. In an obese snake, the scales are spaced out and the skin between can be easily seen. The skin looks stretched and the snake appears overstuffed.

Note that a gravid female snake may exhibit many of these obese symptoms naturally.

amounts of food (basically as much as they can safely consume) prior to their mating cycle. The stores that the female builds up before breeding will be crucial in supplying her with all of the nutrients she needs to properly develop her brood and maintain her own health during her fast. Now let's consider a sickly or recently injured snake. If my snake has been in quarantine and is suffering from or recovering from some illness or other, it obviously needs to eat more to regain strength, regain lost body weight and mass, and boost its immune system. Plenty of food, water, warmth, and possible vitamin and mineral supplements are necessary for ailing snakes, so you can see how an accelerated feeding regimen can be in order for a recovering snake.

SPECIES

The next thing to consider is the species of the snake in question. Previously in this chapter, I laid out the feeding regimen I give my rat snakes. I can feed my snakes that often, in part, because rat snakes are active species that are frequently on the move, and as such, they have a relatively high metabolism. Some snakes, like the racers and coachwhips, have higher metabolic rates than do rat snakes and need to eat even more often. Others, however, have much slower metabolic rates and may comfortably go long periods between meals. Two classic examples of this are the ball python, which may go six months to a year between meals with no signs of discomfort or substantial weight loss, and the highly venomous gaboon viper (*Bitis gabonica gabonica*), which holds the world record for fasting: two and half years between meals with no weight loss or ill effects. Knowing everything you can about your chosen snake species is, yet again, critical to the feeding regimen and long-term health of your pet and the overall success of your serpentine endeavor.

For most of the commonly kept species, offer a meal once per week. Some of the large boas and pythons that eat really big meals (e.g., several rabbits or a small goat) need to feed only every two weeks or even less frequently. The diet of the species in question also plays a role. Snakes that eat insects or fish need to eat more frequently than those that eat rodents—about every three to four days.

TEMPERATURE

The final factor that will affect your snake's feeding regimen is the temperature at which it is housed. If your snake is kept cooler (as many colubrids are kept in the wintertime), it will need to eat less often, or in the winter, not at all. If, conversely, your snake is kept warmer and you frequently take it out of its terrarium and let it slither about for an hour or more at the time, then it will need to eat more often because its metabolic rate will certainly be accelerated under these conditions and it will burn precious calories faster. A good rule of thumb for feeding your snake is to establish a regimen and stick to it. If you notice your snake gaining weight or getting a little round looking (this will vary based on the species in question, but typically when a snake starts to look stuffed like a hotdog, it's eating too frequently), cut back on the feedings. If, however, your snake noses around the tank and seems antsy whenever you come near or open the tank lid, it is likely hungry and needs to be fed.

If you choose to feed live prey, watch to be sure that the food animal doesn't attack your pet.

Power Feeding

There is a practice among herp hobbyists known as power feeding. It is the practice of giving your young snake the absolute most food it can devour and digest during the first 18 to 24 months of life, when it is naturally in its fastest growth period. The logic behind this is to make your snake grow as large as it can possibly become. Power feeding is also used by unscrupulous breeders to make their stock attain breeding size in the shortest time possible. Although power feeding works to some extent, it is a heinous practice. The snake's muscle tissue and skeleton do grow very large and very rapidly, but there is a critical downside to this practice that most hobbyists who engage in power feeding do not take into consideration: The organs and brain of the snake do not grow at the same accelerated rate as the muscle tissue. Thus, the resulting snake is what is known as a "pinhead" snake—the body is enormous (length, girth, musculature, etc.), while the head and internal organs remain the appropriate size for a snake of that age. So the final product of power feeding is a sort of Frankenstein snake that is disproportionate and biologically out of synch with itself.

Power-fed or pinhead snakes seldom live even half as long as do their normal counterparts because their heart and organs cannot adequately supply blood

The Brown-Bag Method

Some hobbyists prefer to feed their snakes freshly pre-killed prey. They may do this out of concern about the freshness of frozen mice or because their snake won't take f/t prey. If you ever need or desire freshly killed, you can use the brown-bag method (which does not refer to your own lunch). To do this, place the mouse in a paper bag (plastic will work if you have nothing else) and twist the mouth of the bag shut. Find a corner of a wall, a bare stud in your attic or basement, or maybe even a counter or tabletop (not in the kitchen). Hold the bag containing the mouse firmly in hand, rear back, and whack the bag as hard as you can on the corner, stud, or counter. Your bag now contains one genuine pre-killed mouse. Although this may sound terrible, and while I may sound like an ogre for suggesting it, this method is instant and is probably the most pain-free and humane way to dispatch a rodent. Don't be squeamish, however, when you conduct a brown-bag pre-killing. If you hit the bag against the counter or stud weakly, you'll only hurt or injure the rodent, and then you've done the one thing you set out not to do. Hit hard, hit fast, and follow through. You definitely want to get it right the first time. Take note, however, that larger mice and certainly rats will have to be double bagged, as you don't want a freshly slain rodent to come flying out of a burst-open bag.

and oxygen to, nor filter poisons and other impurities out of, so much body mass. I once saw a 9-foot-long (2.7-m) Florida kingsnake at a reptile expo in Birmingham, Alabama. Its body was as thick as my forearm and longer than any kingsnake should ever grow to be. Its head, however, was no larger than that of a normal adult Florida kingsnake. Power feeding costs most snakes years off their life, and to knowingly make a freak of nature out of your snake, just for your pleasure in having an unusually large pet snake, is shortsighted, irresponsible, and totally unethical. As responsible pet owners, we should neither engage in power feeding nor knowingly purchase power-fed specimens.

Feeding Methods

So with type of prey, size of prey, and frequency of meals behind us, let's now tackle the matter of feeding methodology. How will you go about feeding the prey to your snake? You can feed live prey or you can feed pre-killed prey—either freshly killed or frozen and thawed. Note that in some areas, it is illegal to feed live vertebrates to other animals.

LIVE PREY

Live fare is natural. Constrictors have been wrapping their prey in their coils and squeezing the life out of it for eons now. Many hobbyists view feeding pre-killed prey as unnatural. If you do choose to feed live prey items to your snake, be aware of one thing: Prey fights back. Many snakes have lost eyes or received a bad cut from the razor-sharp teeth of a struggling rodent. As a responsible pet owner, you must ensure the safety and well-being of your pet, and many would argue that feeding live prey—and thereby placing your snake at undue risk to its health—is an irresponsible thing. Other hobbyists would argue that snakes are adapted to live prey, and hunting down their food gives them the opportunity to use their full range of behaviors and exercises their bodies and brains.

There is one critical matter that you must never do when feeding live: Never leave living rodent prey with your snake unattended. Rodents, especially rats, are omnivores, and if left to their own devices, can inflict deep, bloody, and potentially lethal bite wounds on your snake. Don't risk it! Make sure that your snake has subdued, killed, and begun to swallow its living prey items before you leave the room. Other prey items, such as small lizards or minnows, on the other hand, obviously pose no threat to your snake. See Chapter 5 for more information about the potential hazards of bite wounds inflicted by live prey.

PRE-KILLED PREY

The alternative to feeding live is feeding pre-killed fare. Usually this means f/t rodents, but you can also offer freshly killed animals. Buying a frozen mouse, thawing it for a couple of hours in a tub of warm water, and then drying it off

Scenting is used to convince a snake to feed on rodents when it only feeds on some other item. Here, a pinkie is being scented with a leopard frog.

and offering it to your snake is a humane and surefire way to feed. There is no risk of injury to the snake, and the mouse is spared a slow and dreadful death. Many hobbyists prefer to offer pre-killed fare for a host of reasons, these among them. Another reason is that many types of snakes actually become tamer and easier to handle when fed a diet of pre-killed fare; simply put, a diet of only pre-killed fare helps staunch its hunting instincts and predatory drive to kill its prey. It has long been known among reptile enthusiasts that a pet that still has to wrestle with and kill its prey is typically a less handle-friendly pet.

Feeding f/t prey items is also convenient for you, the hobbyist. If your spouse or parent will let you keep it in the freezer, a bag of frozen feeders means that feeding time is never more than a couple of hours away. Simply pop a mouse out of the bag, let it thaw throughout, and it's feeding time. Although I have and do practice both live and pre-killed feedings, I personally favor the lower cost and immeasurable convenience of feeding pre-killed, and my snakes are all the tamer for it, so there really is no reason not to feed pre-killed. However, some snakes— especially wild-caught individuals—will not accept pre-killed prey. This is rare, and how to deal with this situation is covered a little later in this chapter.

Reluctant Feeders

Sometimes a snake comes along that refuses to feed for one reason or another. It may be a hatchling that has not yet taken its first meal; it may be a sickly individual that needs prompt veterinary attention; or it may be a wild-caught specimen that is unwilling to feed in captivity. Whatever the reason, most hobbyists will run into a snake that refuses to feed. There are a few immediate measures to take to help cure this culinary crisis:

- Check the temperature. Snakes that are too cool will frequently refuse food.
- Check to ensure that you've established the proper environment type for the species in question. Establish and maintain proper humidity, habitat, and water supply for the snake in question.
- Eliminate all needless sources of stress for the snake. Cover the sides of the tank, turn down or off all loud televisions or radios, and leave the snake in a room by itself. Stressed-out snakes are infamous for refusing food.
- Make sure that your snake has several species-appropriate hide boxes.
- Separate all tank mates. Snakes housed communally may refuse food.

Scarlet kingsnakes may be difficult to feed in captivity. They often will only eat lizards and snakes.

Wild Prey: Not Worth the Risk!

Sometimes our wallets get a little thin, or the pet shop is closed, or some other reason will come along that plants an idea in our mind: I could just feed my snake something I catch out of the wild. Within my own pet snake endeavors, I've trapped mice (little field mice that get into the kitchen and garage), shot birds (with my BB gun as a kid), and caught lizards and other small fare from the woods around my childhood home for my pet snakes. Although you can save a little money in the short term,

the long-term risk to your snake's health is not worth the short-term gain. I have an example that you might find both interesting and convincing. I once owned a ball python named Hercules. Little Herky was doing just fine on a diet of white mice from my local pet shop until that fateful day when I heard a loud *snap* in the kitchen cabinet. Rushing into the kitchen, I whipped open the cabinet doors and found a small gray and tan field mouse still kicking in the metallic jaws of the snap trap. Figuring to save some money that day, I pried the trap open, removed the mouse, and tossed it in the terrarium with Hercules. He ate it with much gusto.

In the weeks that followed, however, he turned his nose up at store-bought mice. He had tasted a wild Georgia field mouse, and now that was all he would accept. To make a long story short, it took me nearly a year of braining his meals and even scenting them with a dead field mouse before I finally weaned him back onto store-bought rodents. What I saved in a little bit of money I more than spent again in time, effort, and heartache in setting little Herky's diet right-again.

The other big issue with wild food is the possibility of introducing parasites and other diseases to your snake. For both of these reasons, it's wise to not feed wild-caught prey.

- Separate all mating snakes. Prior to or in anticipation of copulation (e.g., a potential mate is housed in a nearby terrarium), many snakes will refuse to feed.
- Offer the correct food type; a piscivorous species may sooner starve to death than consume a mouse or a lizard.
- Offer food at the proper time of day or night. Many nocturnal specimens will utterly refuse food—no matter how hungry they are—if it is offered exclusively during daylight hours.
- Leave the pre-killed prey item in the terrarium overnight. Many snakes are nervous, and they may not eat with their handler standing over them.

Once you have performed these checks and made any needed corrections, your snake should start eating with gusto. If it doesn't, consider using the jiggle method. Get a pair of long feeding tongs (available through herp-supply websites) or kitchen tongs reserved for this purpose, and grip the rodent by the tail. Lower the dangling rodent into the terrarium and lightly, gently jiggle it in front of your snake. Make the dead rodent crawl along before the snake, bump the snake on the body or nose, and generally make the pre-killed rodent seem to be alive. Most hobbyists are surprised at just how often this trick helps induce fussy feeders into taking pre-killed prey items.

You can also try putting the pre-killed prey inside a hide box. This works quite often, especially if the opening is on the top of the hide. This simulates a rodent burrow, allowing your pet to perform natural foraging behaviors. Another option is to put the snake and the pre-killed prey inside a closed container. This can be a pillowcase, small critter cage, or plastic shoe box, depending on the size of your snake. Just be sure that the snake cannot escape and that there is enough ventilation so that it can breathe. Leave the snake and food alone for a few hours, and quite often the reluctant feeder will eat.

If none of these methods work, however, there is one more trick that I will recommend: braining. Braining is the fine art of splitting open the skull of the pre-killed prey item with a knife (an old steak knife with a serrated edge works well), scooping out a tiny amount of brains, and smearing this material all over the head of the prey. Yes, this is a macabre practice, but many starving snakes have found their first meal in weeks through this trick. Why does braining work? The smell of blood and brains has some near-magical property that awakens a snake's hunger and predatory instinct like nothing else. Just like all the legions of shambling dead in those 1970s zombie-apocalypse films, the smell of brains just drives snakes crazy!

FORCE-FEEDING

The best advice with regard to when to force-feed a snake is don't. The average herp hobbyist should not force-feed his snake. In most cases, it is too risky and not necessary. Over the years of working in pet shops and veterinary clinics,

Good Snakekeeping

Blood Pythons and other inactive species are prone to become obese when kept as pets.

counseling my friends and readers, and generally being involved with the pet snake industry, I have seen so many snakes suffer and even die unnecessarily because their keeper knew too little about reptile husbandry and viewed force-feeding as an easily understood and easily conducted method of getting food in a snake's belly. All too often, the end result was a severely injured or dead snake. I've seen hobbyists pack a rodent down into a snake's lung rather than into its stomach. I've seen snakes with a cut or ruptured esophagus from where the rodent's exposed teeth were accidentally pushed through its throat. And what good does it avail your snake to force a rodent down its throat only to be vomited back up soon thereafter? I've seen hobbyists whose snakes don't even need to feed, yet they start cramming meals down their gullets just because they feel that the time is right and the snakes need to feed (for example, after not having eaten in a week or two). In actuality, a snake's refusal to feed may, in fact, be a symptom of a more grievous problem that demands remedy: illness, inappropriate conditions, being full of eggs, etc. By force-feeding, the hobbyist is missing clues that something is wrong with the snake that needs to be addressed.

In short, I have never known force-feeding to go well when conducted by individual hobbyists. Veterinarians and other herpetological professionals know how to induce feeding or force-feed an animal that is otherwise starving to death.

Normally, they will use pinkie pumps, syringes that liquefy pinkie mice into a highly nutritious goo. These can be fitted with narrow tubes that are carefully and gently inserted down the snake's esophagus, and the liquefied mouse can be slowly pumped into the stomach. If your snake is starving, emaciated looking (a very concave stomach or ventral surface is a surefire sign of advanced starvation), or otherwise seems in dire need of food but will not willingly eat, it is time to take your snake to a qualified veterinarian. When it comes to force-feeding, don't go it alone.

That being said, there is one tactic that may be classified as force-feeding but most careful hobbyists could perform. If a snake is reluctant to feed, try braining a small prey item, gently prying the snake's mouth open, and inserting the brained prey item's head in the snake's mouth. This is usually called assist feeding. As the scent and flavor of the blood and brains oozing out of the prey item's head flood the snake's mouth, it may well decide "Hey, this thing tastes good!" And it may just begin feeding on its own. This trick works surprisingly often and is especially useful with hatchling or juvenile snakes. Just make sure that you never force the prey any deeper into the snake's mouth than merely anchoring it in the teeth. Bear in mind also that no type of force-feeding is appropriate in the case of recently hatched snakes; no species of newborn or newly hatched snake needs to feed until after it sheds its skin for at least the first time.

Obesity

Reptile obesity is, for all intents and purposes, exactly like human obesity. It has all of the same causes, all of the same symptoms, and all of the same cures. Obesity occurs in snakes that are fed nonwhole-organism meals (beefsteak cut into strips, stew meat, chicken pieces, etc.) and snakes that are generally fed too much and exercised too little. Signs of obesity include lack of muscular definition (again, this may vary considerably based on the species in question; a rigid, muscular Amazon boa will have differently defined musculature than will a short, thick-bodied blood python), lethargy, and a general chunky appearance. The long-term ill effects of obesity may include death.

Cure obesity by way of a twofold approach: Alter your snake's diet (i.e., cut back on the frequency of feedings, offer whole-organism meals only), and increase the amount of exercise it receives. Take the snake out and play with it more often. Let it slither about your arms, your hands, and whatever surface you have prepared. Raise the temperature in the terrarium by a degree or two (which will increase metabolism and help burn those stored-up fat calories more quickly). Remember, unchecked obesity can drastically shorten your snake's life. Obesity doesn't have to be a major problem, however, and by monitoring what you feed your snake and actively engaging with it on a regular basis, obesity can be a thing of the past.

Gray-banded kingsnake

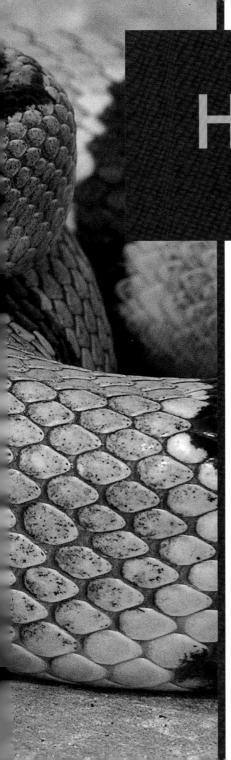

Chapter Five

HEALTH CARE

"And the Lord said unto Moses, 'Craft thee a venomous serpent out of bronze, and set it upon a staff, and it shall come to pass that whosoever is bitten, when he looks upon this snake, shall live.' And Moses fashioned a serpent out of bronze, and he set it atop a staff, and it came to pass that if a serpent bit any man, that man, when he beheld the serpent of brass, was made well and lived."

~**Numbers 21:8–9**

The knowledge of how to prevent and treat the illnesses, wounds, and general maladies that might one day afflict your pet snake is critical, and it is best if all hobbyists understand the basics of disease prevention and treatment prior to buying their pet snake. In nearly three decades of snake keeping and breeding, I've lost my share of pet snakes, and it is through my own failings that I can better direct you away from the pitfalls and common mistakes that frequently plague the newcomer to the hobby. So without any further ado, let's be about the business of treating wounds and preventing any dread disease from ever afflicting our beloved serpentine friends.

An Ounce of Prevention

As is true with the health and well-being of ourselves and any other pets we may own, an ounce of prevention is worth a pound of cure in the case of pet snakes. Prevent disease from taking hold by maintaining clean living conditions and an appropriate

Good Snakekeeping

Maintaining your snake in the appropriate captive environment and keeping it clean will prevent many health problems. A diamond carpet python in its hide is shown here.

environment for your snake. Most diseases that could ever threaten your snake will stem from unsanitary or inappropriate living conditions: inadequately low temperatures, filthy substrate, excessive moisture, or feces and other organic debris left lying about the tank. Simply by maintaining high standards of hygiene within the confines of the terrarium, you can prevent a large number of diseases.

By nature, snakes are hardy animals (which is partly the reason that they make such great pets), and they have durable constitutions. When disease does strike, a snake seldom shows any signs of injury or ailment until it is too late. The result is that an ailing snake may appear healthy, and the novice or unobservant hobbyist may not notice that anything is wrong until the snake takes a sudden (and to the hobbyist, baffling) turn for the worse and expires soon thereafter. Also, medication and physical treatment of snakes can be difficult and expensive, depending on what type of snake you are treating, what disease you are dealing with, how large the specimen is, how advanced the ailment is, etc. Prevention, therefore, is the hobbyist's best bet. Change bedding or substrate regularly, spot clean or scoop out all visible wastes, change the drinking water daily, and always keep the terrarium within acceptable temperature and humidity levels. Likewise, at the first sign of illness, perform additional habitat checks, as an ailing snake will quickly degenerate in health if its housing is unsanitary or excessively cold or damp.

Quarantine

In *The Lizard Keeper's Handbook*, herpetological expert Philippe de Vosjoli says of the quarantining process: "Many people ignore the quarantining of [new] animals and later deeply regret this when most of their collection becomes ill and/or is wiped out. Please heed the advice [of quarantining]." I agree with Mr. de Vosjoli's sentiment here, and I second his advice: The act of quarantining new arrivals is frequently overlooked or ignored by hobbyists, and many come to sorely regret that decision in later months. The matter of quarantining, however, is not as critical if you are only purchasing a single snake specimen and do not have any other reptile pets at home. Bringing one diseased snake into your home will have no more ramifications beyond that specimen's demise. Most hobbyists, however, quickly find themselves falling so in love with their serpentine companion that they begin exploring other species and bringing home new specimens. Before they know it, they've amassed a collection of numerous snakes. When this is the case, as it often is, quarantining all new arrivals is critical to the long-term health of all of your animals.

Establish a quarantine terrarium, and if at all possible place it in a room in your home well away from any other reptile or amphibian pets you already own. Have a set of tools (gloves, lids, terrarium fixtures, heating apparatuses, etc.) that is strictly unique to the quarantine tank; i.e., these are husbandry items that will never come into contact with any specimens in the rest of your collection. Cross contamination or the spread of disease can be curbed by ensuring that no physical tools or husbandry items come into contact with both infected and uninfected specimens.

Likewise, always make sure that you yourself never function as the agent of cross contamination.

Your Snake's Night Watchman

Although you can vary a great many aspects of the quarantine terrarium to accommodate the exact species of snake you'll be housing, remember that one major goal of quarantine is to closely observe your newly acquired animal for any signs of illness or injury. Depending on the species in question, nocturnal observation may also be necessary. So while a diurnal snake can be observed living its life by daylight, you may require special aids to monitor your snake's movements at night. Night-cycle lightbulbs (incandescent with colored glass and low wattage filaments), which come in red, blue, or purple, can illuminate your quarantine tank enough to allow you to witness and observe the movements of a nocturnal species but not so much as to disrupt or disturb its natural rhythms.

123

Good Snakekeeping

Many hobbyists believe that it is sufficient to simply wash their hands with disinfectant soap between handling or caring for quarantined specimens and then handling or caring for specimens already in the collection population. This is a false belief that has led to many an episode of cross contamination. At least three hand washings with disinfectant soap and 24 hours should occur between handling quarantined specimens and population specimens. If you must use a husbandry tool in common between quarantine and population terrariums, either boil the tool first (in the case of metal implements) or scrub it with a sterilizing iodine solution.

Most experts agree that the quarantine period should last for 30 to 60 days, while others recommend quarantining for as long as 90 days. During this period, monitor for mites and ticks, odd movements (indicative of internal injuries), and any changes in appearance or behavior. Also, have your snake's stool inspected for evidence of internal parasites. Bloody stool is a key sign that something is seriously amiss. Many experts like to keep weight records of their specimens during the quarantine period as well. A good digital scale, which measures in grams as well as ounces and pounds, can help you keep track of your snake's weight. An adult snake should maintain its weight, with some small daily or weekly fluctuations, while a juvenile should steadily increase in weight. A snake that drops its weight is not eating enough. If you are feeding it as you should and the specimen still loses weight, something is wrong. Some of the most serious ailments to strike snakes, such as cryptosporidiosis, are accompanied by inexplicable weight loss. Curable internal parasites, such as worms or flukes, will cause a snake to lose weight despite the fact that you've been feeding it on a regular basis. In any case, regular readings of the digital scale will help you stay on top of things and monitor the weight status of your snake. A final variable that enters the quarantine equation is the matter of veterinary care. Should your snake show signs of an ailment, you will be faced with the decision of whether or not to take it to a herpetological veterinarian.

It Can't Be too Clean

The items you place in the quarantine terrarium must be clean and sterilized first. Depending on the item, you may need to soak it in a bleach solution, bake it in the oven, or boil it. Everything that enters your quarantine enclosure must be as germ-free as possible— including your hands.

BASIC SETUP

As for the quarantine tank itself, establish an environment that is at once hygienic and that has all of the necessary physical components and environmental parameters to support the snake you are housing. For example, a quarantine tank

Gray-banded kingsnakes in quarantine. The paper towel substrate makes it easy to see mites or abnormal droppings.

for a new corn snake is a simple construction. It should have a substrate of white paper towels, a white water dish, a hide, a heating apparatus (appropriate to the conditions of the tank; i.e., undertank heating pad or ceramic heat emitter suspended a safe distance above the tank), and a screen lid. Very simple, very spartan. The purpose of the whiteness of the substrate and water dish is to make external parasites easily visible. Mites are frequent invaders that tag along hidden between the scales of newly acquired snakes, and newsprint or chipped-bark substrates will conceal the presence of these bloodsucking parasites. However, they will show up clearly on white paper towels and a white water dish. By simply looking closely at the paper towel under a bright light, you should be able to spot a mite infestation. The same is true of the white water dish—any drowned mites (reddish or gray-black in color) should be highly visible against the white basin of the water dish. White paper toweling will also be similarly helpful when and if you have to inspect your new snake's stool for worms or blood. In addition, some young snake specimens can be sensitive to the dyes or perfumes used in some scented paper towels, and the white, unscented variety removes this chemical variable from the equation.

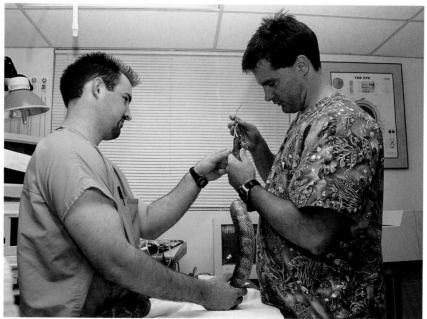

Establishing a relationship with a herp-specific veterinarian before an emergency occurs is a good idea.

VARIATIONS

While a corn snake (and most colubrids) can be housed simply and easily, other species may take a modified environment. Desert animals may require a drier quarantine tank, while jungle and swamp species, like the rainbow boa, will take a much moister habitat. This will require the addition of a modified hide box with a slightly damp layer of paper towels inside. Relative humidity may be raised by covering a portion of the terrarium's lid with cellophane, thereby trapping water vapor inside the tank.

Another modification you may need to consider is the matter of the climbing branch. Adding a branch for arboreal species will go a long way in helping that species live a happy, normal life despite it being in quarantine. Although a simple stick securely erected in one corner of the tank will suffice for many species (rough green snakes, the arboreal rat snakes, etc.), a more securely anchored perch may be in order for more devoutly arboreal snakes. A wooden dowel of appropriate thickness can be anchored with hot glue in the upper reaches of a tank to accommodate the needs of an emerald tree boa, a green tree python, a garden boa, or any other such staunchly arboreal snake. In a large quarantine tank, multiple such perches may be erected.

Likewise, some snake species will require high densities of vegetative cover; the aforementioned arboreal snakes, as well as a host of terrestrial colubrids, need the mental comfort that comes with being able to fully conceal themselves in naturalistic vegetative cover. Notice I say "naturalistic" and not "natural" vegetative cover because there is little room in the quarantine tank for living plants. Live plants (and their accompanying soil) can introduce a host of unforeseen variables into the otherwise sterile and controlled environmental conditions of the quarantine terrarium. Fungi, bacteria, and external parasites can all accompany living plants and their substrate and enter your snake's domain as unwanted hitchhikers. Although such components seldom present any real problem, it is counterproductive to the quarantine period to take any chances. I recommend, therefore, that any clumps of vegetative cover comprise strictly artificial plants: silk, plastic, acrylic, nylon, and other synthetic plants will work fine for this purpose. Avoid piling the vegetative cover too densely, as this will inhibit your ability to observe your specimen.

The Herpetological Veterinarian

This subject is a sticky one for me and for a lot of other hobbyists because humane treatment of our snakes comes into direct contrast with the matter of fiscal sensibility. Put simply, many hobbyists are not willing to invest the kind of money that a veterinarian's bill demands for an inexpensive snake. Although no one can be expected to bankrupt themselves to save a pet snake's life, I believe that if finances allow, the hobbyist should be responsible and ethical enough to provide for his pet's medical needs. Failing that, at the very least have the snake professionally and humanely euthanized rather than allowing it to suffer a prolonged and painful decline.

FINDING A HERP VETERINARIAN

Despite the tough decisions often associated with veterinary care, there are two points of good news when it comes to the people who practice herpetological medicine: Both the number of herp-savvy vets and the ability to locate them have skyrocketed. Until the early 1990s, a vet who treated snakes was virtually unheard of; vets treated cats, dogs, and horses and little else. But since the herpetological hobby has blossomed into a multibillion-dollar international industry, the allied trades have evolved as well. As a result, virtually every major city throughout the United States has at least one veterinary practice that deals with snakes, lizards, and turtles.

Vets Online

One way to locate a reptile veterinarian is to consult the website of the Association of Reptile and Amphibian Veterinarians (ARAV). You can find a directory of their members at www.arav.org.

With the advent of the Internet, the average hobbyist's accessibility to these "snake doctors" has also spiked. Simply type your city and needs in a search engine, and you'll be that much closer to finding the veterinarian you are searching for. Another way to find veterinarians specializing in herps is to contact local pet stores, zoos, and herpetological societies and find out who these organizations recommend.

DON'T WAIT

You and your snake will be better off if you locate and contact a herp-specific veterinarian *before* you have need of his services. Find a vet in your area who deals with herps, and contact him to make sure of the *exact* animals he is willing to treat. Many herp-specific vets may advertise that they treat snakes but may have a safety policy barring them from treating venomous species. Likewise, a vet may take out an ad in the telephone book proclaiming that he deals with reptiles, but the word "reptiles" may, in fact, be limited to a few boas, pythons, and other large or commonly kept species. It's always wise to make sure that a potential vet can—and is willing to—treat the species you will be keeping. Also, note the office hours and the procedure for after-hours emergencies. By identifying a herpetological vet early, you can have a game plan for when your beloved scaly friend is in need. Just as is true of human emergencies, every second counts when your pet's life is on the line.

PRELIMINARY CHECKUP

One of the best uses of veterinary care for your herp is the preliminary checkup. By taking your new snake to the vet for an initial examination, you can identify and begin treating any ailments that it may have immediately, rather than waiting and watching for symptoms during the quarantine period. Blood scans, stool sample evaluations, and a host of other inspections can go a long way in ensuring that your snake is in topnotch health from day one.

The Hospital Tank

A hospital tank is basically a quarantine tank that allows you to remove a sick snake from the rest of your collection. A hospital tank and quarantine tank are, for all intents and purposes, interchangeable. A hospital tank is a sparsely yet adequately furnished terrarium hospitable to the recovery of an ailing snake. It is a warm place, warmer by a couple degrees than the home terrarium because ailing snakes in the wild will bask in the sun to combat ailments. Because they are exothermic—drawing most of their bodily heat from their environment— snakes will seek out warmer temperatures to stimulate their immune systems and fight off infections. Basking in warmer temperatures is the equivalent of a snake running a fever.

Newspaper is a good substrate for the hospital tank because it is sterile and easy to clean.

A hospital tank should also be comfortable for your pet and should be a largely stress-free environment. This means that the room in which the hospital tank is kept should be free from excessive human traffic. It should be free of loud, low-pitched sounds, which will reverberate through the snake and cause it considerable stress. And the hospital tank should be a place of observation for you; as the snake's primary caregiver, you must be able to monitor its actions, movements, symptoms, and overall condition if it is to make a successful recovery under your care. I find that a warm tank (appropriate for the species) outfitted with two hide boxes (one situated directly over a heating pad and one situated elsewhere to accommodate the snake's need for a thermal gradient), a triple layer of white paper towel substrate, and a water dish is totally adequate. These conditions allow me to monitor and inspect my snake at all hours of the day or night, and they grant my snake all the comforts it needs to make a fast and full recovery. It is always best, if your living conditions allow, to have your hospital tank in a separate room of the house from the rest of your collection. This will go a long way in helping prevent the spread of any highly communicable (mites, *Cryptosporidium*, etc.) ailments from infesting your entire snake collection.

The Ailments

What follows is a discussion of some of the most common ailments to afflict snakes in the home terrarium. I have omitted the specifics of some complicated ailments. For example, I do not differentiate here between some types of internal bacterial infections, nor do I split hairs between types of internal protozoa and worm infections. Those finer points of health care are best left for your veterinarian, and this book is a general guide, not a medical journal. However, I do cover the types of ailments to afflict snakes, and because so many related health problems are indicated by similar or identical symptoms, all you need to do is learn to identify the symptoms indicative of the presence of any one of numerous members in each ailment group. After your preliminary diagnosis that your snake is sick, your veterinary practitioner will make the final call and identify the exact bacterial strain or worm species afflicting your pet. Some ailments, however, can be treated or cured with purely in-home remedies, and for those ailments, I list the treatment protocol and allied medicines.

A mouse has chewed on the tail of this California kingsnake. Feeding pre-killed prey prevents these types of injuries.

How to Prevent Injuries to Your Snake

- Do not let your snake slither about outside of its terrarium unsupervised.
- Handle your snake away from other pets, especially cats, dogs, and ferrets.
- Make sure that all terrarium furnishings are fixed securely in place and have no sharp edges.
- Never handle your snake above stone floors or other hard surfaces.
- Never handle your snake while under the influence of drugs or alcohol.
- Never let a child handle your pet serpent unsupervised.
- Never taunt or scare someone with your pet snake; this is dangerous to both the person and the reptile.
- Perform handling sessions away from hot stoves, electrical sources, running machinery, etc.
- Put away all sharp or heavy objects before handling your snake.

INJURIES

BITES

Bites occur when a snake is fed living prey items, such as mice, rats, gerbils, guinea pigs, or rabbits. Most bites occur when a constrictor bites the prey, coils about it, and begins to squeeze. Understandably willing to fight for its life, the prey attempts anything it can to ward off the snake, including biting at its eyes, mouth, or body. Wounds inflicted on your snake this way are usually minor, but they can be severe. Severe bites most often come from larger, stronger prey items with proportionally larger teeth. Rats are particularly prone to inflicting deep wounds with their chisel-like teeth, and when wrapped in the coils of a large snake, they can do some serious damage. Likewise, rats are especially prone to nibble on a snake if left unattended in the terrarium. If your snake is not hungry, it will neither see the rodent as a prey item nor strike and kill the pest. Instead, the rodent will have free reign of the terrarium. At best, its movements will annoy and stress your snake, and at worst, it will get hungry and seriously injure or even kill your beloved pet.

Prevent these wounds from occurring by only feeding pre-killed prey items to your snake. If you do choose to feed live items, absolutely never leave that live prey item unattended in your snake's terrarium. Keep an eye on your snake at least until it has killed and begun to consume the rodent.

Minor bites are best treated with a topical antibiotic cream, while deeper, bloodier bites may require a regimen of veterinarian-administered antibiotic shots and stitches or other surgical aid. Always consider a bad bite wound an emergency and act accordingly.

It is important to note that rats and mice are not the only prey items that can bite and injure your snake. Insectivorous species, such as those snakes of the genus *Opheodrys*, may also suffer bites from their intended prey item. A host of hungry crickets can quickly and easily swarm over a green snake or small garter snake and nibble the life out of it. This may sound far-fetched to some hobbyists, but when mobbed by a swarm of insect life, a snake will most often try to flee. Of course, when locked in an enclosure, there is no place for your snake to go, and it is, by and large, at the mercy of the insect horde. The result is a stressed and probably injured snake—snakes have died from insect attacks. Hobbyists who are used to keeping insectivorous lizards often fall into this scenario. Many insect-eating lizards will feed heavily when presented with a host of crickets, gobbling up one cricket after another when several are dropped into the terrarium at once. Yet insectivorous snakes are not at all like this and will lose interest in feeding if they are presented with too many insect prey items

Emergency!

Sometimes our snakes need veterinary care and sometimes they need emergency care. What's the difference? In the same way that an auto-accident victim doesn't make an appointment with a family physician and wait two weeks for the appointment, our snakes sometimes suffer injuries that need to be dealt with at once. The car-crash victim needs an ambulance and a hospital immediately. When your snake is seriously injured, it requires immediate emergency medical care as well. Although obesity, ticks, and mild bouts of skin and scale infections may wait over a weekend until you can get your snake to the vet on Monday morning, other issues demand more immediate attention. Your snake needs vet care right away if it exhibits the following signs:
- bitten by a rat, mouse, cat, dog, or other pet/prey item
- bleeding from mouth or vent
- discharge from nose or mouth
- most burns
- open wounds
- partly crushed or pressed
- suffered a bad fall
- unable to move or unable to right itself when turned over
- uncontrollable writhing or rolling movements, especially accompanied by a gaping mouth

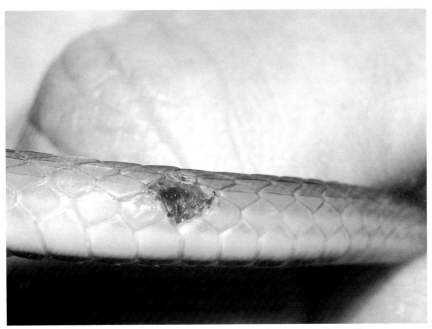

Partially healed burn on a rough green snake. Most burns in snakes will require veterinary treatment.

all at once. The result is the same as in the mouse or rat scenario: The snake will become ill at ease and refuse to either kill or feed on the insects, and the intended prey will turn against the predator. For this reason, never leave an insectivorous snake alone with lots of prey items in its terrarium. Instead, put a few prey items in the tank, and then wait a few days to add more. Never dump a week's worth of crickets in the terrarium of an insectivorous snake.

BURNS

Another common malady to afflict snakes in the home terrarium is the topical burn. Most often caused by faulty heating apparatuses, these wounds are painful for your snake and may, in extreme cases, prove fatal. Until recently, the most common source of topical burns was the hot rock. (The problems with these devices are discussed in the heating section of Chapter 2.) Thankfully, most of the old-school hot rocks have been replaced by modern heating devices, which rarely present such problems in the home terrarium. But burns still occur because cheaper hot rocks are still manufactured by some companies. Likewise, mishaps also occur, not because of the apparatus itself but because of an oversight on the part of the keeper. Proximity is the culprit here—a ceramic heat emitter, an incandescent bulb, or another heat source is suspended too closely above the tank, or in some cases, is even placed inside the terrarium.

Incandescent bulbs and ceramic heat emitters can get hot, easily reaching temperatures in excess of 180°F (82.2°C). These heat sources need to be kept well away from both your snake and anything that can melt or catch fire. Simply placing such heat sources atop the screen lid of your tank and thinking that the metallic screen won't melt is not enough to guarantee your snake's safety. Arboreal and semi-arboreal species are particularly at risk, as a snake that climbs to the upper reaches of the tank could get dangerously close to the heat source.

Prevent burns by buying name-brand heating fixtures, replacing old or worn-out fixtures, and never situating heating bulbs or emitters too close over the terrarium. A good rule of thumb is to turn on your heat lamp or and place it over the tank. Now put your hand atop the screen directly beneath the emitter/bulb. Can you keep your hand there, or is the heat uncomfortably or painfully hot? If it is too hot to hold your hand beneath it comfortably, the emitter/bulb is likely too close to the tank. Back it away from the tank a couple of inches (cm) at a time until you can repeat this test and keep your hand comfortably yet warmly beneath the emitter/bulb. If your terrarium setup does not afford you the room to back the emitter/bulb away from the tank, switch to a smaller wattage heat source. Wiring a dimmer switch or thermostat into the socket holding your heat source is also a good way to regulate the amount of heat it gives off.

If your snake does become burned from a heating apparatus, begin by removing the offending heat source. Once the problem is remedied at its source, it's time to treat your snake. Severe burns frequently require euthanasia. The massive tissue damage caused by deep burns makes for serious wounds, and they seldom heal. Secondary infection often takes hold quickly, and the snake is ultimately doomed. Third-degree burns that cover a large area of the snake's body may also warrant euthanasia. It is often best to simply euthanize the afflicted animal and humanely spare it a painful, protracted ordeal. Your veterinarian will euthanize the snake.

Blister Prone

Garter, ribbon, and water snakes seem to be particularly prone to blister disease. This occurs because while all of these snakes need a humid terrarium and preferably a large water bowl, they also need to be able to dry off and warm up. Too many keepers house them without adequate basking areas, which enable these species to dry themselves. If you keep one of these species, house your snake properly, clean the terrarium regularly, and keep an eye out for blister disease.

Inclusion Body Disease

Inclusion body disease (IBD) is a serious and mysterious disease of boas and pythons (seen most often in red-tailed boas and Burmese pythons). Its name comes from the dark spots—the inclusions—it leaves in various bodily cells. IBD possibly is carried by mites, but the actual cause is not known. It is highly contagious.

Signs include regurgitation, anorexia, and head tremors. As the disease progress, severe neurological symptoms develop, including holding the head and neck in strange positions, paralysis, and a behavior called stargazing, in which the snake holds its head so it is looking straight up. There is no cure for IBD and it is always fatal. Infected snakes should be humanely euthanized by a veterinarian.

Of course, not all burns are fatal. Small, localized, minor burns may be treated successfully. Treat minor burns by applying a topical antibiotic and anti-inflammatory cream, such as Neosporin (with pain reliever is best) to the affected area. Also, provide your snake with plenty of clean, fresh drinking water, as it will drink more water than usual during the healing process. Be aware that most burns will require veterinary care. If the wounds are treatable, your vet will likely begin a regimen of antibiotic injections coupled with topical applications of a prescription-strength antibiotic cream.

FALLS AND OTHER ACCIDENTS

As the saying goes, "accidents will happen," and these are the wild cards of snake health—you never know exactly when they will happen or exactly what will cause them. A heavy terrarium lid can fall shut on a snake's tail as you are putting the animal away. Your snake may fall from a high countertop when you turn your back for a second. Your young child or younger sibling may squeeze too tightly when playing with your snake. These falls and crushing injuries usually come when you let your guard down, and they may cause no, little, or severe damage to your snake. Many times, these type of accidents cause spinal injuries and necessitate having the snake humanely put down. When less severe, these types of injuries still usually require veterinary care. It is much better to prevent them by avoiding situations that put your snake at risk. For example, never leave it unattended when it's outside the terrarium, never leave it on a surface that's far above the floor, make sure that all terrarium furnishings are securely fixed and cannot fall on your snake, and be vigilant.

INFECTIOUS DISEASES

BLISTER DISEASE

Blister disease occurs when snakes are kept in excessively humid or wet conditions. When housed on moist or soiled substrate, a snake's belly scales will begin to canker, split, and turn foul. Otherwise sturdy belly scales will turn yellowish to gray, crinkle around their edges, and develop small white to yellowish bumps or blisters along or underneath their edges. These blisters are the visible effects caused by bacterial colonies thriving just beneath the surface of the skin and scales. The fluid inside these pimple-like bumps often has an extremely foul odor. Blister disease is a virulent, fast-progressing ailment that will only worsen as time passes. Small, innocuous blisters will develop into open sores and may eventually cause the muscle and other tissue beneath to become necrotic. If not treated quickly, blister disease can kill a snake.

Once blister disease is detected, remove your snake to quarantine and fix the offending environmental conditions at once—change the substrate in the home terrarium, raise the temperature, and cut down on ground moisture. Oftentimes,

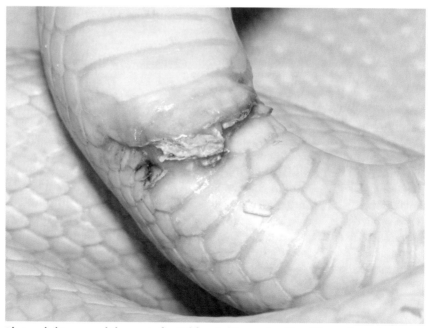

Blistered skin around the vent of a California kingsnake. Most blisters in snakes are caused by the enclosure being dirty and too damp.

snakes will develop blister disease because they have been spending copious amounts of time soaking or submerged in their water dish. Blister disease is especially likely to result if the snake is soaking in filthy or fouled water. If the water dish, clean or otherwise, is the culprit, replace it with a much smaller one—one in which the snake cannot immerse its body—although you should also address the reasons why your snake may be soaking so much, such as mite infestation or improper temperature.

While in quarantine, which you should keep warm round the clock (as described in the section on mouth rot), your snake will enter a rapid shed cycle. This is its body's natural attempt to quickly replace the damaged scales with fresh, new scales. During this period, your snake may refuse food or it may eat more than normal. Attempt to feed it often. Topical rinses of hydrogen peroxide, followed by applications of antibiotic ointment, will help speed along the healing process. It is important to note, however, that only mild cases of blister disease should be treated in this fashion, and it is always best to involve a veterinarian in the treatment of this illness. Cases in which the blisters on your snake's belly have burst or in which the belly scales have rotted completely away to expose the flesh beneath certainly require a veterinarian's care, as exposed flesh is a prime area for secondary infection. Because the bacteria that cause blister disease are so virulent and persistent, a long-term treatment regimen, administered by your veterinarian, may be in order. Full recovery may take several months, depending on the severity of the case.

LESIONS AND ABSCESSES

Lesions and abscesses are both forms of infected wounds, but they present different signs and have different treatments. Generally speaking, lesions are sores or open wounds that refuse to heal for some reason. Fungal infections, bacterial infections, or some other physiological malady (such as an immune system ailment) may prevent an existing wound from healing properly. Lesions may be treated initially as would normal wounds: washing with clean water or iodine solution and applying topical antibiotic ointment. If the lesion swells, shows excessive redness about the edges (often accompanied by a whitish or gray center), produces pus, or doesn't seem to be healing, then topical solutions will not be sufficient treatment. Veterinary attention will be necessary. The vet will usually clean and debride the area and possibly administer injections of an antibiotic and prescribe antifungal or antibiotic ointments. A lesion must be treated quickly because a perpetually open wound is both a source of great physical pain for your snake and an open invitation for secondary infections.

Abscesses are internal maladies that are, for all intents and purposes, beyond the treatment of the average hobbyist, and they always demand professional medical attention. An abscess typically occurs when some injury becomes infected after it has superficially healed. A good way to think of an abscess is that it is a wound that topically scabbed over but is infected inside. Pus will form under the skin or scales, and because it cannot flow out of the wound, will form a pustule under the skin. This pustule will usually be in the form of a hard knot or tumor-like lump under the skin, which is painful for your snake. (In rare cases, the pus will be more liquid, as in mammals.) Because an abscess can leak bacteria into the bloodstream, it must be dealt with by your veterinarian as soon as you notice its existence. Your vet will treat an abscess by surgically removing the lump (or lancing and draining, in the case of a more liquid abscess) and administering antibiotic injections to combat the internal infection. Always have your veterinarian inspect any mysterious or newly arisen lumps under your snake's skin and scales.

Corn snake with mouth rot in a relatively early stage.

MOUTH ROT

Known to veterinarians as infectious stomatitis, mouth rot is an oral disease usually brought about by unsanitary or otherwise inappropriate—usually too cold—living conditions. Additionally, vitamin C deficiency is sometimes related to this condition. As the immune system of your snake weakens due to the stress of living in a suboptimal terrarium, opportunistic pathogens begin to infect the gums. A yellowish, cheesy substance will begin to form in the affected area of the gums. If left untreated, this cheesy exudate will spread throughout the teeth and gums, and bits of it may become dislodged and end up in the digestive tract or even the lungs. Some may move up into the sinus within the skull. Untreated, mouth rot is fatal.

Caused by a bacterial (or sometimes fungal) infection, mouth rot has some noticeable symptoms, although these are often not apparent until the illness is advanced. These include swollen gums, holding the mouth open, loss of appetite or refusal to feed, frequent working of the jaws back and forth (trying to shed itself

Pueblan milk snake with advanced mouth rot. Mouth rot this severe will be difficult to treat successfully.

of the exudate), swelling of the mouth and throat, and blackening or rotting of the teeth. If you handle your snake often, you may also notice exceedingly foul breath, as the flesh inside its mouth is going necrotic.

Inspect for infectious stomatitis by gently grasping your snake behind the head and inserting the clean, rounded, dull edge of a credit card or driver's license into its mouth. Push gently but firmly backward, starting at the tip of the snout. (Don't insert from the side, as this can break out the snake's teeth.) As the card starts to slip in, the snake should open its mouth widely in an attempt to expel the card. As it does so, look for any discoloration inside the mouth or any whitish or yellowish cheesy material in the gums and around the teeth. A healthy mouth will appear to be pinkish or red with veins and capillaries visible just beneath the surface of the skin, and healthy teeth will appear whitish to clear or translucent, depending on the size of the snake in question. (Smaller, younger individuals typically have clearer-looking teeth.) If you spot any type of gunky or cheesy buildup, discolored or blackened teeth, or reddish, swollen areas within the gums, then mouth rot is likely the culprit.

Treat mouth rot by removing your animal to quarantine. Increase the temperature in the quarantine tank by 2 to 4°F (1.1 to 2.2°C) higher than the daily recommended average for your species, and maintain this temperature

Good Snakekeeping

Fighting Crypto

Disinfectants that contain quaternary ammonium seem to be the most effective at killing *Cryptosporidium* cysts on surfaces. Applying strong bleach solutions and baking items do kill crypto but not as effectively. At this time, no disinfectant is 100 percent effective against this pathogen.

around the clock. For example, if you own a snake whose daily recommended high temperature is 80°F (26.7°C), raise the temperature inside the quarantine tank to 82 to 83°F (27.8 to 28.3°C) and keep it there. The purpose of this increase is to help your snake's immune system fight off the bacterial infection.

Experienced keepers may also wish to gently flush their snake's mouth with hydrogen peroxide or some other mild antiseptic. Have someone knowledgeable show you how to do this before attempting it on your own. You may also wish to pry open your snake's mouth (as explained earlier) and gently swab away any noticeable cheese or exudate. Some hobbyists have experienced great success with squirting an eyedropper full of dilute antiseptic mouthwash in their snake's mouth; the snake will certainly not like the harsh alcohol burning in its mouth, but the infection will typically yield under this disinfectant wash. Again, have someone show you how to avoid getting the mouthwash into the snake's digestive or respiratory tract. It is always advisable to take your snake to the veterinarian when the threat of mouth rot looms because proper diagnosis and treatment (advanced or intermediate cases often call for antibiotic injections) is your best defense.

RESPIRATORY INFECTION

Ailments affecting a snake's respiratory tract are particularly dangerous because most snakes only have one functioning (and typically, one vestigial) lung, and unlike cats and dogs, their life literally depends on the sustained health of that single lung. Serpentine pneumonia is, much like mouth rot, brought about by unsanitary and excessively cool living conditions. Some cases of respiratory infection are caused not by incorrect temperatures but by incorrect (i.e., excessive) levels of humidity within the terrarium. Desert species, such as rosy boas, sand boas, and rat snakes of the genus *Bogertophis*, are prone to respiratory infections, especially if housed in poorly ventilated or excessively humid terrarium environments.

Once it starts, a respiratory infection will spread quickly and can kill in a surprisingly short period, so quickly initiating treatment is essential to prevent disaster. Symptoms include loud and repeated hissing, frequent opening of the mouth, frequent and long spells of holding the mouth agape, holding the head and forequarters up (at a 90-degree angle to the floor of the terrarium) for long periods, mucus or saliva bubbling from the nostrils or corners of the mouth, wheezing, or generally struggling to breathe. Once you witness any of these symptoms, or if you otherwise suspect your snake to be suffering from a respiratory infection, begin by removing it to quarantine and raising the temperature as described for mouth rot. This will help your snake's natural immune system fight the disease until you can get it to a veterinarian for a proper, long-term cure. Prevent this illness by maintaining proper temperature and level of relative humidity within your snake's terrarium.

PARASITES

With the exception of mites, parasites are normally seen only in wild-caught snakes, although captive-bred individuals can contract them if they come in contact with infested snakes. Internal parasites usually require veterinary treatment, while external parasites can be eradicated by a diligent hobbyist.

INTERNAL PARASITES

Known to veterinarians as endoparasites, internal parasites are a dangerous group of organisms that are often difficult to treat. These include nematodes

Frequent soaking in the water bowl can be a sign that your snake has mites, but it can also mean that the enclosure is too hot.

(various roundworms), protozoa (coccidia, amoebas, etc.), and flatworms (flukes, tapeworms, etc.). Such internal devils typically accompany recently imported snakes from the tropics and are particularly problematic with large, wild-caught boas and arboreal colubrids, including the Asian rat snakes. Often it is impossible to diagnose the exact parasite you're dealing with without the skilled eye of a herpetological veterinarian.

There are some general symptoms that frequently accompany an internal parasite load:

- frequent regurgitation of meals or vomiting of recently drunk water
- excessive appetite with no accompanying weight gain
- intensely foul-smelling stool
- intensely sweet-smelling stool
- lack of appetite
- presence of tiny living or deceased worms or their eggs in the snake's stool
- runny, watery, or bloody stool
- sudden and extreme weight loss

Any one of these signs may point to an internal parasite infection. A combination of these symptoms almost certainly means internal parasites are at work. It has often been said of snakes, "resistant to disease, sensitive to medication." This maxim is very true. Although snakes can be medically treated for internal maladies, I do not recommend that most hobbyists attempt to do so. For all the same reasons that I do not fill my own cavities or remove my own tonsils, we who are unskilled in the application and practice of veterinary medicine need not attempt it on our pet snakes. Although there are some basic topical treatments that virtually any hobbyist can and should apply when the situation warrants, the application of internal medicines is much more difficult and complex than the application of topical medicine. It has been the experience of myself and other keepers and breeders that unskilled hobbyists often do more harm than good when attempting to cure internal maladies. Misdiagnosis of the parasite, inadequate or excessive dosages of the medicine, or inappropriate application of treatment (subcutaneous injection versus intravenous injection, for example) can all result in the untimely and unnecessary demise of your snake. Additionally, there is the risk of not completely wiping out the parasites and leaving behind some that are now resistant to the medication you

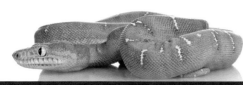

The Telltale Tick

If you find ticks on a snake being sold as captive bred, you should be skeptical. Captive-bred reptiles rarely carry ticks, and finding them may be your first clue that the vendor is not on the level.

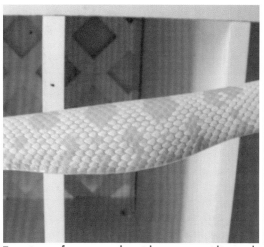
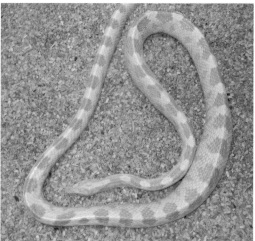

Two views of a corn snake with cryptosporidiosis, showing the mid-body swelling commonly seen in this illness.

used and are consequentially harder to treat..If you are unskilled with internal herpetological medicine, do not attempt to treat an internal parasite load on your own.

If you suspect your snake to be suffering from internal parasites, take either the animal and/or a fresh stool sample to your herp vet at once. Your veterinarian will microscopically inspect the stool and properly identify, diagnose, and treat your snake's ailment. Doing otherwise is simply ill-advised.

CRYPTOSPORIDIOSIS
The most dreaded of all snake ailments, cryptosporidiosis (known as crypto to most hobbyists) is the technical term for a disease caused when the *Cryptosporidium* protozoan infests the snake's digestive tract. Symptoms include mid-body swelling, bloating, and rapid weight loss. There is currently no known cure for cryptosporidiosis, but there are some promising new medications that keep the infection in check. (These treatments seem to only be effective in snakes, not lizards and other herps). However, crypto can spread rapidly through your entire snake collection, and infected animals are likely to be carriers for the rest of their lives. Therefore, most hobbyists and breeders euthanize infected specimens.

Despite the fact that cryptosporidiosis is lethal and causes its victims to suffer immense pain in the later stages of the infection, these are not the worst parts of the infection. The *Cryptosporidium* protozoan's most deadly attribute is the fact that it can live, undetected and without causing any symptoms, for as long as two

143

Too Many Ticks

If you have a snake specimen that is heavily laden with ticks (numerous individuals around each eye and clustered around the mouth and cloaca, for example), you may want to remove the little bloodsuckers piecemeal—remove a few one day, then wait a day and then remove the rest. Pulling off ticks can be stressful for your snake, and it's better to complete the process over a few days than to cause needless and overwhelming pain and stress to your pet all at once. Fortunately, tick infestations of this magnitude are quite rare.

years in a snake's gut. This can lead a hobbyist to inadvertently infect his entire collection. Crypto resists most disinfectants, so even keepers who practice excellent hygiene can spread it around their collections. Any infected animal's enclosure, fixtures, climbing branches, heating apparatus, etc. (i.e., anything with which the infected snake came into contact with on a regular daily basis), should be destroyed. Many snake keepers have infected later specimens with *Cryptosporidium* by attempting to reuse old, infected terrariums and furnishings.

TICKS AND MITES

The most common external parasites (sometimes known collectively as ectoparasites) to afflict pet snakes, ticks and mites are bloodsucking arachnids—kin to spiders, crabs, and scorpions. Ticks and mites are similar organisms, but hobbyists must treat snakes affected by them differently. Ticks are normally found singly or in small groups, while mites occur in enormous numbers.

Much like the ticks that attack cats and dogs, reptilian ticks feed by attaching their mandibles to the softest tissue that they can find—usually around the eyes, mouth, under the chin, or around the cloaca. In snakes that have heat-sensitive pits, ticks will attach inside these. Ticks are typically easily spotted. They resemble tiny flaps of flesh hanging off an otherwise smooth, streamlined animal. In color, reptilian ticks may be reddish, brown, gray, black, or even whitish. Most frequently, they are a rusty or earthy color. Captive-bred snakes and those that have been in captivity for a long time are seldom afflicted with ticks. Ticks almost exclusively enter the pet trade attached to the delicate parts of wild-caught adult snakes from the tropical regions of the world. Wild-caught boas and pythons often sport at least a few ticks clustered around their eyes or cloaca. Their presence can hint at more serious internal infections. A snake that has numerous ticks attached to its body has usually been shipped under hostile conditions and frequently suffers from infections or external parasites.

Once you have identified a tick problem, treat by carefully and gently plucking each tick off your snake with a pair of tweezers. This is delicate work, as you must pull the whole tick free and be careful that the tick does not tear or break in half. If you successfully remove the back half of the body but leave the head attached, you have only made the problem worse. A head and mandibles that remain attached to your snake will almost surely cause a localized secondary infection. Avoid breaking or tearing a tick in two by dabbing a bit of mineral oil, cooking oil (vegetable, corn, peanut), rubbing alcohol (do not use near the snake's mouth), or petroleum jelly on the tick for ten minutes or so prior to removing it; this chemical wash will starve the tick of oxygen or make it uncomfortable and may force it to loosen its hold on your snake.

Begin the removal process by gently but firmly grasping your snake. Large or temperamental snakes may require two people to safely hold it to keep it from squirming, thrashing, and potentially injuring itself or biting you. Once the snake is safely restrained, carefully grasp the tick fully inside the jaws of the tweezers and pull backward slowly but firmly. Do not jerk or twist the tick, as this will almost certainly rip off the head or mandibles. Simply apply firm, constant pressure until the tick pulls free from your snake. After removing all of the ticks from your snake, dab each attachment point with a bit of antibiotic ointment to help prevent secondary infection.

The second type of external parasite is the mite. Mites are minuscule

Tick embedded in a ball python. Wild-caught snakes commonly have ticks, but captive-bred ones rarely do.

bloodsuckers that closely resemble tiny fleas. Normally dark in coloration, mites typically appear on a snake as tiny moving flecks of pepper or specks of dirt. Mites are a prolific pest, and therein lies their most threatening facet: Within the home terrarium, mites can reproduce to plague-like proportions within a surprisingly short period. A single female may lay several scores of eggs over the course of her life span, and those eggs may hatch in a short period. A typical mite infestation can grow from a few individuals to more than a few hundred mites in a week's time.

Determine whether your snake has mites by inspecting it physically. Bathe it in a tub of lukewarm water; the tub should be white or very light in coloration. Are there any tiny, dark insects kicking about atop the water or sunken on the bottom of the tub? If a tub is not available, take a white paper towel and soak it in warm water. Swab the snake's body, making sure to massage the scales under the lower jaw, around the eyes, behind the jaws, and near the cloaca, as they are areas where the blood flows close to the surface, and blood-hungry mites will congregate in these locations. After swabbing the snake, closely examine the paper towel for tiny, crawling flecks of pepper—these are mites.

If mites are present, you must tackle the problem from a number of directions all at once. Begin by removing your snake to quarantine. Remember, because mites are so insidious and can move from tank to tank, an infection that starts out in one terrarium can quickly spread to any and all other terrariums in a collection. For this reason, *all infected snakes and accompanying husbandry items and terrariums must be isolated at once!*

Once your snake is in quarantine, it is time to purge the terrarium of mites. Do so by disposing of all substrate matter. Sand or gravel may be put in a bucket and scoured with boiling water and then dried out and reused, but all earth, woodchips, coir, orchid bark, and any other organic or shredded substrate must be totally disposed of, preferably in a trash can outside the house. Any terrarium carpet must be disposed of as well. Moving on to the fixtures in the tank, all organic items such as cork bark slabs or climbing branches must be heat purged in the oven if they are to be salvaged at all. Merely washing these wooden items in hot water—even boiling hot—will not kill the eggs and mites that are likely to be anchored deep within the cracks of these wooden items. Heat purge wooden items by wrapping them in aluminum foil and placing them in your oven for one hour at 300°F (149°C) as described in Chapter 2. Natural stones may also be heat purged, but artificial or acrylic hides, caves, bowls, etc., must be washed in a chlorine bleach and water solution, which may be mixed at five parts water to one part bleach. After cleansing with the bleach solution, rinse the fixtures well (by soaking and scrubbing) with clean, pure water until no smell of bleach remains.

Once the materials in the terrarium have been either disposed of or purified, you must now set about the task of cleaning the terrarium. Accomplish this by scrubbing the entire tank with a warm water and chlorine bleach mixture. Very hot water, such as that which was recently boiling, can either crack the glass of some terrariums or may cause the silicon sealant, which cements the walls of the tank together, to weaken or separate. Use a bleach solution mixed as described earlier. Swab the inside of the tank liberally with this solution; immerse the tank entirely if at all possible. Take your time while cleaning the tank and fixtures, making sure to get bleach into every nook and cranny, under every plastic lip and in every crevice, as any eggs or mites that remain will simply reinfest your snake and its terrarium. Anyone who has ever combated a mite infestation will tell you one thing: You want to kill them all the first time!

While your fixtures are heat purging in the oven and your mite-free terrarium and acrylic fixtures are drying, it is time to free your snake of its parasitic attackers. Old-school practice was to wash the snake in a faint mixture of water and flea killer or tick and flea shampoo, as is used with dogs. This is no longer a common practice—it is potentially hazardous to a snake, and I do not recommend using any such product. Instead, swab your snake down with a light coating of vegetable or corn oil, such as that used for cooking. This oil will cause the mites, which are buried beneath your snake's scales, to release their hold. After your snake has been wearing the oil for about 30 minutes, wash it in

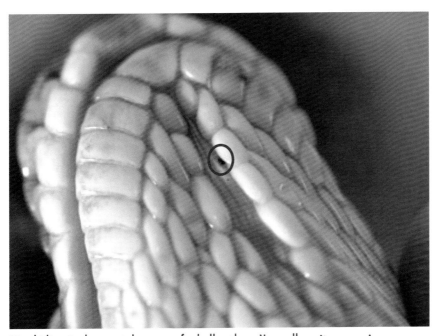

Mite hiding in the mental groove of a ball python. Normally, mites occur in great numbers.

Florida kingsnake with cloudy eyes, indicating it is starting a shed cycle.

a tub of lukewarm water, carefully massaging the snake and flushing mites out from under the jaws and near the cloaca, where they typically congregate en masse. Another great mite-bath solution is to create a dilute mixture of water and povidone-iodine, which is available in any drugstore. The mixture should be about the color of weak tea. Soak your snake in the mixture for 15 to 20 minutes at a time; repeated soakings may be necessary. During these soaks, make sure that your snake's head goes under the solution, but obviously do not leave it unattended in its bath, as drowning is a possibility. Juvenile snakes or very young snakes are at greater risk of drowning in bathwater than are larger, stronger, adult specimens. Destroy mites in your quarantine terrarium by spraying or treating it with Provent-a-Mite, a highly effective mite killer that is safe for use in the snake and lizard terrarium. (Follow the manufacturer's instructions exactly.) Once all mites have disappeared from your snake, and after your terrarium has been properly disinfected, you may return your snake to its former home. Hopefully, the infestation is over, but eradicating mites often requires several treatments.

It is always best to prevent mites from ever entering your home snake collection, so inspect any snakes and any terrarium items (caves, wooden logs, climbing branches, etc.) carefully prior to bringing them home.

OTHER AILMENTS

DYSECDYSIS

Commonly known as shedding problems or a bad shed, dysecdysis is the medical term for any mishap that occurs during a snake's skin-shedding cycle. Shedding problems can occur in a wide range of severities, but most are relatively minor. Most episodes of dysecdysis pose no threat to your serpentine pet. There are instances, however, in which a poor shed can cause considerable complications and affect the health of your snake.

A normal shed happens thusly: Your snake's color will begin to go dull. Afterward, its eyes will take on a smoky or milky hue (typically bluish or gray; herpers often say that their snake is "in blue" at this time), and its vision will be distorted or limited during this time. After a couple of days, the smokiness will disappear and the snake's eyes will once more be clear. Another couple of days will pass and the snake will begin rubbing its nose on rough surfaces in the terrarium. Once your snake has found a suitably rough surface, its skin will begin to peel away at its nose, and as the old skin clings to the rough surface, your snake will slowly crawl or wiggle out of its old skin (by slithering slowly and flexing all of its muscles in a rhythmic cycle and pulling away from the old skin). Ideally, your snake will shed its skin in one long, continuous piece, and what will emerge will be a brightly colored, vibrantly patterned snake. Of course, this ideal shed is not always the case. A number of things can go wrong.

An incomplete shed, or a piecemeal shed in which the old skin peels away in chunks, is emblematic of dehydration. It is likely that your snake is living under excessively dry conditions. Under properly moist and hydrated conditions, your snake will shed in one piece and its newly emerged skin will be slightly damp to the touch (much like when you get a sunburn and peel, the skin underneath is slightly moist). When either the environmental conditions are too dry or the snake's internal hydration level is too low, the moisture layer that exists between the emergent skin and the outer, older skin will become too low to allow the two layers to separate efficiently. Remedy this problem in the short term by soaking your snake in a lukewarm bath for a few minutes; this will loosen the skin, which should now simply slide off the body in your grasp. Correct the issue in the long term by increasing the levels of relative humidity in your snake's terrarium and providing it with more ready access to drinking water.

I do not recommend trying to peel away the outer skin while your snake is still dehydrated, as this is much

Shed Aid

When you see that your snake is getting ready to shed, you may want to mist the cage lightly each day until it is finished shedding. The added humidity will help prevent problems with the shedding process.

Yellow rat snake with retained shed. Although this is not immediately dangerous, retained shed will cause health problems if not corrected.

akin to pulling off a human's sticky bandage—it is irritating and painful for your snake. For most species, it does no harm to provide a little extra moisture when your snake is getting ready to shed. You can lightly mist the enclosure once a day or provide a larger water bowl, for example.

Another common shedding problem is the retained scale. This occurs when a single scale or a small cluster of scales are left clinging to the body after a shed. This typically occurs over the eyes or at the tip of the tail. Because any retained portions of the old, shed skin are no longer living, growing cells, these transparent items begin to dry and shrink on the snake's body, thus becoming like manacles or restraints. If not removed promptly, they can cause some serious problems. The scales retained on the tip of the tail will tighten and constrict blood flow to the tip of the tail. The end result is that the tip of the tail, so starved of blood flow, will dry up and eventually fall off. This process can take a long time and may be painful for your snake. In extreme cases, the constricted area can turn infectious due to poor circulation, becoming a threat to your snake's life. If you notice that the tip of its tail is duller or darker in coloration than the rest of the body immediately following a shed, it has likely retained some scales there (you can make sure by checking the shed skin and seeing if the old skin on the tip of the tail is present or absent), and you'll need to carefully remove these retained scales with tweezers. Soaking your snake in lukewarm water will make this removal much easier.

Scales retained over the eye, however, present a considerably more entailed and dangerous problem. When a cuticle or spectacle (names for the scale covering your snake's eye—the eyelid is actually a transparent scale and is renewed along with every other scale during a shed) is retained during a shed, that scale will stay atop the new scale growing beneath it. In the short term, the old scale will inhibit the snake's vision, and it can be the source of terrible discomfort. In the longer term, this retained scale may give rise to secondary infection in the soft tissue or scales surrounding the eye. After a cuticle has been retained once, the tendency is for future sheds to retain that cuticle as well; once the oldest scale hardens and forms a tight "seal" around the eye, subsequent layers of developing scales are trapped beneath this top scale.

Long-term eye-cap retention can result in the total loss of an eye due to constriction or infection. If your snake retains a cuticle, bathe the animal in lukewarm water and gently dab at the edge of the retained scale with a cotton swab or pair of tweezers. If the eye cap comes away easily, problem solved. If, however, you are having difficulty in removing the cap, it is probably tightly attached to the scales beneath it. In this case, or if your snake is too aggressive for such delicate work, you'll need to make a trip to your herpetological veterinarian

Ball python with a retained eye cap. This is one of the most common shedding problems and one of the most serious.

Blind Fury

When I was working in a local pet shop during my junior year of high school, the store acquired a small blood python. A gorgeous animal with striking markings, the snake was sold to us by a man who no longer wanted it because the animal had turned brutally aggressive about six months prior. When I pulled it out of the bag to inspect it, I noticed that it had a silver eye. I wondered how this could be, and I started to inspect the eye. After a bit, I noticed that the silver eye had a flap of old shed skin hanging from its corner. I gently pulled on the flap with a pair of tweezers, and an entire eye scale came away. I repeated this action, and another scale came away. And another. And another. In all, seven eye caps had been retained. When I pulled the last one away, a gush of fluid spewed from the eye socket, and a small black eye emerged. After a couple of days, the shrunken eye was back to normal and the snake lost its aggressive disposition altogether. The retained eye caps had been causing the snake considerable pain and blindness for some time. When the blindness and pain were alleviated, the snake was once more a happy, healthy animal.

to get the problem remedied. When dealing with a retained cuticle yourself, be extremely careful. You could blind your snake permanently if you slip or if you pull off the bottommost scale.

NOSE RUBBING

Nose rubbing is a behavioral issue that results in a physical health problem. In this situation, the snake continually moves within its terrarium and rubs its nose or snout along the screen lid and glass walls of the terrarium. This condition can be fatal if left untreated. It begins when the rostral scale (the scale on the tip of the snake's nose) is rubbed raw, turning pink in color. As the snake continues to probe for a way out of the terrarium, the condition worsens—pink becomes red and red becomes bloody and scabby, eventually leading to exposed bone along the snout, inflammation, and secondary infection around the wound. In the final stages, permanent maxillary or facial disfigurement or even death (by secondary infection) can occur. Typically brought about by a critical environmental flaw within the terrarium, nose rubbing is both easily prevented and easily eliminated simply by evaluating and adjusting the conditions inside the terrarium.

Size is a major consideration. Is the tank big enough for the snake? Large snakes need large quarters. Although a snake's space needs will vary considerably based on the species in question, a good rule of thumb is that the tank should be large enough to allow the snake to fully stretch out. I recommend keeping a snake in an enclosure that is 1.5 times the length of the snake. A 48-inch-long (1.2-m) snake, therefore, would have plenty of slithering room in a 72-inch-long (1.8-m) terrarium. By giving your pet space to stretch out, you can curb a lot of the stress it might feel in an exceedingly cramped environment.

Excessive heat is also a major cause of nose rubbing. In nature, snakes regulate their body temperature by entering or exiting locations of higher or cooler temperatures. If your tank is excessively hot, your snake will nose around the cage in earnest, desperately seeking a cooler retreat. I've often seen amateur hobbyists overheat their pet's terrarium by using an overly large bulb or ceramic heat emitter. Remedy this by lowering the temperature in the tank. Use a heat lamp of lower wattage, move the ceramic heat emitter back several inches (cm) (a foot [30.5 cm] or so at first, then farther if necessary), or provide your snake with a cooler escape. Simply heat one end of the terrarium but do not heat the other end. This will afford your snake the thermocline (temperature gradient) it requires.

One of the most common sources of nose rubbing is an improper level of moisture in the terrarium. Excessively damp substrate can be extremely irritating

African rock python with a snout injured from nose rubbing.

for your pet, and it will forego food, drink, and sleep in its attempts to flee the damp, raw confines of the terrarium. Read up on the moisture requirements of your chosen species and make sure that your terrarium supports these requirements. If you are unsure whether your tank is too moist, try replacing the substrate with a simple layer of dry paper towels. If the snake soon calms down and quits rubbing its nose around the lid, then you know your former setup was too moist.

A lack of appropriate hiding places can also contribute to nose rubbing. Snakes are naturally secretive and feel most comfortable when they are concealed from predators. A captive snake without an adequate hiding place often will spend its time searching for one. In the process, it will be rubbing its snout against the surfaces of the enclosure. Always include at least two hiding places—one at the warm end of the terrarium and one at the cooler end—in your snake's enclosure. Also, make sure the hide is appropriate for the size and species of your snake.

Remember, it is the environmental conditions that you maintain within your snake's habitat that will determine whether its terrarium is a paradise or a prison. In nearly 30 years of intense snake husbandry, I've seen countless cases of nose rubbing that have their roots in some variable of the environmental conditions that existed inside the terrarium. Begin treating your snake's nose-rubbing behaviors by thoroughly cleaning and properly maintaining its habitat. Once the unsuitable conditions are remedied, the snake will almost always settle down and cease its nose rubbing behavior within a matter of days or even hours. Bear in mind, however, that sometimes the cause of the nose rubbing is the snake itself; some species are ill suited to life in the captive terrarium because of their ceaseless nose rubbing. If you know that a species is prone to nose rubbing, I recommend not attempting to house it unless you can give it vast amounts of space and a habitat in which nose rubbing is simply not a viable option (such as in a zoological park or nature center).

What if you cannot identify and fix the environmental factors in time, and your snake has rubbed its nose bloody raw? If no bone is visible beneath the rostral scale, then apply a topical antibiotic ointment, preferably the type with a pain reliever inside. Because the bloody wound is so painful for a snake, the pain-relieving ingredient is a humane addition to the antibiotic salve. Continue dabbing small amounts of topical salve on the affected site until it heals completely. Scabbing over of the wound should take place shortly after treatment begins and after active nose rubbing stops, but the new rostral scale may not come into being until after multiple sheds. If the nose rubbing has been more severe, however, and the rostral scale is missing, or if there is substantial inflammation around the nose (a possible sign of secondary bacterial infection), then an internal antibiotic given by your veterinarian may be necessary in addition to topical treatments. Scarring and disfigurement may occur in the aftermath of severe nose rubbing.

MALNUTRITION

Although overfeeding is the more common problem, underfeeding snakes is also an issue. Hatchlings and juveniles are especially at risk. Young snakes are in a stage of rapid growth, and they need their vitamins (not to mention enough protein, minerals, and calories). Vitamin D3 is particularly important to the proper development of a young snake's skeleton. Improper skeletal development is usually detectable by odd bends or zigzags in the spine and tail or a failure of the mouth to close properly. (The jaws may appear crooked.) If caught early and treated with vitamin supplements, these deformities may be either halted, or in some cases, reversed. See Chapter 4 for more on vitamin supplements.

Feedings should correspond in frequency and size to the age and size of your snake. Signs that you're feeding your snake too infrequently are a concave ventral surface or sunken belly, a light body weight,

Obese blotched kingsnake. Obesity shortens the life span of snakes, just as it does in humans.

listlessness, sunken eyes, decreased movements, frantic nosing around the lid or walls of the tank, and excessive vigor when feeding. If your snake eats quickly and is obviously searching for more food immediately after feeding, it may be trying to tell you that you are feeding it too infrequently. An excessively slow growth rate may also be an indicator that you need to step up the feeding regimen.

OBESITY

Although we tend to think of obesity as a mammalian problem, reptiles and amphibians can certainly suffer from it as well. Obesity in snakes always stems from overfeeding. Sometimes hobbyists indulge their pet too much, and the snake eats more than it can effectively metabolize. The excess food then goes into storage in the form of fat cells. An obese snake will likely live a much shorter life than will its lithe counterpart, and its mobility may be seriously restricted.

Detect obesity in your snake by inspecting him physically. Most colubrid snakes should have a body profile that closely resembles a loaf of bread: flat bottom, vertical sides, and a rounded top or back. You should also be able to discern the musculature beneath the scales and skin of your snake. If your colubrid snake is totally round (with a body profile that more closely resembles a hotdog or sausage link than a neatly defined loaf of bread) or if you cannot discern muscles or lateral lines beneath the skin, your snake is obese. Remedy this by taking your snake out and exercising it (allowing it to slither about, swim in the bathtub, etc.) while reducing the frequency of your feedings.

STRESS

Although we humans are acutely aware of the negative effects of stress on our bodies, we tend to forget that our pets can also suffer physically from the anxieties that they experience in their lives. Despite their relatively simple brains, snakes—perhaps more so than any other type of reptile—can suffer from serious bouts of stress. Stress occurs when your snake is in a living environment in which one or more of its basic requirements are going unmet. Stress typically stems from:

- excessive human traffic in the room
- excessively cold or hot temperatures
- filthy living conditions

- handling too frequently or improperly
- improper levels of relative humidity
- infrequent or nutritionally insufficient feedings
- insufficient hiding places within the terrarium
- internal or external parasite infections
- loud noises or percussions nearby
- overcrowding (in some cases, this can be just one other snake in the same terrarium)
- retained scales or other sources of physical discomfort
- threatening species housed too closely to one another (kingsnakes, which are natural predators for most other North American species, can cause serious stress in nearby snakes, as those other snakes smell the kingsnake and recognize that scent as indicative of a natural predator)

A highly stressed snake will be very active, nosing around the tank or pushing up against the lid, refusing to feed, or offering to bite when you approach the terrarium. Remedy the stressful situation by first identifying the source of the stress. Snakes that are scared of human traffic (colubrids in the racer family tend to suffer from this, as do garden boas and members of the *Opheodrys* genus) do better when housed away from the major areas of activity in the home. Many hobbyists make their snakes feel more secure by covering or painting over the outside—*never* the inside—of three sides of the terrarium. This gives the snake a more enclosed feeling, and with that feeling comes a much greater sense of stability and security. Remember, most snakes have a terrible natural fear of wide-open places—with total exposure comes the threat of predators. Most snakes feel most comfortable when they can hide and when they feel hidden and protected from potential predators.

Once you've identified the source of your snake's stress and taken all of the necessary steps to correct it, the problems that typically come along with stress—aggression, unwillingness to feed, frantic or escapist behaviors, etc.—should soon vanish as well.

Again, none of us can see the future, and there is no way of totally preventing an injury or ailment from striking your pet snake, but by following a few simple rules and using your best judgment when it comes to the habitat and environmental conditions you provide, the type of food and frequency of feedings you offer, and the cleanliness and hygiene level at which you maintain your pet, you can go a long way in curbing any would-be disasters or diseases from afflicting your pet snake. As I said at the beginning of this chapter, an ounce of prevention is worth so much more than a pound of cure when it comes to keeping your pet snake in peak mental and physical health.

Stripe-tailed rat snake

Chapter Six

SELECTED SPECIES

"Old obsoleta's…head wagged slow, benevolent and sad and sage, as though it understood our human limitation, and forgave all."
~**Robert Penn Warren,** *Brother to Dragons*

Perhaps the most critical element to a successful snake-keeping endeavor is the selection of both the right individual snake as a pet and the right species of snake. Not every snake owner is able, willing, or equipped to deal with every species of snake. Indeed, the general care and maintenance of some snake species can be so different from the care of other species that they seem like entirely different pets. A small North American milk snake, for example, will require vastly different keeping conditions than will a 17-foot-long (5.2-m) reticulated python. On paper, the two are snakes, and snake lovers might take an interest in either one. But the fact of the matter is that the person who is well equipped to provide years of healthy, safe, and loving care for a 3-foot-long (0.9-m) milk snake may be unprepared to tend to the spatial, dietary, and heating requirements of the titanic reticulated python for even one day.

But size, of course, is not the only consideration in matching the right snake with the right keeper. Over the years, I have kept a personal collection of several venomous species, including copperheads and rattlesnakes. It goes without saying that these snakes were pets in name only. I never handled them unless it was absolutely necessary, and even then I used all of the appropriate tools and accessories (snake hook, bite-resistant gloves, etc.) to ensure that my pets' fangs and my flesh never crossed paths! It

Good Snakekeeping

Not every available snake is suitable for every hobbyist. Baby green tree pythons are expensive, delicate, and often aggressive snakes suitable only for experienced keepers.

also goes without saying that such hazardous animals are not to be handled or played with as pets. On the other hand, I have also owned several rosy boas, which are some of the most handle-friendly North American snakes I've ever encountered. They would spend hours quietly coiled around my wrist or within the palms of my hands when I handled them; they absolutely loved soaking in my 98.6°F (37°C) body heat, and I absolutely loved the gentle, temperate nature of those beautiful, docile reptiles. These two scenarios, therefore, represent yet another yawning divide between the suitability of a particular snake species with a potential keeper. Do you want a snake you can handle and interact with frequently, or will it be fine with you if you only handle it when necessary, enjoying your snake for its beauty and behavior only?

I could go on and on with polar opposites when it comes to matching the right snake species with the right keeper, but I think the point is clear: You must know as much as you can about the species of snake you desire before getting one. Buying before you have a working, in-depth knowledge of your preferred species can end in calamity; your snake will likely receive inadequate care or attention, and you will be displeased with your investment (and you just might turn sour on snake keeping as a whole). The good news is that such a scenario is easily prevented, and it is the purpose of this chapter to thwart just such circumstance from ever coming to pass.

Organization of This Chapter

Contained in this chapter are the basic nuts and bolts of a wide selection of frequently encountered species. Although all of the standard pet shop snakes are covered here, you'll also find information on more obscure or less frequently kept animals as well. These species profiles are organized in a fashion that offers both a broad range of information (on the family level) as well as specific information (on the species level). So, for example, the information covering a Columbian red-tailed boa will be at once specific to that animal while at the same time offering keen insight into the keeping of other subspecies of red-tailed boas (such as the Surinam red-tailed boa or the Dominican clouded red-tailed boa—considered a separate species by some authorities).

Each profile further breaks down into several categories, each of which gives crucial information about the animal in question.

- **Range:** *Range* refers to the animal's natural range in the wild; this can give you a good feel for the biome or habitat in which your chosen species will thrive.

- **Size:** *Size* gives a general estimate of how large/long the average specimen will grow. It is important to note, however, that both sex and diet can be major determining variants in the size of an individual snake. In returning to the red-tailed boa, for example, males of the species seldom exceed 8 feet (2.4 m) in length, while females may attain 10 feet (3 m), or in rare cases, 14 feet (4.3 m) in length—that's an additional 50 to 75 percent the size of the males. Likewise,

Beginner's Best Bets

Here is my "Ten Best Beginning Pet Snakes" list. Although the general care and maintenance vary widely among these species, the following chart represents some of the hardiest, most docile, and most commonly kept snakes in the trade today. It's hard to go wrong with any one of these excellent starter animals.

The Ten Best Beginning Pet Snakes

- Baird's rat snake (*Pantherophis bairdi*)
- California kingsnake (*Lampropeltis getula*)
- corn snake (*Pantherophis guttatus*)
- garter snake (*Thamnophis sirtalis*)
- Honduran milk snake (*Lampropeltis triangulum hondurensis*)
- Kenyan sand boa (*Eryx colubrinus loveridgei*)
- rosy boa (*Lichanura trivirgata*)
- rough green snake (*Opheodrys aestivus*)
- twin-spotted rat snake (*Elaphe bimaculata*)
- western hognose snake (*Heterodon nasicus*)

The ball python (*Python regius*) could be added to this list, provided you obtain a well-started, captive-bred juvenile.

diet (nutritional quality of feedings, frequency of feedings, etc.) can also play a major role in the growth rate and maximum size of your captive snake.

- **Subspecies and Similar Species:** The category of *Subspecies and Similar Species* gives details on similar snakes you may encounter in pet stores and at expos. The snakes covered here require the same or very similar care as the species in question. Recent taxonomic changes are covered here.

- **Description:** *Description* is just that, a succinct description of that species and the particulars of its behavior in captivity; this category will give you a short yet concise overview of that species.

- **Captive Diet:** The next category is *Captive Diet*, which gives all of the necessary information on that animal's particular dietary demands in the home terrarium environment.

- **Longevity:** *Longevity* provides a general timeline for how long your chosen species will live when kept under ideal conditions. Like *Size*, this category is subject to substantial variation, as there are any number of factors that can end even the seemingly healthiest snake's life prematurely. Paying strict attention to *Longevity* is a definite necessity, as your purchase may well hinge on how long lived your investment will be. Are you purchasing a snake for your child, who may make an excellent hobbyist for the five or so years that

Some snakes have numerous subspecies. The common garter snake has 13, including the valley garter snake (*Thamnophis sirtalis fitchi.*)

Pet Suitability Guide

1: An easily cared for and good beginner's snake

2: Best for someone with some snake experience or a very conscientious novice

3: Somewhat challenging species best suited for experienced hobbyists

4: Challenging and/or somewhat dangerous species. Expert hobbyists only.

5: Extremely challenging and/or dangerous species. Best suited for zoos and other professionals

that his rough green snake is alive? Or are you buying a red-tailed boa as a long-term addition—several decades long—to your personal collection?

- **Habitat and Terrarium:** The next category, *Habitat and Terrarium*, will give you a good idea of both the natural environment a particular species comes from, as well as what manner of habitat to construct for your new pet snake. A desert-dwelling species, for example, will require a desert-type environment with low relative humidity, warm air, bright basking lights, and rocky hideaways, while a jungle-dwelling species will thrive best with dense foliage, climbing branches, and humid conditions.

- **Temperatures and Humidity/Lighting:** The next two sections, *Temperatures and Humidity* and *Lighting*, give specifics on how warm and humid and how bright your snake likes its surroundings. Diurnal species, for example, may enjoy a basking light, while nocturnal animals may avoid bright basking lights at all costs.

- **Reproduction**: *Reproduction* is a category that provides only basic information about that species' reproductive cycle; breeding snakes is an advanced aspect of husbandry that is not covered in depth within this book. Many species-specific books contain complete information on breeding when that information is known.

- **Pet Suitability:** The final category is *Pet Suitability*, which is a no-nonsense breakdown of just how easy or difficult it is to care for that species. An everglades rat snake, therefore, may rank high on the suitability scale; it is relatively small, mild mannered, undemanding, and hardy. An emerald tree boa, however, will rank low on the suitability scale because this species is sensitive to humidity and temperature, and its temperament is such that few casual hobbyists would purchase one. Using a numbered system ranging from 1 to 5—5 being a species that is difficult to care for and best left to professionals and 1 being an absolutely wonderful pet for hobbyists at any experience level—the *Pet Suitability* category is the bottom-line advice that addresses the question: Is this species right for me and my experience level and budget?

All things considered, the following profiles are intended to give you the basic information necessary to both make an informed purchase and to give your animal all the necessary care in the captive environment. However, I urge you to become as knowledgeable as you can about both your chosen pet as well as snake husbandry as a whole. At the end of this book, therefore, I include a suggested reading list of some of my favorite texts on the captive care and maintenance of snakes. Knowledge is power; the more of it you have, the more your snake will flourish under your care and the more positive and rewarding your pet snake endeavor will be.

Boidae: The Boas and Pythons

The family Boidae contains all of the snakes collectively known as the boas and pythons. This family is, however, frequently broken down into three subfamilies: the Boinae (the boas, mostly found in the New World), Pythoninae (the pythons, found in the Old World), and Erycinae (the sand boas, of North America, Africa, and Asia). Many hobbyists keep the two straight in their minds by remembering that boas are Central and South American animals, while pythons inhabit the Middle East, Africa, Asia, and the Pacific Islands. Although this Old World/New World divide is not a perfect fit (the boas of the South Pacific islands, for example), it does provide a general overview of the geographic ranges of the two subfamilies.

Splitting Up the Family

Much debate exists within the scientific community as to whether the pythons, boas, and sand boas are all one family or three different ones—or even two families (pythons in one and boas and sand boas in the other). This is not at all critical to the care of these snakes, but don't be surprised if you see Boidae, Pythonidae, and Erycinidae treated as full families in other books and articles.

Large, nonvenomous snakes, the boas and pythons (sometimes collectively referred to as boids) dispatch their prey by constriction. The supratemporal and quadrate bones in the skull of the boids are elongated, which allow them to swallow extremely large prey items. Despite their muscular power and lightening speed in making a kill, many boids make docile, hardy captives. As such, they are highly in demand within the exotic pet trade (and in Hollywood, where

The Boidae includes the largest living snakes. The green anaconda (*Eunectes murinus*) is the heaviest known snake reaching a weight of 300 pounds (136 kg) or more.

directors frequently film a reticulated python, a species native to southern Asia, slithering along a bough in a movie set in South America!). Sadly, the rich colors and intricate patterns of these snakes also make them marketable in the skin and exotic leather trade; every year, countless wild and farm-raised boids are slaughtered for their beautiful skins.

The Boidae comprises some 70 species ranging across the globe's forests, savannas, jungles, and deserts. Of these diverse species, most are found in the tropical jungles and rainforests of the world; only a few species live in Europe, and only two are found in the United States. Curiously, most subfamilies of boids have ranges that do not overlap; boas and pythons seldom coexist. In the areas where the two subfamilies do overlap, they tend to thrive in different habitats. The most likely reason for this inability to coexist comes from the fact that the two would be in direct competition with each other for food, space, and general ecological niche.

Both boas and pythons are primitive snakes and have spurs located on either side of the cloaca. Actually vestigial hind limbs stemming from a pelvic girdle (that's right, boid snakes still have remnants of hind legs), these spurs are now used in mating behaviors. Some male boids will, when aligning with females just prior to copulation, stroke the female with these spurs to stimulate her. Many species of boids also have heat-sensitive pits in their faces, usually between or within the scales of the upper lips. These pits, which can detect even slight variations in temperature, aid the snake in both subduing prey and avoiding predation. The situation of these pits in the face is another good way to distinguish boas from pythons. Boas have pits located in broad gaps between the labial scales, while pythons' pits are generally on or more adjacent to those scales. Likewise, all but one of the boas are ovoviviparous, meaning that they give birth to live young, while all of the pythons are oviparous, meaning that they reproduce by laying eggs. Female pythons often coil about their eggs until they hatch and generate body heat by rapidly contracting and relaxing small muscles.

AFRICAN ROCK PYTHON
PYTHON SEBAE (GMELIN, 1788)

Range: Wide ranging throughout central and southern Africa. Has been driven to extinction throughout much of its range due to urbanization and overhunting.

Size: Enormous. One of the true giant snakes alive today, the African rock python may grow to lengths in excess of 20 feet (6.1 m) and may weigh more than 150 pounds (68 kg).

The African rock python is an enormous and usually aggressive snake. Although captive breeding of this species occurs, it is uncommon.

Subspecies and Similar Species: There is much conflict over the subspeciation of this snake, although no other subspecies occur regularly in the pet trade.

Description: A very large snake adorned with cryptic brown, black, tan, and other earth tones, the rock python is a quietly handsome animal. Novice hobbyists frequently mistake this species for its close ally, the Burmese python, because the two are similarly marked. The dorsum of the rock python is a mosaic of chocolate blotches atop a darker base, thereby forming a loose chain-link pattern. Lateral surfaces are tan to yellowish gray with brown adjoining blotches, forming a zipper-like pattern. Longer stripes of dark and lighter chocolate colors adorn the head and neck. The head is large and strapped with powerful jaw muscles. Despite its large size, a hungry rock python can strike with alarming speed. As is true with all giant snakes, large adult rock pythons pose a potential threat to domestic pet and human life. Always be cautious when working with or around this species.

Captive Diet: In the wild, African rock pythons consume anything and everything that they can subdue: rodents, birds, small mammals, and wild pigs. Large adults may take deer, crocodiles, monkeys, and domestic livestock. Mehrtens reports a 13-foot-long (4 m) specimen containing a "small leopard." Captive diet may include pre-killed mice, chicks, and hamsters or gerbils for hatchlings, and pre-killed rats, guinea pigs, quail, chickens, rabbits, and small goats for larger adults.

Longevity: Although it is the topic of some dispute, the African rock python may easily exceed 20 years of age, and reports of 30-year-old specimens are not unheard of. In either case, the purchase of this snake is a long-term commitment.

Habitat and Terrarium: Large environs. More subterranean in its habits than many of the other giant snakes, the rock python needs three major components to thrive in captivity: room to slither, a basking spot, and a deep, dark hideaway. Juveniles may be housed in 55-gallon (208.2-l) terraria, while larger adults will require specialized or custom housing. Many hobbyists report great success with outdoor greenhouses or a room within the house dedicated to the snake.

In the wild, these snakes thrive in savannas and open grasslands, so their home terrarium should replicate this environment. Obviously, the space to slither is

One Rock Python or Two?

Most authorities recognize two subspecies of African rock pythons, *P. sebae natalensis* and *P. sebae sebae*. *P. s. natalensis*—sometimes called the lesser rock python or the Natal rock python—occurs in the southern part of the range of the rock python, from southern Kenya and Angola to southeastern South Africa. Small numbers are available in the pet trade. Because of differences in head scales, coloration, and range, some biologists consider the Natal rock python to be a separate species, and in 1999, Donald G. Broadley officially elevated this snake to a full species, *Python natalensis*. However the status of the Natal rock python remains controversial.

key feature and can be difficult to satisfy in the case of a snake as large as rock python. Half-buried lengths of appropriately sized PVC pipe work well ides. Access to pools of water is also paramount because these pythons are ost always found in or near bodies of water in nature. However, the substrate uld not be permanently moist because this species is prone to contract skin respiratory ailments.

iperatures and Humidity: Rock pythons like it hot: daily ambient temperatures of 80° to 83°F (26.7° to 28.3°C) with a basking spot up to 90°F (32.2°). Cooler retreats are needed, and nightly drops into the mid 70s F (23.6° to 24.5°C) are acceptable. Maintain a moderate relative humidity and consider using a humidified hide box.

Lighting: Although they are primarily nocturnal, rock pythons are prone to late afternoon basking (the warmth obtained will fuel the snake's metabolism through the cooler hours of the night) and should be provided with a full-spectrum bulb.

Reproduction: Egg layers. Females will coil about and vigorously defend their clutches, which may consist of well more than100 eggs. Young hatch after three months and may exceed 24 inches (61 cm) at hatching.

Pet Suitability: 5

The African rock python is an infamously ill-tempered species. Couple this strike-happy disposition with its enormous stature, and it's easy to see that this snake is fit only for the most dedicated and advanced hobbyists and zoological professionals. That said, it is also important to note that with patience and regular handling, this snake can become somewhat tame to human touch. I definitely do not recommend it for beginning or intermediate enthusiasts. Even if you are desirous of keeping your first "giant" snake, I recommend the red-tailed boa or Burmese python before recommending the rock python.

BALL PYTHON
PYTHON REGIUS (SHAW, 1802)

Range: Central and western Africa, from Mauretania to Uganda.

Size: Although reports of 6-foot-long (1.8-m) specimens exist, common adult lengths are 3 to 4 feet (0.9 to 1.2 m). Despite its short length, this species is quite heavy bodied.

Subspecies and Similar Species: None. The Angolan python (*P. anchietae*) is the closest relative to the ball python, but it is quite rare in the pet hobby.

Description: A short, earth-toned snake, the ball python (alternately named the royal python because Cleopatra was allegedly fond of wearing this species around her wrists) wears a base color of chocolate brown to black with lighter brown, tan, sandy, or yellow irregularly shaped blotches along the flanks and dorsum. Smaller black spots or ocelli frequently occur within these lighter blotches. Many hobbyists have noted that the markings on the backs of ball pythons are as variable and as unique as human fingerprints. The head and snout is broad, and the tail is moderately short. A primarily terrestrial snake, the ball python spends considerable time occupying old mammal or tortoise burrows.

This species derives its common name from its unique habit of curling itself into a tight ball—its head hidden deep within its protective coils—when a predator approaches. When the threat has passed, the snake will abandon its defensive ball posture. The belly scales are very narrow, making this snake unsuited for extensive climbing. Within its native Africa, the ball python is a significant animal, raised and skinned for the leather trade by some, revered as the symbol of an earth god by some religious factions, and sold for the commercial pet trade by wildlife entrepreneurs.

Captive Diet: Mice and small rats. Wild specimens take a variety of rodent fare.

Longevity: 20 years or more. One zoo-kept specimen was recorded as living for almost half a century, thereby making the ball python the longest-lived snake ever in captivity.

Habitat and Terrarium: In the wild, ball pythons thrive in grasslands and open or sparsely wooded savannas. Captive habitats should mimic this setting: lots of

Ball python demonstrating the defensive behavior from which the common name derives.

Breeders produce a staggering number of ball python morphs. Here are four out of the many dozens available: (clockwise from top left) pinstripe, albino, caramel albino (also called xanthic albino), and piebald.

Most ball pythons are docile and easy to handle.

open floor space, a few climbing branches, and numerous hides. Aside from this, your ball python will thrive in virtually any type of tank: glass, ABS plastic, or the classic sweater-box style used by breeders and importers. In general, ball pythons are not picky in their environs.

Temperatures and Humidity: Maintain daily temperatures between 79° and 82°F (26.1° and 27.8°C) with a hot spot that reaches between 85° and 90°F (29.4° and 32.2°C). Establish a definite gradient through which your snake may regulate its bodily temperature. Maintain a mid-range relative humidity, about 50 to 70 percent. Good ventilation is paramount, and a moist spot under a hide is also a good idea.

Lighting: Some keepers recommend using a full-spectrum bulb with the ball python, although this is not necessary.

Reproduction: Mates in spring (after a period of slightly reduced temperatures) in captivity. Females deposit small clutches, seldom exceeding a half-dozen large, ovate eggs. As do all pythons, the female will coil about her brood until they hatch some three months later. However, most breeders opt to incubate the eggs artificially.

Pet Suitability: 1

Because it is so widely available, this snake can often be purchased for a low price. Avoid buying wild-caught specimens at all costs, as all imported specimens come with heavy internal parasite loads, as well as mites and ticks. Wild-caught ball pythons are infamous for being picky eaters, and a finicky ball python may not eat for months at a time. If this happens, monitor your pet to ensure that no radical weight loss occurs. Ball pythons can also be particular in the color of their fare; I've owned snakes that will only eat black mice and snub white mice. Conversely, I've seen specimens that will only take gray or white mice while refusing to accept black or brown rodents. Despite the wide availability of this snake, I do not recommend it for beginners. However, novice hobbyists can succeed with captive-bred, well-started juveniles.

BLOOD PYTHON
PYTHON BRONGERSMAI STULL, 1938

Range: Southern Malay peninsula, Thailand, Sumatra, and adjacent areas.
Size: The blood python is a short but very heavy-bodied species. Males may attain 45 to 50 inches (114.3 to 127 cm), while females may reach 6 feet (1.8 m). Reports of 9-foot-long (2.7-m) specimens are unconfirmed. The weight of such specimens is astronomical, however, with a 5-foot-long (1.5-m) snake easily weighing some 35 pounds (15.9 kg) or more. Such bodily structure—

Blood pythons have a reputation for being nasty, vicious animals. However, captive-bred ones can be docile when handled consistently.

The three species of blood python are the stockiest of the pythons. They are bulky, powerful snakes.

huge girth with a short tail—distinguishes the blood python as a primarily terrestrial species, although short ventures into low-growing, stout-limbed vegetation are common.

Subspecies and Similar Species: The blood python has long been considered to be divided into three subspecies: *Python curtus curtus*, *P. c. breitensteini*, and *P. c. brongersmai*. However, papers published in 2000 and 2001 (see References section) elevated all three subspecies to full species. Hobbyists have been slow to adopt these changes and often treat the blood python as being three subspecies of *Python curtus*. Because *P. brongersmai* is the only form that gets the deep blood-red coloration—although not all specimens are this color—it is the one that should be called the true blood python. Various common names are used for the others. *P. curtus* is often called the black blood python because it is the darkest in color; it is also called the Sumatran blood python. *P. breitensteini* is usually called the Borneo short-tailed python but may also be called the Borneo python or the Borneo blood python. All three occur in the pet trade, and ill-informed buyers (or importers) are often confused about the exact identity of the snake they are considering for purchase. Most hobbyists agree that *P. curtus*

Borneo short-tailed pythons are endemic to Borneo and are the only one of the blood pythons found there.

the easiest to handle of the subspecies, but captive-bred specimens of any species may be docile if handled properly. Color and pattern morphs of *P. breitensteini* and *P. brongersmai* exist, including albino and ivory *P. brongersmai*.

Description: A breathtakingly beautiful snake, the blood python wears a base coat of sandy gray to yellow. This base is heavily mottled with irregular blotches of orange, maroon, black, red, brick, or blood color, depending on the species in question. A dark band extends from the snout back through the eye and down the neck. In the wild, these asymmetrical markings help grant the blood python a surprisingly effective camouflage. Bodily, the blood python is very thick; its jaws are powerful, and an angry specimen can strike with alarming speed and accuracy. The head is extremely broad and tapers to a much more slender neck, and the tail, which is not very prehensile, is short.

Captive Diet: Blood pythons prey almost exclusively on rats. Juveniles may be reared on pinkie or fuzzy rats, while larger prey is appropriate for larger specimens. Attempts to supplement the diet with the occasional chick meet with varied levels of success.

Longevity: Exceeds 20 years.

Habitat and Terrarium: Natural habitat includes forests, marshes, and riverine areas. They are also found in plantations. Captive terrariums should strive to simulate such conditions. Substrate may range from jungle-mix or natural (sterilized) soil mixtures to such artificial materials as recycled newspaper or paper towels. Many hobbyists report having met with great success by using folded newsprint. Daily mistings to the naturalistic terrarium are in order. Keep a large (and not easily tipped) dish of water at your python's disposal at all times, as this species may safely spend long periods submerged underwater.

Whether opting for a naturalistic terrarium or a spartan enclosure, ventilation is a must. Even though blood pythons thrive in humid environments, they can still suffer under perpetually damp conditions, and supplying ample ventilation (attained by a screen lid) is a necessity. Because it is terrestrial, the blood python needs a tank that stresses lateral dimensions over vertical height. Many keepers report that an ABS plastic or polyethylene cage is preferable over an all-glass, fish-tank-style terrarium for housing this species. I recommend a tank that provides no less than 3 x 3 feet (0.9 x 0.9 m) of floor space for moderately sized animals and a larger enclosure for very large adults. A cage with an area 4 x 4 feet (1.2 x 1.2 m) would be ideal for long-term housing. One of the most common mistakes that blood python keepers make is establishing a tank for their pet that is too small.

Temperatures and Humidity: 80° to 85°F (26.7° to 29.4°C) ambient with slight drops at night. Maintaining a relative humidity of 60 to 70 percent is preferable.

Lighting: No specialized UV lighting is necessary.

Reproduction: Females deposit small clutches of rather large eggs and will coil about their brood until it hatches. Some two-and-a-half to three months after deposition, the young should emerge from their eggs. Young may be pale or washed out in coloration. As they mature, however, these snakes will take on the brick-red or bloody coloration for which they are famous. The young are 11 to 13 inches (27.9 to 33 cm) at hatching.

Pet Suitability: 3

The blood python has experienced a massive surge in popularity within the last few years or so, and as a result, is much more widely available than it was just ten years ago. Considering its need for floor space and its semi-aggressive disposition, this animal is not recommended for the beginning hobbyist. However, someone who is skilled in python husbandry and wishes to up the ante on his experience might want to keep this gorgeous reptile. I recommend purchasing captive bred over wild caught, as wild blood pythons are notoriously ill tempered. If hatched in captivity, however, young will come to thrive in the home terrarium and will even enjoy gentle handling.

BURMESE PYTHON
PYTHON MOLURUS BIVATTATUS KUHL, 1820

Range: Extensive throughout southern China, Burma, Thailand, some Indonesian islands, and surrounding areas.

Size: Enormous. Documented accounts of 25-foot-long (7.6-m) specimens are accurate. Typical adult lengths do not exceed 17 to 20 feet (5.2 to 6.1 m), with females being considerably larger than males.

Subspecies and Similar Species: Two subspecies occur, but only the Burmese python ("burm" to most hobbyists) is seen in the pet trade. The Indian python (*P. m. molurus*) is the nominate race but is rarely bred or imported, as trade in this animal is tightly regulated. When it appears in the pet trade, it fetches an accordingly high price. The pythons of Sri Lanka were once considered a separate subspecies and called Ceylonese pythons (*P. m. pimbura*). However, they are now treated as a local variant of the Indian python.

Description: A pretty snake, the Burmese python wears a base coat of tan to cream or yellowish with rich cinnamon- to chocolate-colored saddles and dorsolateral blotches. The chain-link pattern between the blotches on the dorsum may be sandy to champagne in color. Very popular also are albino,

Due to irresponsible hobbyists letting their Burmese pythons go when they become too large to handle, this snake has become an invasive species in several areas.

Timor Pythons

The Timor python (*P. timoriensis*) was once considered a subspecies of the Indian python but is in fact a separates species. It is a mysterious snake that rarely appears in the pet trade. It almost never exceeds 6 to 7 feet (1.8 to 2.1 m) in length but may reach almost 10 feet (3 m). It ranges in color from amber yellow to dark brown. It has irregular darker blotches that are often more abundant on the rear half of the body. Timor pythons only occur on the islands of Timor, Flores, and Lombien, although it is possible that they occur on other islands in this understudied part of Indonesia.

patternless (often called green), and other designer variants of the Burmese python.

Juveniles are strong, accomplished climbers, while adults tend to stay terrestrial. All specimens are devout swimmers and may even hunt underwater. (In the wild, deer or aquatic rodents stand little chance of escape when taking to water.) Capable of striking with blinding speed, the Burmese python can inflict a painful, bloody bite on its keeper, but with patience and gentle, regular handling, this snake typically tames to human touch.

Captive Diet: Pre-killed rodents and chicks for juveniles and larger fare for adults: rabbits, guinea pigs, small goats, and small pigs will be taken with relish. Wild Burmese pythons accept any prey they can subdue. As is true of all giant snakes, a large Burmese python may pose a threat to domestic pets and human life. All precautions must be taken when dealing with large specimens.

Good Snakekeeping

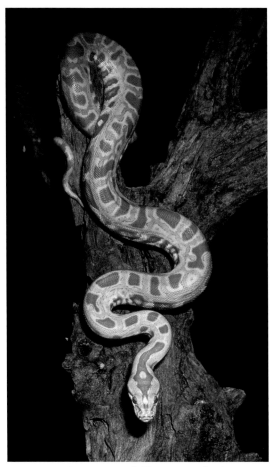

Burmese pythons are available in several color morphs. The albino is the most popular morph.

Longevity: 20 years or longer.

Habitat and Terrarium: Large environs are a must. Captive terrarium conditions should stress longer and wider dimensions for adult snakes and taller dimensions for juveniles, as the young snakes will climb, while the older, heavier-bodied adults seldom leave the ground. Snug-fitting hide boxes are a must, as is plenty of room to slither about. These snakes may bask. A large pool of water is a must; either supply a large tub within the terrarium or soak the animal regularly in a bathtub or kiddie pool. Substrates of mulch mixed with leaf litter work well if naturalistic conditions are desired, while recycled newspaper bedding is a great choice for the spartan terrarium. Many hobbyists dedicate an entire room or outdoor shed or greenhouse to their Burmese pythons.

Temperatures and Humidity: Warm temperatures, in the range of 78° to 84°F (25.6° to 29°C), and humid conditions (about 70 percent or lower if you use a humidified hide box) are just what the doctor ordered for a healthy burm. These snakes are rainforest animals by nature and seldom stray far from a permanent source of water. As such, they are tolerant of humid conditions but can still fall victim to blister disease if denied a place to dry themselves.

Lighting: Most experts agree that full-spectrum lighting is advantageous for this species, but this is more personal opinion then it is proven fact. I have found that natural sunlight (unfiltered) is also beneficial.

Reproduction: Of all the giant snakes, the Burmese python is perhaps the most fecund and the most willing to reproduce in captivity. Females deposit up to 100 eggs and defend them vigorously during their 90-day incubation period. Young are 24 inches (61 cm) at hatching and grow quickly.

Pet Suitability: 4

Owing to its beautiful pattern and semi-docile nature, the Burmese python makes for a congenial and attractive pet giant snake. Because of its tremendous

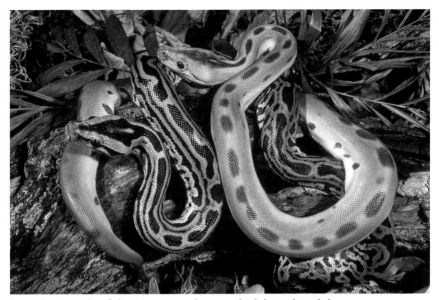

Two other morphs of the Burmese python are the labyrinth and the green or patternless morphs.

size as an adult, however, this is not a pet to be purchased lightly or on a whim. As is true with all of the giant snakes, this animal represents a serious, long-term, and potentially dangerous endeavor and must be met with corresponding responsibility on the part of the keeper. As far as the giants go, however, the Burmese python is an agreeable species; it is hardy, attractive, usually docile, and readily bred in captivity.

DIAMOND PYTHON
MORELIA SPILOTA (LACÈPÉDE, 1804)
Range: Australia and New Guinea.
Size: May exceed 12 feet (3.7 m) in length, although this is highly unusual. Common adult lengths seldom exceed 8 feet (2.4 m).
Subspecies and Similar Species: The carpet python (*M. s. variegata*) is far more common than the true diamond python (*M. s. spilota*) in the pet trade. Lacking the typical diamond or rhombic pattern, the carpet python wears a zigzag or zipper-like pattern of alternating or interwoven bars of white or cream and black or gray. The jungle carpet python (*M. s. cheynei*) is another popular subspecies. It is marked similarly to the carpet python, but the jungle carpet is much brighter in color, typically being black or dark brown with bright yellow markings. The

Close-up and full-body views of the diamond python. Pure diamond pythons are rare in the pet trade and are often crossed with the other subspecies. The snake on the right shows some evidence of not being a pure diamond in the blotchiness of its pattern.

carpet python is the most common subspecies because it occurs in Papua; this province of Indonesia allows the export of its fauna, unlike in Australia, where the rest of the subspecies occur.

Although nomenclature and exact classification are confused for these snakes (especially in areas where populations overlap and breed into integration), the care for the subspecies is nearly identical. The various subspecies have been interbred extensively in the hobby. Jungle-diamond crosses are particularly common.

Description: An absolutely gorgeous snake, the diamond python takes its common name from its pattern: an alabaster to ivory base color with heavy black flecking and mottling dorsally. Dominant dorsal markings usually consist of a pattern within a pattern—some scales are two toned, creating a tight, minute pattern of contrast, while other black scales form rhomboids or diamonds (with all-white centers) along the midline of the back. Irregularities within this double pattern only increase the snake's unique beauty. The ventral surface is white, and larger diamonds frequently occur along the lateral surfaces. Some particularly handsome specimens have an overall greenish tint to them. Pronounced labial pits are present; the nostrils are situated toward the top of the snout. Carpet pythons tend to wear less clearly defined colors and markings, the black and white on each scale being less two toned and more muddy or blended in appearance.

Captive Diet: Diamond and carpet pythons thrive on a rodent-based diet:

pre-killed mice, rats, and gerbils are accepted with relish, as are chicks and small quail.

Longevity: May exceed 15 years.

Habitat and Terrarium: Equally at home in low shrubs, bushes, and thick-limbed trees and on the ground, these pythons thrive in both wooded and grassland areas in the wild, and they require some elements of both in the home terrarium. A sturdy outcropping of rockwork, plenty of snug hideaways (buried PVC piping works well for this purpose), and a host of stout and sturdily anchored climbing branches will make for one happy, healthy diamond python. Sandy substrate or a mixture of sand and organic mulch substrate is recommended, although many breeders recommend a paper substrate.

Temperatures and Humidity: Maintain ambient temperatures of 75° to 84°F (24° to 29°C) with a basking spot of about 88°F (31.1°C). Light, daily mistings of lukewarm water are highly beneficial to this species, as it can suffer from dysecdysis in captivity. A humidified hideaway is also recommended, although the substrate should not be wet to the touch.

Lighting: I have housed a number of diamond and carpet pythons through the years, and it has been my experience that these snakes fare better with at least two hours of exposure to full-spectrum lighting each day than with no exposure at all. Colors seem brighter, shed cycles seem quicker, and metabolism and scale quality seem finer and healthier.

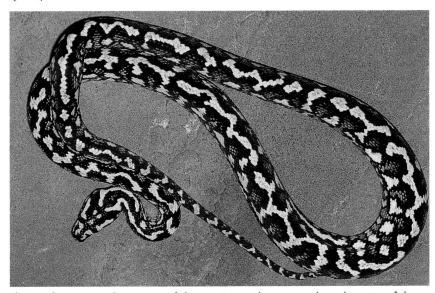

The jungle carpet python is one of the prettiest and most popular subspecies of the diamond python.

Reproduction: Egg layers. Large females may lay about 18 eggs and will incubate them until they hatch. Young are 12 inches (30.5 cm) long at emergence, and incubation lasts roughly 40 to 60 days. Young *M. spilota* are noted for being very nippy, but most calm down with proper handling.

Pet Suitability: 2

Ever popular with zoos and experienced collectors, these snakes are hardy and beautiful, large but still manageable, and typically quite docile. A handling session with a diamond python is an exercise in amazement because this species truly combines all of the best qualities of snake keeping in a single animal. Although I recommend the diamond and carpet pythons highly, you should learn as much as you can about these animals before making the investment. Even though they are hardy and easily cared for, these snakes still require an experienced hand in their everyday maintenance.

DUMERIL'S BOA
ACRANTOPHIS DUMERILI JAN, 1860

Range: Southern and western Madagascar.

Size: To 8 feet (2.4 m), although 6 to 7 feet (1.8 to 2.1 m) is more common.

Subspecies and Similar Species: The Malagasy ground boa (*A. madagascariensis*) is a larger relative and may reach lengths of up to 10.5 feet (3.2 m). It is often more reddish than Dumeril's boa and has a reduced or absent pattern on the dorsal surface.

Description: A heavy-bodied and cryptically colored snake, the Dumeril's boa is an infinitely attractive animal. It features a base coloration of brownish to gray with rosy hues and coral tinting along the head and the midline of the back. Pattern is especially cryptic: Dorsolateral ocelli and rhomboids ("rhombs" to some hobbyists) are dark and accented with white to cream color ovals and flecks. Along the midline of the back, the pattern is less distinct and may take an hourglass shape in some specimens, a zigzag pattern in others, or a series of ovals in others. Black to brown lines may adorn the head and neck.

Captive Diet: Rodents and pre-killed chicks are greedily taken. Captive feeding is seldom a problem with the Dumeril's boa. Larger specimens may take guinea pigs or small rabbits.

Longevity: May exceed 15 to 20 years.

Habitat and Terrarium: Dry forest and semi-arid areas of Madagascar. Requires a large, horizontally oriented tank with lots of ground cover and plenty of hides. A devoutly terrestrial species, the Dumeril's prefers leafy substrate and plenty of vegetative cover. A couple of large, flat stones or fallen logs are also recommended. A thick substrate of mulch and leaves is recommended.

Temperatures and Humidity: Maintain 75° to 81°F (24° to 27.2°C) ambient

Dumeril's boa is one of the easiest large snakes to maintain. It is usually not at all aggressive.

temperatures, with warmer basking spots of about 90°F (32.2°C) or so. Relative humidity levels are not crucial throughout the tank. Drier conditions may prevail atop the leafy substrate, while a humid hideaway (such as a half-buried length of PVC) is a must. This allows for a humidity disparity that allows the snake to occupy either drier or more humid environs as it desires or needs.

Lighting: Many hobbyists report success with full-spectrum lighting, while others insist that they see no difference in their snake's appearance or health, regardless of lighting.

Reproduction: Mates in July to August (spring season in the southern hemisphere) in the wild, although captive breeding can be conditioned around the climate of the northern hemisphere (usually July to August under controlled conditions). Young are born from four to six months after mating and are 18 to 24 inches (45.7 to 61 cm) at birth.

Pet Suitability: 1

The Dumeril's is a hardy, gorgeous, and easily kept boa. Most are docile. The only drawback is its size. Formerly an extremely expensive snake, captive breeding has brought down its price considerably.

EMERALD TREE BOA
CORALLUS CANINUS (LINNAEUS, 1758)

Range: Amazon Basin and the Guiana Shield: Ecuador, Peru, Guiana, Brazil, Bolivia, and surrounding countries.

Size: One of the heaviest bodied of the strictly arboreal boids, the emerald tree boa may exceed 7.5 feet (2.3 m) in length.

Subspecies and Similar Species: None.

Description: A large, heavy-bodied snake, the emerald tree boa is a strikingly beautiful animal. Adult coloration is emerald dorsally with a lemon-yellow belly and jaws. White wedges or triangles distend from the midline of the back. Labial heat-sensitive pits are extremely well developed and can detect a fraction of a degree in temperature difference even at a distance of several feet (1 m) away. The pupils are elliptical, as is common with nocturnal species. The scales are smooth, and the tail is highly prehensile. Musculature is well developed; this

Because of their high price and exacting requirements, emerald tree boas are best left to experienced hobbyists.

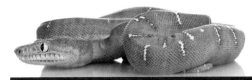

snake may, after striking and latching onto a bird or bat, hang completely upside down while devouring its prey. To this end, the teeth are very long, sharp, and inward curving; a bite from an emerald tree boa is a bloody, painful ordeal.

Captive Diet: Pre-killed chicks, finches, and rodents are taken with relish. Most keepers recommend that you feed the emerald tree boa with long feeding tongs, as a hungry or overanxious specimen can inflict a deep, bloody, and painful bite wound if it accidentally strikes you instead of its intended meal. This species has a slow metabolism and only needs food every 10 to 14 days.

Longevity: May exceed 20 years.

Habitat and Terrarium: Jungle. Specifically, this species is found in tropical lowland rainforests. Habitat is as described for the garden boa: a large, vertically oriented enclosure with ample ventilation and lots of sturdy climbing branches and suitable living or artificial vegetation for a canopy effect in the tank. Substrate is of little importance because this species may live its entire life without ever touching the ground.

The Puddle as a Substrate

Emerald tree boas and green tree pythons are arboreal snakes that need high humidity. Because they don't use the bottom of the cage often, some keepers use a small amount of water as the substrate; this helps maintain the high humidity these species need.

Temperatures and Humidity: Maintain daily ambient temperatures of 78° to 84°F (25.6° to 29°C) with drops to 72° to 75°F (22.2° to 24°C) at night. Lightly mist with warm water daily or every other day, and maintain suitably high levels of relative humidity within the enclosure. During the day, humidity levels should reach at least 80 percent; small drops at night may be beneficial and mimic the daily cycles the boas experience in nature.

Lighting: Most experts agree that at least a couple of hours of full-spectrum lighting do wonders for this snake's appearance and mental well-being.

Reproduction: Breeds during a mild cooling period. Many breeders provide seasonal variations in the humidity and photoperiod along with the temperature. They are live bearing, with young that are reddish, maroon, orange, or in some cases, bluish green to blue-gray in coloration. As the snake matures green splotches will appear randomly on its body and begin to increase in size until they meet and its entire body takes on its adult emerald hue.

Pet Suitability: 5

In *Living Snakes of the World*, John M. Mehrtens says of this snake: "not an 'easy' snake to maintain." Nothing could be truer; the arboreal boas of the genus *Corallus* are best suited to advanced hobbyists, and the emerald tree boa is, arguably, the most difficult species of that entire genus. Not only are its environmental conditions exacting, but the emerald tree boa is infamous for

Separated at Birth?

You might go to the zoo or a high-end pet shop and see a snake that you identify as an emerald tree boa (*Corallus caninus*), yet the sign beside the terrarium reads green tree python (*Morelia virids*). The fact of the matter is that, although these two snakes look almost identical, they are not that closely related. The green tree python is native to New Guinea, Australia, and many surrounding islands, while the emerald tree boa lives several thousand miles away in Central America. This is an example of convergent evolution: Two species occupy the same niche in their habitats and evolve similar anatomy and behavior to fit their environmentally identical conditions. Green tree pythons are often called chondros by hobbyists, referring to the fact that they used to be placed in their own genus, *Chondropython*.

It can be difficult to tell the two apart, but you can do so by looking at the head. The snout of the green tree python is covered by tiny granular scales, while the tree boa has larger, more plate-like scales. Additionally, the scales around the nostrils of chondros are often enlarged, giving them a sort of pug-nosed look. Caring for the green tree python is like caring for the emerald tree boa—both require large, lofty environs, sturdy perches, avian or mammalian fare, and warm, jungle-like conditions.

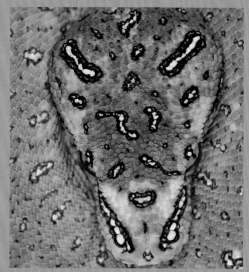

Note the scalation differences between the green tree python (top) and the emerald tree boa (bottom). The python has only small, granular scales on its head, while the boa has larger, plate-like scales on the snout.

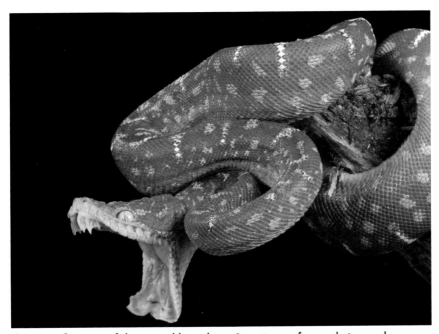

The scientific name of the emerald tree boa, *C. caninus*, refers to their greatly enlarged teeth. This one still has the juvenile colors and the normal tree boa attitude.

being picky in what it will and will not eat—some specimens will take light-colored mice but not dark-colored ones, or vice versa. Additionally, constipation, gut impaction, and regurgitation are common problems (often cured by forcing your snake to swim in a tub of lukewarm water until it defecates). This is one of the most difficult and expensive species to care for in this book.

GARDEN BOA/AMAZON TREE BOA
CORALLUS HORTULANUS (LINNAEUS, 1758)

Range: South America from southern Venezuela and Colombia to Bolivia and Peru.

Size: May reach 7 feet (2.1 m), although 6 feet (1.8 m) is more common.

Subspecies and Similar Species: The slender arboreal boas found from Costa Rica to Bolivia and on some Caribbean Islands were long considered to be one species, *Corallus hortulanus*. Now these boas are considered to be four different species: *C. cookii* from St. Vincent in the Caribbean, *C. grenadensis* from the Grenadines and Granada, *C. hortulanus* from South America, and *C. ruschenbergerii* from Costa Rica south to northern Venezuela and Colombia plus

Garden boas are beautiful and interesting snakes, but they are normally too aggressive to handle.

Trinidad and Tobago. The garden boa is the one most commonly found in the pet trade. *C. ruschenbergerii* is sometimes sold as the Central American tree boa. The other two species are rare in captivity. Because of the confusion over the identity of the various tree boas, it is possible that some of the ones in the pet trade are hybrids.

Description: A wildly variable snake in appearance. Colors may range from muddy brownish to rich orange to vibrant banana yellow. Darker specimens may be patterned with black to gray rings or a net-like pattern, asymmetrical blotches, or a loose zigzag pattern, while lighter specimens may be devoid of pattern altogether. The body is compressed laterally and is extremely muscular. The tail is prehensile, and the bulldog-like head is stocky and strapped with powerful jaw muscles. These features, coupled with its inward-curving teeth and ill disposition, have earned this species its German moniker, *Hundskopfboa* (literally, "hound-head boa"). The eyes have elliptical pupils, indicative of a nocturnal lifestyle. The body scales are small, giving the snake a velvet-like texture.

Captive Diet: In the wild, these devoutly arboreal boas prey heavily on birds and bats as adults and on frogs and lizards as juveniles. Well-developed labial pits in the face indicate their sight-free hunting prowess; these snakes can snare bats on the wing in near-total darkness. Captive diet may include finches and quail, but the main staple can be pre-killed mice. Buying captive-bred specimens is recommended, as they will more readily accept rodents. Such animals may be weaned on pre-killed chicks.

Longevity: May exceed 15 years.

Habitat and Terrarium: Jungle. The home terrarium should be as tall as possible, and it should have many lofty perches, limbs, forks, etc. Vertically oriented environs are a must for this species, as it is almost exclusively arboreal. Substrate is of little importance if no living plants are anchored directly in the substrate. Many hobbyists experience great success with simple housing: a network of climbing branches with artificial leaf clusters scattered throughout for a jungle canopy effect.

Temperatures and Humidity: Maintain ambient temperatures of 75° to 82°F (24° to 27.8°C) with a basking spot to 85°F (29.4°C). Nightly dips to no lower than 73°F (22.8°C) are acceptable. Relative humidity should be 65 percent, but good air circulation is also paramount. A light morning misting of lukewarm water is also advised.

Lighting: Although this snake is semi-nocturnal in its movements, a full-spectrum bulb is recommended. Full-spectrum lighting helps the snake physiologically and aesthetically; these snakes' color is more vivid through exposure to natural sunlight or full-spectrum lighting.

Reproduction: Live bearing. Young are 12 to 13 inches (30.5 to 33 cm) at birth. Wild variety in color may occur within a single litter; it is possible for no two siblings to be colored and/or patterned like one another.

Pet Suitability: 4

This is a specialized snake that, while aesthetically gorgeous, is foul-natured and infamous for striking at anything that moves. (Remember, those heat-sensitive pits in the face make this snake able to sense you no matter how slow moving or careful you are). Capable of inflicting deep, bloody wounds, this snake is definitely not for beginners. Advanced hobbyists, however, may find a

What Is *Corallus enydris?*

For years, the garden tree boa was known as *Corallus enydris*, and that name is still used for it occasionally instead of *C. hortulanus*. This confusion with the names happened because Linnaeus described two snakes in the same publication: *C. enydris* and *C. hortulanus*. Of course, these are actually the same species. For complete details on how this happened and why *C. hortulanus* is the correct name, see McDiarmid, Toure, and Savage, 1996, *Journal of Herpetology*, 30 (30): pgs. 320–326.

beautiful, low-maintenance centerpiece for their snake collection in the garden boa. I've personally owned a number of garden boas through the years, and I find them to be hardy and interesting, if not handle friendly.

KENYAN SAND BOA
ERYX COLUBRINUS LOVERIDGEI (LINNAEUS, 1758)

Range: Subspecies range throughout Egypt, Niger, Kenya, Sudan, Ethiopia, Yemen, and surrounding areas; range discontinuous in northeastern Africa.

Size: Heavy bodied and stocky. Males may reach 15–16 inches (38.1–40.6 cm) while females can attain lengths of nearly twice that; 28–30 inches (71.1–76.2 cm) is possible.

Subspecies and Similar Species: There are more than 12 described species and subspecies of sand boas. Care and maintenance for all are virtually identical, although only a few have any following in the pet trade. These are the Egyptian sand boa (*E. colubrinus colubrinus*), the Indian or brown sand boa (*Eryx johnii*), and the rough-scaled sand boa (*E. conicus*).

Description: A thick-bodied, cylindrical snake with very stubby tail. Scalation is smooth over most of the body, with the tail scales being quite rough and granular. Dorsal base coloration is chocolate brown with yellowish- to tangerine-colored asymmetrical or zigzagging splotch-like patterning across the back. Vent

Kenyan sand boas vary quite a bit in color. These three were all collected in a small area of Tanzania.

The rough-scaled sand boa is another popular species of sand boa. Captive-bred babies of this species are not difficult to find.

and lower sides are creamy white to ivory. Owing to its habit of lying in ambush for prey just beneath the surface of the sand, the sand boa has eyes that are situated toward the top of the skull. The head is wedge shaped and aids the snake in burrowing.

The sand boa stalks its prey by lying motionless in the sand for hours on end; when prey unwittingly draws near, the boa erupts from the sand with blinding speed, loops its coils around the prey, and constricts its victim to death. May seek refuge below large, flat stones or deeper in the ground when surface temperatures get too hot. Albino and other color morphs have been created through selective breeding and are frequently available.

Captive Diet: Wild Kenyan sand boas take rodents and lizards and seem especially fond of raiding rodent nests to prey upon newborn or young rodents. Juvenile boas are also reputed to kill insects. Offer a captive diet of pre-killed mice supplemented with occasional feeder lizards. Feeding frozen prey with tongs—jiggling the prey item to simulate life—may be necessary; this is most frequently the case with juvenile or newly imported sand boas.

Longevity: May exceed ten years.

Habitat and Terrarium: All subspecies of sand boas require dry, warm environs. These animals are obligate burrowers and need at least 6 inches (15.2 cm) of sandy substrate in which to burrow. Large objects, such as climbing logs, basking rocks, etc., are of little value in the sand boa terrarium, as the boa's burrowing will

Sand Boa Taxonomy

Some authorities place several of the sand boas in a different genus, *Gongylophis*. The species included in this genus are *colubrinus*, *conicus*, and *muelleri*. The Arabian sand boa (*E. jayakari*) may belong in its own genus (*Pseudogongylophis*) because of its distinction of being the only boa that lays eggs.

undermine and topple these items unless they are situated on the very bottom of the terrarium. Long, wide tanks make better enclosures for sand boas. Height is an irrelevant dimension, considering the subterranean lifestyle of these snakes.

Temperatures and Humidity: Hailing from tropical and subtropical Africa and Asia Minor, these snakes like it hot. Daytime highs should range between 84° and 87°F (29° and 30.6°C) with nightly dips to the upper 60s (19° to 20.5°C). Maintain low levels of humidity—less than 45 percent relative humidity.

Lighting: Although lights may be employed to attain proper ambient temperatures within your sand boa's enclosure, basking or UV lamps are not necessary, as this species is almost totally subterranean and seldom basks.

Reproduction: Sexual maturity at 24 to 30 months. Mating occurs in the spring; 6 to 18 young are born alive after four to five months of gestation. Young are typically 5 to 6 inches (12.7 to 15.2 cm) long at birth.

Pet Suitability: 1

Although the Kenyan sand boa is a hardy, long-lived, and attractive snake, many hobbyists steer clear of it because of its subterranean lifestyle. This animal spends virtually all of its time buried beneath the sand of its terrarium; its beautiful coloration and intricate markings stay perpetually hidden from sight. The Kenyan sand boa is typically a very handle-friendly snake and is bred in captivity with relative

ease. It's a great snake for beginners, provided the novice chooses a well-started juvenile. Getting neonates to feed can be tricky. The Kenyan sand boa can be a bit nippy if pulled suddenly or roughly from its terrarium. In the wild, natural predators to the sand boa strike from above, so this species reacts adversely to contact from above. Remove your sand boa from its terrarium by slowly running your fingers through the sand of the tank to locate your snake, then gently grasping it from below and lifting it out of the sand. Once out of its sandy environment, the Kenyan sand boa should respond well to handling.

PACIFIC ISLAND BOA
CANDOIA CARINATA (SCHNEIDER, 1801)

Range: Papua New Guinea, Fiji, Solomon Islands, and nearby archipelagos.
Size: Depends on the subspecies. The nominate subspecies rarely grows longer than 2 feet (61 cm). For *C. c. paulsoni*, about 3.5 feet (1.1 m) is average, but some reach 5 feet (1.5 m).
Subspecies and Similar Species: Biologists seldom agree on the taxonomy of the Pacific island boa and the other species of *Candoia*. Two subspecies of *C. carinata* are usually recognized: *C. c. carinata* and *C. c. paulsoni*, known as the Solomon Island ground boa. There are at least two other species of *Candoia*, and several authorities believe that there are more waiting to be discovered and described. The two other species—both present in the hobby in small numbers—are the Fiji Island boa or Pacific tree boa (*C. bibroni*) and the viper boa (*C. aspera*). The viper

All three species of *Candoia* are present in the hobby, but none are very common. From left to right: *C. carinata carinata*, *C. bibroni australis*, and *C. aspera*.

193

boa is so named because of its similarity in appearance to the lethal death adder (*Acanthophis* spp.). *C. bibroni* is the longest species, capable of growing up to 7 feet (2.1 m) long. Viper boas rarely exceed 30 inches (76.2 cm) in length.

Description: Wearing earthen colors and cryptic patterns, the Pacific island boa is perfectly camouflaged amid the leaf litter of its forest habitat. Coloration is highly variable between subspecies and varies by locality and individual as well. Some wear marbled gray and black or tan mid-dorsal striping, while others are almost uniformly brown, sandy, and rusty in coloration with minimal pattern. Zigzag dorsal markings are prevalent. The muscular body is slightly compressed, forming a roughly triangular shape, with a noticeable ridge along the midline of the back. The head is set off from a thinner neck. Shy and retiring, these snakes spend their days hiding amid fallen debris or under logs on the forest floor, and they forage by night. The pupils are elliptical.

Captive Diet: Captive-bred specimens readily accept pre-killed mice of appropriate size, although imported specimens may only take lizards and nontoxic frogs. Wean on anoles and house geckos. Neonates usually require lizards and/or frogs for their first few meals.

Longevity: Ten years or more.

Habitat and Terrarium: Ground cover is essential; substrate should consist of leaf litter, organic mulch, orchid bark, coir, etc. Hides and climbing branches are a must, as is a permanent source of water. Adults may be housed in a 55-gallon (208.2-l) aquarium, and juveniles may thrive in accordingly smaller terrariums. Pacific island boas are one of the few species that seem unaffected by tank mates, and many hobbyists report great success housing these snakes communally.

Temperatures and Humidity: Maintain temperatures between 76° and 83°F (24.4° and 28.3°C) with a warmer basking spot and a cooler retreat. A pool of water large enough for the snake to fully immerse itself is mandatory.

Lighting: No specialized lighting is necessary, as the Pacific island boa is devoutly nocturnal. Night-cycle bulbs accommodate nighttime viewing without disturbing the snake's natural behaviors.

Reproduction: Live bearing but not easily bred in captivity; females may ovulate only triannually. Numerous rain showers stimulate breeding cycles. The Solomon Island variety is, by far, the easiest member of the species to breed in captivity; females may birth as many as three dozen young per litter. Males are recognizable by their elongated cloacal spurs. Young are tiny and somewhat challenging to rear.

Pet Suitability: 2

A hardy, quietly attractive, and often docile snake. Relatively inexpensive and able to be kept in considerably smaller environs than most of the other Boidae species, the Pacific island boas can be good snakes for beginning hobbyists, if they start with captive–bred, well-started juveniles.

Pairs or trios of them make good breeding projects for advanced hobbyists and zoological institutions.

RAINBOW BOA
EPICRATES CENCHRIA (LINNAEUS, 1758)

Range: Costa Rica south to Paraguay and Argentina east of the Andes.

Size: A mid-sized boa. Adults seldom exceed 5 to 6 feet (1.5 to 1.8 m) in length, with very large specimens measuring closer to 7 feet (2.1 m). Some specimens never grow any longer than 3 to 4 feet (0.9 to 1.2 m), however. A slender species, the rainbow boa should not, at even its longest, weigh more than 8 to 10 pounds (3.6 to 4.5 kg).

Subspecies and Similar Species: Ten (or nine, depending on which authority you ask) subspecies of rainbow boas have been described; only two of these subspecies occur frequently in the pet trade, however. The nominate Brazilian race (*E. c. cenchria*) hails from the Amazon River Basin and northern South America. The slightly less vividly patterned Columbian race (*E. c. maurus*) occurs from Costa Rica to northern South America. Some authorities consider the Colombian rainbow boa a separate species (*Epicrates maurus*), an idea that is growing in popularity. Many habitats in which the rainbow boa thrives are currently inaccessible (either by political or environmental boundaries), and

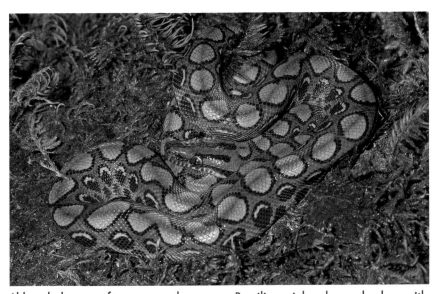

Although they are often snappy when young, Brazilian rainbow boas calm down with consistent and gentle handling.

While the Colombian rainbow boa lacks the sharp pattern of some of the other subspecies, it does have the brilliant iridescence that gives the species its name.

many experts speculate that within these untamed wildernesses, new subspecies of rainbow boas are waiting to be described. The opposite is also true: More scientific study is likely to reveal that some subspecies are not distinct enough to warrant their own taxonomic status.

Description: The rainbow boa is a slender species, with the two most common subspecies differing greatly in color and pattern. Both of them sport an iridescent sheen, like the rainbow produced by sunlight striking an oil slick. It is from this multicolored sheen that the snake derives its common name. All of the subspecies have five dark lines on the head (at least as babies). The Brazilian rainbow boa wears a base coat of reddish to maroon with similarly colored ovate saddles straddling the midline of the back. These saddles are edged in dark brown to black. Eye-like markings (called ocelli) with lighter edges and dark centers flank the lateral surfaces of the snake. The Colombian rainbow boa begins life looking similar to the Brazilian but with the reddish base color replaced with brown. As the snake matures, the pattern fades and the color darkens until it becomes a brown snake with faint traces of the original pattern remaining. The distinctive five-lined pattern on the head often remains visible. Heat-sensitive pits are present on the labial scales. Body scales are smooth, and the muscular tail is highly prehensile. A nocturnal species, the rainbow boa spends the lion's share of the daytime under forest debris but emerges at night to forage for rodents, fledgling birds, bats, and other warm-blooded fare.

Captive Diet: Pre-killed rodents. Juveniles will take mice, while larger adults may take small rats or hamsters. Feed juveniles every ten days, and offer fare to adult snakes every ten days to two weeks. If your rainbow boa refuses to feed, remove the rodent and offer food again in a couple of days. Low humidity and high temperatures are the most frequent causes of refusing food.

Longevity: Rainbow boas are long-lived snakes. Reports exist of specimens surviving in captivity for more than 21 years. Average life expectancy ranges from 15 to 18 years.

Habitat and Terrarium: In the wild, rainbow boas thrive in woodlands, swamps, bogs, and other moist areas with dense foliage and thick underbrush. You must keep these environmental conditions in mind when constructing a habitat for this species. The same spartan terrarium setups that will accommodate some species of snakes will not meet this boa's specialized needs. Rainbow boas must be able to hide beneath fallen debris, climb high into the treetops, and slither over long distances. Thus, the ideal terrarium will be generous in all of its dimensions: tall, wide, and long.

Outfit the tank with a moisture-retaining substrate, such as orchid bark, cypress mulch, sphagnum moss, coconut husk, or a mixture of these. Newspaper or paper toweling has also been known to work, but I do not recommend it. Plenty of hides, retreats, and heavy leaf cover are a must, as are one or more sturdy climbing branches. When shopping for climbing branches, get some with boughs jutting at a 90-degree angle from the main trunk because your rainbow boa will enjoy coiling and resting within the nook created by the adjoining of the trunk and the bough. A secure lid is absolutely necessary.

Temperatures and Humidity: This is where the matter of keeping a rainbow boa gets tricky. Being natives of swamps and bogs throughout the tropics of Central and South America, these snakes need very humid conditions if they are to thrive in the captive environment. Because these snakes are extremely sensitive to humidity and are prone to death by dehydration, high relative humidity and continual access to standing water are absolutely paramount. Maintain a high relative humidity (most experts recommend 70 to 80 percent and up to 95 percent for neonates up to a year old) by covering a portion of the terrarium's lid with cellophane or some other impermeable substance. Daily misting of the terrarium is recommended, as is keeping a bowl of fresh water at your boa's disposal at all times. This bowl should be both large enough for your snake to totally immerse itself but shallow enough that even a juvenile snake cannot get trapped inside and potentially drown. Your rainbow boa will also relish a half-buried hide under which the substrate is both cool and moist. Drier hideaways and perches are also mandatory.

As for the matter of temperature, the daily temperature gradient should run from about 85° to 75°F (29.4° to 24°C), with nighttime temperatures around

Including a humidified hide box in your rainbow boa's enclosure helps to meet its need for high humidity.

75°F (24°C). Colombian rainbows can handle slightly higher temperatures. A thermal gradient is critical to success with any rainbow boa—most inexperienced hobbyists keep this species too hot.

Lighting: Because the rainbow boa is a devoutly nocturnal animal, no specialized UV lighting is necessary. Most hobbyists prefer incandescent bulbs to heat the tank, fluorescent bulbs for extended viewing of the tank, and red, purple, or "moon-glow" bulbs for nocturnal viewing.

Reproduction: Copulation occurs from late fall to early spring, with females bearing small litters of considerably sized young; juveniles may be 20 to 22 inches (50.8 to 56 cm) upon emergence. Both sexes attain sexual maturity at around 36 months old.

Pet Suitability: 4

This snake is best left to experienced hobbyists who are adept both at general snake husbandry and naturalistic terrarium maintenance. The rainbow boa is an expensive animal that has demanding temperature, humidity, and habitat needs that must be meticulously met if it is to thrive in the home or institutional terrarium. Any dedicated hobbyist who is confident in his skills at maintaining a suitable terrarium and who is interested in this species, however, may well enjoy housing the rainbow boa. This animal's benevolent disposition, cryptic pattering, and iridescent sheen make it a desirable and rewarding species. Bear in mind that rainbow boas must be handled gently and regularly if they are to tame to a keeper's touch—babies often bite defensively. Rainbows that are infrequently held may forever be edgy and nippy.

RED-TAILED BOA
BOA CONSTRICTOR LINNAEUS, 1758

Range: Extensive. The nominate race is found over much of South America, including Brazil, Bolivia, Colombia, Venezuela, and surrounding nations. The numerous subspecies occur throughout South and Central America, offshore islands, and parts of Mexico.

Size: Large; male red-tailed boas may reach 9 feet (2.7 m) or a little more in length. Females may reach 14 feet (4.3 m) as the maximum adult length. Keep in mind, however, that the vast majority of *Boa constrictor* specimens do not attain these gargantuan dimensions. The average red-tailed boa ranges from 7 to 9 feet (2.1 to 2.7 m) in length. The size depends somewhat on subspecies and feeding regimen.

Subspecies and Similar Species: There are ten subspecies of *B. constrictor*, and three of these appear regularity in the American, European, and Japanese pet market: *B. c. constrictor* (the true red-tailed boa), *B. c. imperator* (Colombian boa), and *B. c. occidentalis* (Argentine boa). The other subspecies range from uncommon to very rare in the hobby: *B. c. amarali* (Amaral's boa), *B. c. longicauda* (long-tailed boa), *B. c. melanogaster* (black-bellied boa; probably not a valid subspecies), *B. c. nebulosa* (clouded or Dominican boa), *B. c. orophias* (St. Lucian boa), *B. c. ortonii* (Peruvian or Orton's boa), and *B. c. sabogae* (Pearl Islands boa). By far the most commonly available subspecies sold in pet shops and from online wholesalers is *B. c. imperator*, which tends to be less vividly colored than a true *B. c. constrictor* and also tends to be more aggressive. Note also that the Argentine boa is listed as an Appendix I species on Convention on International Trade in Endangered Species of Wild Fauna and Flora (CITES). Most Argentines are captive bred, but you should still be careful that you are not buying an illegally collected one.

Description: A large, heavy-bodied species. Base coloration is tan to dun or creamy gray. The large, triangular head is set off from a thinner neck. Coloration varies greatly from one subspecies to the next and also by locality and individual, as does pattern. Most wear dorsal saddles of brown mottled with cream-colored to whitish ovals at the edges. In particularly handsome specimens, these saddles are reddish to maroon in color. The saddles at the anterior end of the body are thinner and hourglass shaped, while those toward the posterior are ovate and trimmed in lighter bands outlined in black. The saddles on the tail range in color from reddish brown to orange to deep red.

Good Snakekeeping

Recommended Reading

Captive breeding of red-tailed boas can be a surprisingly difficult feat to accomplish for such a common snake. If you are serious about undertaking a breeding project with any boa or python species, I highly recommend that you read *The Reproductive Husbandry of Pythons and Boas* by Richard A. Ross and Gerald Marzec.

Captive Diet: Pre-killed rodents. Juvenile specimens should be offered a mouse or fuzzy rat once weekly. Larger specimens will take larger rodent fare—medium-sized snakes will take rats, while adults may be offered small rabbits or guinea pigs. Quail and chickens will also be taken. Bear in mind that most *Boa constrictor* specimens are gluttons and will eat any time you feed them. Avoid the temptation to overfeed.

Longevity: A red-tailed boa is a long-term investment; it is no rare feat for one of these snakes to live for more than 20 years, with 30- to 35-year life spans being recorded. Take this into consideration before making a purchase.

Habitat and Terrarium: Red-tailed boas are tropical, forest-dwelling snakes, and their terrarium should reflect this fact. Outfit the tank with hides and plenty of sturdy, well-anchored climbing limbs, foliage (I recommend artificial plants), and heating equipment necessary to maintain the snake's optimum temperatures. Security is also paramount, as these snakes are master escape artists and adults are very powerful, easily able to break through small-gauge screen or push open weighted lids. Locking lids with heavy-gauge screening is always necessary.

A jungle-mix-type substrate works well in a naturalistic terrarium, while shredded/recycled newspaper makes an excellent choice for the more spartan enclosure. Never house your red-tailed boa on aquarium gravel or cedar/pine shavings, as both of these agents can be irritating to its labial scales and pits.

Temperatures and Humidity: Maintain a relative humidity of 60 percent, but supply ample ventilation as well because boas are subject to respiratory infections. Temperatures should also be accordingly high—keep daily highs around 80° to 82°F (26.7° to 27.8°C), with nightly dips into the mid 70s F (23.3° to 25°C). Basking spots should reach 90°F (32.2°C), although cooler retreats within the terrarium are also necessary. All in all, your red-tailed boa's terrarium should feel like a tropical forest.

Lighting: In the wild, *Boa constrictor* is a crepuscular or outright nocturnal species and seldom basks. Although many enthusiasts, therefore, will say that no specialized UV lighting is necessary, I highly recommend that a full-spectrum bulb be suspended above your boa's enclosure and your snake be exposed to about two hours daily of UV lighting. In my specimens, I have noted a distinct clarity and vividness in color when exposed to such a lightbulb.

Of the giant snakes, red-tailed boas probably make the best pets. They don't get as big as the others and tend to have good temperaments.

Good Snakekeeping

The Argentine boa is one of the most distinctive of the subspecies of *Boa constrictor*. It has a reputation for aggression.

Reproduction: Females become sexually mature at 36 to 48 months old. Captive mating is best conducted in late December, when terrarium temperatures are at their lowest—boas breed best when provided with seasonal temperature variations. After fertilization, females will give birth to 25 to 100 live young, which may be 14 to 22 inches (35.6 to 55.9 cm) at birth.

Pet Suitability: 3

The red-tailed boa is a staple of the pet trade, and for the right hobbyist, it can make a wonderful long-term captive. These snakes are definitely not for everyone, though, and many hobbyists have made a snap decision in purchasing an 18-inch-long (45.7-cm) juvenile *B. constrictor*, only to regret the 8-foot (2.4-m) adult specimen it became. If you are an experienced hobbyist, however, and you fully understand that your snake will eat relatively expensive meals once each week, produce copious feces once that meal is digested, need a very large enclosure, and live until your kids are old enough to graduate college, then a *Boa constrictor* just may be the pet for you. Bear in mind also that these snakes can be temperamental. True *B. c. constrictor* tend toward gentle handling and a calm disposition, while the far more common and less expensive *B. c. imperator* can be a bit "bitey" if not handled regularly. If you are willing and able to accommodate this snake's dietary and habitat needs, it is a beautiful, long-lived, and easily maintained serpent.

RETICULATED PYTHON
PYTHON RETICULATUS (SCHNEIDER, 1801)

Range: Southern Asia from Bangladesh to Indonesia and the Philippines.

Size: Enormous. Wild specimens have been reported in excess of 25 feet (7.6 m) long, with the record being 28.5 feet (8.5 m) or possibly 33 feet (10.5 m). Captive lengths frequently exceed 18 feet (5.5 m). This is the longest snake species in the world.

Subspecies and Similar Species: In 2002, two subspecies of reticulated pythons (or "retics," as hobbyists often call them) were described, *P. r. jampeanus* and *P. r. saputrai*. Both of these are smaller than typical retics and are from specific islands in Indonesia. As of this writing, they are rare in the hobby and expensive.

Description: The largest snake in the world, the gorgeous reticulated python wears a base coloration of yellowish to dun or gray with a darker chain-link pattern and diamond-shaped dorsolateral blotches of white to cream or golden to silvery and even a gunmetal color in some particularly handsome individuals.

The reticulated python in the longest known species of snake. These gigantic animals are a poor choice for almost any hobbyist.

203

One of the most popular reticulated python morphs is the tiger. It is reported to be less aggressive than the normal form.

Iridescence covers the entire body but is particularly pronounced in the darker regions of the body. Dark bars run from the eyes down the jaws and into the neck. Eyes are golden to orange or red. Thinner than some of the other giant snakes of the world, the reticulated python is a powerful constrictor.

A whole host of aberrant color and pattern morphs have been selectively bred in this species. Such designer morphs include the albino, tiger retic, and super-tiger retic.

Captive Diet: Pre-killed rodents and chicks as a juvenile but quickly graduating to guinea pigs, rabbits, and even small goats when an adult. Wild specimens also consume monitor lizards and other pythons. Caution: Large specimens pose a serious threat to domestic pet and human life! *Never* trust a large reticulated python or leave someone alone around one.

Longevity: 20 years or more.

Habitat and Terrarium: As large as possible. Juveniles may be successfully housed in large terrariums, while adult specimens may require a secure greenhouse or room within the house of their own. Juveniles like leaf litter, sturdy climbs, and plenty of hideaways, while adults seem to prefer large pools of water and dense clusters of vegetation under which to hide. Reticulated pythons are excellent swimmers.

Temperatures and Humidity: Maintain temperatures in the low 80s F (26.7° to 28°C), with hot spots reaching 88°F (31.1°C) and nightly drops into the mid 70s F (23.3° to 24.4°C). Hot spots should be big enough to fit the entire specimen. As a jungle species, the reticulated python requires high levels of relative humidity but can also develop skin problems (blister disease) if left on excessively moist substrate. Aim for humidity of about 60 percent.

Lighting: No specialized lighting is required beyond that necessary for viewing. Some hobbyists do report success with full-spectrum bulbs, however.

Reproduction: Egg layers. Females deposit large clutches of up to 100 eggs, which often must be incubated in an incubator. (The female retic will likely abandon the eggs instead of coiling about them.) Young are 2 feet (61 cm) long at hatching.

Pet Suitability: 5

"-nae" or "-dae?"

In taxonomy, animal families generally end in the suffix "-dae," while subfamilies end in the suffix "-nae." So depending on your opinion, you may talk about Pythonidae or Pythoninae when you discuss pythons.

If I could rank a snake higher than 5, I would do so in the case of the reticulated python, as this animal is only fit for zoological institutions and accomplished private collectors. Every year, thousands of unwanted reticulated pythons (bought on a whim because of their startling beauty and manageable size as juveniles) wash up on the shores of animal shelters and reptile rescues because they either outgrew their terrarium or the hobbyists who bought them could no longer afford to deal with such a large and powerful reptile. Bear in mind that the purchase of a reticulated python is a life-changing decision. This reptile will live for a long time, will grow to *very* large dimensions, and is frequently an aggressive snake. Only purchase a reticulated python if you are 100 percent certain that you have the skill, resources, and dedication to take care of it for the long haul.

ROSY BOA
LICHANURA TRIVIRGATA COPE, 1861

Range: Southern California, southwestern Arizona, south to northwestern Mexico.

Size: Adult specimens may reach 40 to 43 inches (101.6 to 109.2 cm), although most individuals do not exceed 36 inches (91.4 cm). Some specimens may only reach 18 to 22 inches (45.7 to 55.9 cm) at adulthood. Females are typically the larger of the two sexes.

Subspecies and Similar Species: Many varieties of rosy boas have been described; virtually all have some manner of following in the pet trade. Prices will alter based on the rarity and desirability of the variety in question. Commonly encountered varieties include *L. t. gracia*, *L. t. trivirgata*, and *L. t. roseofusca*.

Description: A smooth-scaled burrowing boa. Rosy boas have stocky bodies with short tails, small scales, and a tapering head. Ventral scales are particularly small, and males have pronounced cloacal spurs. Color varies widely based on subspecies and geographic range: The Mexican variety (*L. t. trivirgata*) tends to be ivory with chocolate to black stripes, while the popular coastal variety (*L. t. roseofusca*) wears a bluish base with rosy or rust-colored stripes. Local variants (named based on the geographic location in which they are found) exist and are the subject of much debate. All subspecies and local variants are secretive, retiring creatures that forage and are active primarily by night in the summers and by twilight (late afternoon or early morning) during the spring and autumn months. It may spend days on end buried beneath sand, pebbles, leaf litter, fallen evergreen needles, or within crevices in stone deadfalls.

Captive Diet: Wild rosy boas eat birds, rodents, lizards, amphibians, and even other snakes. Captive fare should include pre-killed mice supplemented by the occasional chicken or quail chick. They also relish feeder lizards (house geckoes or anoles).

Longevity: Rosy boas are long-lived snakes; captive specimens may thrive for 15 to 18 years.

Habitat and Terrarium: Hailing from the rock-strewn hillsides and sage and mesquite bush ravines of southern California and western Arizona, the rosy boa is a desert-dwelling species that thrives in riparian gulches and rocky outcroppings. Rosy boas thrive, therefore, in dry, well-ventilated terraria with

Rosy boas range in color from the very pretty to the very dull, but all of them make great pets.

broad, wide dimensions. These snakes absolutely must be provided plenty of secure hiding areas. Many hobbyists find that their rosies prefer partially buried lengths of PVC pipe more than other hides. Thick, low climbing branches are also recommended, as rosy boas sometimes climb shrubs and low overhangs in the wild.

Temperatures and Humidity: Although the rosy boa thrives in the deserts of the southwest, this animal should not be maintained at excessively high temperatures. Moderate temperatures are best: daytime highs of 80° to 84°F (26.7° to 29°C) with a hot spot reaching about 90°F (32.2°C) and nightly dips to 68° to 70°F (20° to 21.1°C) are preferable. Daytime highs are most easily achieved by way of an incandescent lighting fixture suspended above the terrarium. Due to this snake's subterranean lifestyle, an undertank heating pad positioned directly or partially beneath a hide can also optimize its comfort by providing a thermal gradient. Rosy boas do best at low humidity levels, although some individuals tolerate moderate humidity quite well.

Lighting: The rosy boa does not require intense basking lights or specialized UV lighting because of its nocturnal and crepuscular habits. Moderate lighting, enough to accommodate viewing, is suitable.

Reproduction: Live bearing; females reach sexual maturity at 18 to 36 months of age. Mating occurs in the early spring, with up to ten 8- to 10-inch-long (20.3- to 25.4-cm) young being born in October to mid-November. Young often do not feed until the following spring.

Pet Suitability: 1

An absolute peach of a snake; I cannot recommend this animal highly enough for beginning, intermediate, and advanced hobbyists. The typical specimen is quite docile, slow moving, curious, and all around mild mannered. Rosy boas enjoy gentle handling and are hardy in captivity.

Colubridae: The "Typical" Snakes

In the introduction to his section on colubrid snakes in *Living Snakes of the World*, John M. Mehrtens writes: "Suffice it to say that the colubrids are the preeminent family of 'typical' snakes throughout the world." By "typical" here, I take Mehrtens to mean roughly the same thing I do in expressing the colubrids as a family: lean, muscular, swift, moderately sized, retiring, and agile. A few other typical traits apply to some members of the family but not all: nonvenomous and egg laying apply to a majority of colubrids but certainly not to all, for the African boomslang (*Dispholidus typus*) has a bite that is easily capable of causing human fatality.

Colubrids represent the largest family of snakes by far, with more than 2,500 species known to exist. Diverse beyond any other family, the colubrids thrive in virtually all corners of the globe; only Antarctica, which is home to no snake

Most of the colubrids are harmless to humans. One exception is the deadly venomous boomslang.

of any species, is devoid of colubrids. Colubrids have also adapted to virtually all environmental niches. They thrive in forest floors, jungle canopies, open fields, and murky swamps; they swim, burrow, and climb trees, and some can even "fly" or glide from one branch to another within a dense forest. Colubrids eat at every level of the food chain as well, preying upon rodents, birds, eggs, insects, crustaceans, reptiles, amphibians, mollusks, and fish, and some will even cannibalize others of their own species. Colubrids are considered by most scientists and taxonomists to be highly "advanced" or "evolved" snakes. They differ from the "primitive" boas and pythons in that they lack all traces of a pelvic girdle and vestigial hind limbs (or cloacal spurs) and have only one lung.

By virtue of their biological diversity, these snakes are widely represented in the pet trade. Although colubrids compose the majority of snake species available for purchase, a minuscule fraction of their total species actually enters the pet industry; most are too small, too selective in their diet, too feisty, too aggressive, or simply too delicate of constitution to make a viable pet. Although the popular kingsnakes and rat snakes are colubrids, those groups are unique enough to warrant their own section in a book of this nature. What follows, therefore, are snakes that share little in common but that are readily grouped together as colubrids. By understanding the family as a whole, potential colubrid keepers can come to better understand the individual species they choose to house and maintain.

BULL, GOPHER, AND PINE SNAKES
PITUOPHIS CATENIFER AND PITUOPHIS MELANO-LEUCUS HOLBROOK, 1842

Range: Extensive throughout the United States and Mexico; the bullsnake just enters southern Canada.

Size: Among the largest North American snakes, these species may exceed 8 feet (2.3 m) in length.

The Cape gopher snake is sought after by hobbyists because it is the most vibrant of the gopher snakes.

209

Bullsnakes have a reputation for being pugnacious, but they will calm down when handled consistently.

Subspecies and Similar Species: Many are described, and several appear regularly in the pet trade: northern pine snake (*P. m. melanoleucus*), black pine snake (*P. m. lodingi*), Florida pine snake (*P. m. mugitus*), bullsnake (*P. catenifer sayi*), Pacific gopher snake (*P. c. catenifer*), San Diego gopher snake (*P. c. annectens*), and the vibrantly colored Cape gopher snake (*P. c. vertebralis*). Aside from humidity, which will vary based on the natural habitat of the subspecies in question, all other terrarium requirements are identical for each subspecies.

Description: Very large, powerful constrictors, the bull, pine, and gopher snakes wear earthen colors. Tan, gray, reddish, brown, rust, and sandy colors are marked with extensive interstitial flecking and brownish to yellowish or even whitish or black saddles. Although color intensity and hue vary considerably among subspecies, pattern shows little variation. A starkly contrasting Northern pine snake—which wears black saddles atop an ivory base—is a handsome animal indeed. Some gopher snakes, such as the Baja variety, wear bright colors: bright orange, yellow, lavenders, and all manner of earthen tones. Various color morphs are available. Scales are keeled, and the eyes have round pupils, indicating that this snake is a diurnal, visual hunter.

When cornered, the members of the *Pituophis* genus will not hesitate to vigorously defend themselves; angered snakes will raise their forequarters into a striking "S," hold their mouth agape, and hiss loudly. Be warned that this is not a bluff! These snakes will strike repeatedly if they feel truly threatened. Bullsnakes have a reputation for being aggressive, while the pines and gophers often become extremely docile pets.

Captive Diet: Rodents. In the wild, bull, pine, and gopher snakes will raid active rodent burrows, often eating several rodents at a time. For this reason, many hobbyists feed their adult snakes numerous small rodents rather than singular large rodents; this is especially true of Cape gophers, which often regurgitate large rodents. Most *Pituophis* will eagerly eat birds and eggs as well.

Longevity: May exceed 25 years.

Habitat and Terrarium: These snakes require very long, broad environs to accommodate their terrestrial movements and need for space. A tank of 55 gallons (208.2 l) will work for a small specimen, while larger tanks will be required for larger adults. Outfit the terrarium with a thick layer of substrate; a mixture of coarse sand and garden mulch works well because it is loose enough to allow these snakes to burrow, which they love to do. Numerous PVC pipes buried under the substrate (and with one or more chutes leading upward) will

The northern pine snake has a disjointed range that includes parts of New Jersey, Virginia, the Carolinas, Georgia, and other southeastern states.

simulate a mammal burrow and provide your snake with an excellent place to hide. A large water dish should be kept in the terrarium at all times. Beware of placing heavy or precariously stacked rocks, as your snake's burrowing movements could easily undermine and topple such a structure.

Temperatures and Humidity: Warm and dry conditions are best at the upper levels of the substrate, although more humid retreats will help provide ample moisture for these snakes. Maintain temperatures in a range from about 75° to 85°F (24° to 29.4°C) with a basking spot that reaches the upper 80s F (30.6° to 31.7°C). Nighttime temperatures can safely drop to the low 70s F (21.1° to 22.8°C).

Lighting: No specialized lighting is necessary.

Reproduction: Mating, which occurs in early spring after hibernation, often takes place underground (in old rodent burrows). Females deposit relatively small clutches of large, round eggs about 45 days after copulation. The young, which measure 12 inches (30.5 cm), emerge in about 60 days.

Pet Suitability: 2

Despite their somewhat boisterous disposition in the wild, captive-bred bull, pine, and gopher snakes make excellent captives. Living for a long time and growing to impressive but still manageable proportions, these snakes are one of the most impressive colubrid species available on the market today. Hardy and attractive, they do require large environs and a skilled hand in their husbandry.

CHINESE GARTER SNAKE
ELAPHE RUFODORSATA (CANTOR, 1842)

Range: Eastern China, Korean peninsula, and eastern Russia.

Size: To 30 inches (76.2 cm).

Subspecies and Similar Species: None.

Description: A taxonomist's nightmare, the Chinese garter snake is officially classified as a species of rat snake (genus *Elaphe*), although no one is fooled into believing that a fish- and frog-eating, live-bearing snake belongs in the rat snake group. Clearly, this curious little snake is some manner of garter snake-like animal, although it is not likely to be related to the North American garters.

Coloration is quietly attractive, with a base hue of tan to brown with yellowish to golden longitudinal stripes and oblong blotches. The belly is checkered, and a spearpoint-like mark adorns the crown of the head. Do not confuse this species with *Elaphe bimaculata*, as their superficial similarities belie different husbandry requirements. A diurnal hunter with a short snout, this snake is an accomplished fisher and can quickly subdue its prey underwater.

Captive Diet: Feed on fish, nontoxic frogs, and recently molted crayfish and freshwater shrimp.

Although not closely related to North American garter snakes, the Chinese garter snake requires the same care in captivity.

Longevity: May exceed eight to ten years.

Habitat and Terrarium: As described for the common garter snake. These snakes are highly aquatic in their habits and seldom venture far from a permanent source of flowing water. Thus, a large dish full of clean water should be kept at your snake's disposal at all times. This species, while it does entangle itself in grasses and branches to avoid being swept away by stream-edge currents, is not a frequent climber. Numerous hides are recommended.

Temperatures and Humidity: As described for the common garter snake. It requires moderate to high levels of relative humidity but with plenty of air circulation as well. Maintain temperatures in the mid- to upper 70s F (24° to 26.1°C). If your snake spends all of its time in its water dish, this may be a sign that the terrarium is too hot. Lower the ambient temperature.

Lighting: Known to bask daily. Full-spectrum lighting is recommended. This snake may exhibit nocturnal behaviors as well.

Reproduction: Mates in April to May, with litters of live young birthed in early September. Young are very thin and have to be raised on pinhead crickets and tiny guppies.

Pet Suitability: 3

Despite the little knowledge we have of this bizarre little serpent, it makes a great pet, provided it is treated for internal parasites as soon as possible. Gaining

213

popularity in the pet trade in recent years, the Chinese garter snake (oftentimes sold as an Asian rat snake or Chinese rat snake in pet shops) can be purchased at a reasonable price. A healthy specimen makes a great starter snake. Recently imported specimens, however, may not be in the best shape. Select your Chinese garter carefully.

COMMON GARTER SNAKE
THAMNOPHIS SIRTALIS (LINNAEUS, 1758)
Range: Extensive throughout North America; one of the only snake species to inhabit lands inside the Arctic Circle.

Size: Can grow to nearly 5 feet (1.5 m), although most subspecies do not exceed 3 to 3.5 feet (0.9 to 1.1 m)

Subspecies and Similar Species: Numerous; at least 12 subspecies described and recognized by most taxonomists. Notable subspecies include the strikingly gorgeous blue-striped garter snake (*T. s. similis*), the beautiful and widely available red-sided garter snake (*T. s. parietalis*), and the highly sought-after San Francisco garter snake (*T. s. tetrataenia*), which is critically endangered

The San Francisco garter snake is both one of the most beautiful and most endangered North American snakes. However, a number of European hobbyists breed this subspecies.

The beautiful blue-striped garter snake is endemic to Florida.

in the wild but bred with some regularity within the European pet trade. This serpent always commands an exorbitant price tag. Numerous designer varieties of various garter snakes are also available, although they are quite pricey.

Several other *Thamnophis* species are widely available and have similar care to the common garter snake. Butler's garter snake (*T. butleri*) stays under 2 feet (61 cm) long and is cleanly marked. The checkered garter snake (*T. marcianus*) has a subtlely beautiful pattern and is one of the most frequently captive-bred garters. It is one of the garter snakes that feeds readily on mice. The closely related ribbon snake (*T. sauritus*) may be housed, fed, and cared for in the same manner as the garter snakes.

Description: Thin and somewhat "wiry" or "squirmy" in the hand, these animals are the quintessential colubrid snake. Dorsal coloration varies among subspecies, with the nominate form being black dorsally with three longitudinal stripes of yellow running the length of the body. Interstitial reddish and white flecks are visible on dorsal and lateral surfaces. The vent is cream colored. The eyes are large, with round pupils that are indicative of this snake's nature as a diurnal, visual predator. The scales are heavily keeled. Blue species wear pastel lines dorsally with an accordingly blue vent, and the San Francisco variety has bold red and blue markings dorsally.

Captive Diet: Fish, earthworms, nontoxic frogs, tadpoles, and pinkie mice. One of the few piscivorous species to thrive in the pet industry, the garter and ribbon snakes do well on a varied diet consisting of whole fish, amphibians, and earthworms. Many will also eat insects and slugs.

Longevity: May exceed ten years. Some garter snake subspecies may live considerably longer.

Habitat and Terrarium: One of the most widely kept snakes in the world, the common garter snake needs little to thrive in captivity. Dry conditions, a hide or two in which to feel safe and secure, and a large water dish are all that is critical. Tank size should be enough to accommodate movement and stretching out and should be fitted with a secure lid. (These slender snakes can escape through small holes.) Both the naturalistic terrarium and the spartan habitat will accommodate virtually any species of garter or ribbon snake. That being said, the ribbon snake is considerably more arboreal than the garter snake and does best when housed in a vertically oriented tank with plenty of climbing branches and clusters of vegetative cover. All members of the *Thamnophis* genus seem to love hiding in clumps of Spanish moss.

Temperatures and Humidity: Will vary based on the species in question. All species of garter and ribbon snakes are tolerant of a wide range of relative

Albino checkered garter snakes rank among the most frequently captive bred of the garters.

humidity, although some subspecies like more humid conditions than others (such as the swamp-dwelling blue-striped garter snake of the American South). Likewise, some subspecies enjoy warmer conditions. A good rule of thumb is to learn the exact parameters of your chosen subspecies and replicate those conditions. In the meantime, maintain daily temperatures of 74° to 80°F (23.3° to 26.7°C) with both warmer basking spots and cooler retreats. Although these snakes like to swim, they can be prone to blister disease, so set up the terrarium so that your snake can dry off when it chooses.

Lighting: No specialized lighting is necessary.

Reproduction: After a winter hibernation, up to 100 young are born alive in midsummer, although most litters are smaller. Newborns are very small and need to be weaned on tiny fare: cut earthworms, tiny minnows, etc.

Pet Suitability: 5

Although not always the most personable or handle-friendly snakes, the garter (or "garden snake" as it has long been known throughout the United States) and ribbon snakes do make excellent captives. Many herpetologists and hobbyists got their start with some member of the *Thamnophis* genus. They are truly a beginner's best bet!

Know What You're Getting

The San Francisco garter snake is protected by federal law. If you encounter a specimen of this species available for sale, make sure that it was obtained and is being sold legally. Illegal poaching of this snake for the pet trade threatens to drive its wild populations to extinction. Do not support poaching by buying any illegally collected species.

LONG-NOSED SNAKE
RHINOCHEILUS LECONTEI BAIRD AND GIRARD, 1853

Range: Range is extensive throughout the American West: Texas and Kansas west through Colorado to California and south through northern Mexico.

Size: Adults rarely attain 3 feet (0.9 m) in length, with the record being nearly 3.5 feet (1.1 m).

Subspecies and Similar Species: The Texas long-nosed snake (*R. l. tessellatus*) enjoys popularity in the pet trade and is the only subspecies normally available.

Description: Short and slender, the long-nosed snake is highly variable in its coloration. Dorsally, it may be tricolored: Alternating saddles of reddish orange and black are edged in a yellow to sandy color, which also adorns the snake's sides and vent. Dorsolateral flecks of black cover a yellowish background. Some specimens, however, lack the red coloration and wear only alternating stripes of black and whitish yellow. Such specimens are often mistaken for the California kingsnake. The snout is elongated, and the lower jaw is noticeably shorter than the snout. The scales are smooth.

Captive Diet: Adults take lizards, smaller snakes, reptile eggs, and small rodents in the wild. Captive fare should consist of small pre-killed rodents and lizards. Wild-caught specimens—and this species is rarely captive bred—can be difficult to feed. The editor of this book has had luck enticing long-nosed snakes to eat using rodents scented with baby corn snakes.

Longevity: May exceed ten years, although this species is not noted for its longevity.

Habitat and Terrarium: A desert-dwelling animal, the long-nosed snake thrives in warm, arid environs. Broad, wide tanks are stressed over tall ones, as this snake is a devoutly terrestrial and subterranean species that seldom climbs. Offer loose, sandy substrate and plenty of hides. Most hobbyists have found that lengths of PVC piping half buried in the substrate are relished by this shy, retiring species. The long-nosed snake thrives in either the savanna-style or desert-style habitat.

Temperatures and Humidity: Maintain daily temperatures that range from 75° to about 88°F (24° to 31.1°C) at the hottest spot with a drop to not lower than 65°F (18.3°C) at night. Keep relative humidity low at the upper reaches of the

Butler's garter snake (*Thamnophis butleri*) primarily feeds on earthworms in nature. When keeping one as a pet, feed it mostly earthworms with occasional insects, mice, and fish.

Unfortunately, the beautiful and docile long-nosed snake usually requires lizards as food. Otherwise, it makes a nice pet.

tank, although the sandy substrate should be moistened every few days to keep the snake and its habitat from drying out. Although it is a desert animal, it should be provided with plenty of water at all times because it is prone to dehydration in the captive environment.

Lighting: The long-nosed snake is a powerfully nocturnal animal. No UV lighting is necessary. Many hobbyists recommend using some manner of night-cycle bulb to allow viewing when the snake is at its most active.

Reproduction: Egg layer. This species mates in April and deposits small clutches in June. Young emerge in two to three months. Hatchlings can be difficult to rear on rodent prey; small lizards are recommended.

Pet Suitability: 2

The long-nosed snakes are bizarre colubrids, to say the least. Devout burrowers and subterranean hunters, these attractive snakes put on quite the display when threatened. They coil into a writhing ball while hiding their head at the center, lunging in closed-mouth strikes, vibrating the tail (which may sound like a rattlesnake when vibrating against dry vegetation), and forcibly dispelling on their attacker a bloody, oily fluid from the cloaca. In captivity, these elaborate defensive behaviors quickly disappear, and these snakes readily tame to human touch.

MALAGASY GIANT HOGNOSE SNAKE
LEIOHETERODON MADAGASCARIENSIS DUMÉRIL AND BIBRON, 1854

Range: Endemic to Madagascar and Comoros Islands.

Size: To 6 feet (1.8 m), although 4 feet (1.2m) is more common.

Subspecies and Similar Species: *L. geayi* and *L. modestus*. Also endemic to Madagascar, these species do not show up in the pet trade as regularly as the giant hognose.

Description: A large, muscular colubrid, the Malagasy hognose snake wears a dappled coat of earth tones and lighter whites, creams, and ivory shades. It has askew dorsal saddles. The overall effect is of a zigzagged dark layer laid atop an ivory base; the lateral surfaces bear a sawtooth pattern of dark on light. Dorsal scales may also have tiny spots of reddish to clay color on a darker base. The eyes are large. The rostral scale curves upward to accommodate burrowing and rooting out of toads, frogs, and reptile eggs from forest debris and loose soil.

Captive Diet: Wild giant hognose snakes prey upon all manner of lizards, frogs, and their eggs. Captive fare should consist of pre-killed mice and nontoxic frogs

Although not closely related to the North American hognoses, the Malagasy giant hognose has a similar upturned snout.

(leopard frogs, bullfrogs, etc.) Some individuals may also accept pre-killed chicks. Lizards (anoles and house geckos) will also be taken with relish. Some specimens will only take fare at night. Scenting (with a toad or frog) may induce fussy specimens into taking rodent prey.

Longevity: 10 to 15 years is recorded.

Habitat and Terrarium: All species of the Malagasy giant hognose snake require very large environs. These snakes are devout burrowers who need all the horizontal space they can get in the home terrarium. Native habitats range from coastal to forest, so substrate should allow burrowing. Most hobbyists recommend a cypress mulch or sand mixed with mulch or bark. Many keepers have also reported excellent success with recycled newspaper bedding, which is clean, very loose, lightweight, and fully functional for this species' burrowing requirements. Caves, hides, and lengths of PVC piping, as well as plenty of artificial vegetative cover, are also required. Although small specimens may climb, most adults lead a strictly terrestrial life. Acrylic terrariums are recommended over glass tanks, as the screen lid of glass tanks tends to allow heat to escape, and these snake thrive with warmer air.

Temperatures and Humidity: Maintain daily ambient temperatures in the mid 80s F (29° to 30°C) with a hot spot that reaches about 95°F (35°C), with only very slight drops by night. Relative humidity should range from 50 to 60 percent.

Lighting: Enough for viewing is suitable. Specialized UV lighting is recommended by most experts, although there is some speculation that, owing to the subterranean nature of this species, such lighting is not needed.

Reproduction: Mating occurs in August, with eggs being deposited in November and December. After roughly two months of incubation, the eggs, which may be as many as 15 to a clutch, hatch into 12-inch (30.5-cm) neonates.

Pet Suitability: 3

Although not encountered in the pet trade with any regularity, the Malagasy giant hognose snake has a quiet following among hognose enthusiasts. Not a pet for the beginning hobbyist or the novice, this snake does make a wonderful pet for the intermediate herper and a challenging and rewarding breeding project for advanced keepers.

RED-BELLIED WATER SNAKE
NERODIA ERYTHROGASTER (FORSTER, 1771)

Range: Extensive throughout eastern seaboard west through Texas. Absent at high elevations.

Size: May exceed 5 feet (1.5 m) long.

Subspecies and Similar Species: Many species of *Nerodia* may appear in the captive terrarium for one reason or another. Some make attractive, if aggressive, terrarium subjects, others are attractions in larger ecosystem exhibits at

The blotched water snake is one of many water snakes that show up at pet stores from time to time.

at zoological parks, and still others make their way to the science classrooms of middle and high schools nationwide. Other species and subspecies include the yellow-bellied water snake (*N. e. flavigaster*), the blotched water snake (*N. e. transversa*), the copper-bellied water snake (*N. e. neglecta*), the banded or southern water snake (*N. fasciata*), the common or northern water snake (*N. sipedon*), the Florida green water snake (*N. floridana*) and the brown water snake (*N. taxispilota*). The brown water snake is a particularly mild-mannered member of the genus, which isn't really saying much. All species of *Nerodia* are renowned for their defensive dispositions.

Description: A hardy species with heavily keeled scales, vibrant ventral coloration, dark, muddy dorsal coloration, and an insatiable appetite for fish, frogs, tadpoles, sirens, and baby turtles. The body is heavy and the head is broad, with powerful jaw muscles. This snake loves to bask and is frequently encountered in branches overhanging water by fishermen and exploring children. If cornered or captured, it will resist violently, biting, hissing, thrashing, and expelling its cloacal contents on its molester. Bites from this species are quite painful and bleed profusely because of a potent anticoagulant in its saliva. Although it is frequently mistaken for the dreaded water moccasin, this genus is not venomous and poses no threat to human life or safety. Owners of fishing ponds often kill these snakes indiscriminately because they erroneously believe that these snakes deplete fisheries.

Captive Diet: Fish, crayfish, and frogs (members of the genus *Rana* in particular) are preferred; some will take earthworms and pinkie mice. This species will often eat to gorging in captivity. It may vomit up fare if stressed or tampered with soon after feeding.

Longevity: May exceed ten years.

Habitat and Terrarium: A swamp-style terrarium is required. A large tub of clean, fresh water is mandatory, as are ample dry areas. Sturdy climbing branches will be enjoyed, as will large, flat rocks and deep, dark caves and hides. These are good-sized snakes that need lots of room to slither and swim. As such, they require large terrariums and watery environs. Large, flat rocks situated directly beneath a spot lamp or heat lamp will be used for basking and drying after swimming.

Temperatures and Humidity: Maintain warm temperatures (a range from the low 70s to mid-80s F [21.1° to 30°C]) and high levels of relative humidity. Simply having a large water container for swimming in the terrarium should satisfy the matter of humidity. Good air circulation is paramount, as these snakes are prone to respiratory infections if housed in perpetually damp habitats. Fungal and bacterial skin infections may also be problematic when housed under excessively cool or otherwise inferior conditions. Clean water is a must; soiled or contaminated water will lead to serious infection in your snake.

Many of the water snakes, including the Florida green water snake, are found in both fresh and brackish water habitats.

223

Lighting: All species of *Nerodia* are sun worshippers and love to bask. Full-spectrum UV lighting is required for four hours each day.

Reproduction: Live bearing. Large females may birth several dozen young in the summer months.

Pet Suitability: 4

The genus *Nerodia* is a foul-tempered lot. Characterized by savage squirming, cloacal venting, and repeated biting, these snakes do not like to be handled. Kept primarily for their aesthetic value, they do make nice additions to a large, naturalistic swamp or wetland terrarium. If you buy one, know that this snake is a pet in name only.

ROUGH GREEN SNAKE
OPHEODRYS AESTIVUS (LINNAEUS, 1766)

Range: Eastern United States from central New Jersey south through Florida and west through Texas and northern Mexico.

Size: A small-bodied snake with an incredibly long tail, the rough green snake seldom exceeds 42 inches (106.7 cm); common adult lengths are between 30 and 36 inches (76.2 and 91.4 cm).

Subspecies and Similar Species: Although not seen in the pet trade with as much regularity as their rough-skinned cousin, the eastern smooth green snake

Rough green snakes are excellent subjects for naturalistic terraria. Their small size prevents them from damaging most live plants.

(*O. vernalis vernalis*) and the western smooth green snake (*O. v. blanchardi*) are the other North American green snakes. The largest of the *Opheodrys* species, *O. major*, is an Asian species. Growing to over 4 feet (1.2 m) in length, this montane species occurs sporadically in the pet market.

Description: A small-framed yet long and agile species, the rough green snake is a denizen of low-growing shrubs, the dense forest understory, and streamside vegetation. Diurnal hunters of all manner of insects, these demure snakes are stealthy and swift; they have excellent vision and can spot both predators and prey with proficiency. Their eyes are accordingly large. Dorsal coloration is forest green. Lateral surfaces are yellowish to olive, while the ventral surface is bright yellow to creamy white. Such a color scheme makes this snake extremely difficult to detect in its natural habitat— viewed from above, it takes on the green hue of the leaves around it, and viewed from below, it looks like sunlight filtering through leaves higher in the canopy. As its name implies, this snake is rough; each scale is heavily keeled. Although some specimens are aggressive when startled or caught out of the wild, most tame and adapt well to gentle handling. The rough green snake may coil quietly for hours around its keeper's wrists. The long tail is quite prehensile and helps it move gracefully and safely from branch to branch in the forest canopy.

Captive Diet: Primarily insects, including caterpillars, spiders, grubs, crickets, grasshoppers, cicadas, katydids, and locusts. Captive fare should include gut-loaded crickets supplemented with wax worms, silkworms, and recently molted mealworms. Earthworms are usually taken with relish. Feeder geckos or small anoles may be taken by large adult specimens.

Longevity: Rough green snakes are not known for their longevity, although some specimens may thrive for nearly a decade.

Habitat and Terrarium: A devoutly arboreal snake, the rough green snake should be supplied with plentiful branches. Heavy vegetative cover (artificial or living plants) is a necessity. Height is also a major consideration, so favor a tall, narrower tank over a longer or broader short tank. Ground cover is of minimal concern; hobbyists have reported great success with both natural substrates as well as recycled newspaper and even folded paper towels and newsprint bedding. Hides are also a necessity; hollow logs, curved slabs of cork bark, and lengths of PVC piping left lying atop (or partially buried in) the substrate work well for this purpose.

Delicious Caterpillars

Some newly captive rough green snakes refuse to take crickets and mealworms. If yours is like this try caterpillars. Silkworms, tomato hornworms, and wax worms are some of the commercially available caterpillars you can offer your snake.

Temperatures and Humidity: Temperate. Provide daily temps in the mid- to upper 70s F (23.3° to 26.1°C) with nightly drops into the mid- to upper 60s F (17.8° to 20.6°C) Relative humidity is seldom an issue. If your snake's scales begin to curl at their edges, increase the humidity by misting the tank or partially covering the lid with cellophane.

Lighting: Full-spectrum lighting is required; all insectivorous snakes typically need vitamin supplements and UV lighting. Exposure to natural sunlight is also beneficial, so when handling your rough green snake, take a half-hour walk outside so that it can bask in some natural sunlight. Never place your snake's terrarium in direct sunlight..

Reproduction: Mating occurs in spring and again in late autumn (in the southern extreme of its range). Up to eight eggs are deposited in a communal nesting site. Females may return to the same nesting site year after year.

Pet Suitability: 1

The first pet snake I ever bought from a pet shop was a rough green snake. It is a best bet for the beginning hobbyist and makes an excellent breeding project or subject for a natural terrarium for the more advanced hobbyist. I highly recommend the keeping of a rough green snake to anyone of any experience level. Most rough green snakes in the pet trade are wild caught and may need to be inspected/treated for internal parasites.

WESTERN HOGNOSE SNAKE
HETERODON NASICUS NASICUS BAIRD AND GIRARD, 1852

Range: Nominate race is found from southern Canada south through Oklahoma and the Texas panhandle and west to New Mexico.

Size: To 36 inches (91.4 cm).

Subspecies and Similar Species: There are numerous species and subspecies of *Heterodon* found throughout the central and eastern United States. The most commonly available subspecies is certainly the western hognose, as it is by far the most keepable variety. Other subspecies include the dusty hognose (*H. n. gloydi*, sometimes considered the same as *H. n. nasicus*) and the Mexican hognose (*H. n. kennerlyi*, sometimes considered a full species). The eastern and southern hognose snakes (*H. platyrhinos* and *H. simus*, respectively) are considerably larger snakes, tend to be somewhat bland in coloration (some populations of southern hognose snakes, however, are vibrant red and coral pink in coloration), and often do not thrive in captivity. Both of these species have specialized diets of toads and frogs, and both are considerably more prone to stress and eating disorders. I do not recommend keeping either *H. platyrhinos* or *H. simus* in the home terrarium to anyone who is inexperienced with the *Heterodon* genus as a whole.

The western hognose is the only hognose snake captive bred in any numbers. Normal and albino individuals are illustrated here.

Description: A truly unusual species, the western hognose snake is a stocky animal with a sharply upturned nose to aid it in burrowing through soft soil or in rooting out prey items hiding beneath stones, under loose bark, or in other tight crevasses. Dorsal coloration is a motley blend of earth tones: sandy to tan base with peanut-shaped blotches of light brown down the centerline of the back and a series of smaller, coffee-colored blotches occur laterally. The head is striped in browns and coffee colors, and the vent is cream colored with small, dark flecks. This snake actively forages for prey in the morning and late afternoon.

Hognose snakes are also known for their "death throes" behavior. If accosted by predators, these snakes will put on an elaborate show, flaring their necks like cobras and lunging (with mouth closed) at their attacker, then flipping on their back, holding their mouth agape, and emitting an extremely foul-smelling musk. Most would-be predators lose interest in the suddenly dead and rotting snake in front of them. When the predator leaves, the hognose snake will slither away, none the worse for wear. In the captive environment, this defensive behavior almost never occurs.

Captive Diet: Wild western hognose snakes take all manner of fare: lizards, small

The upturned snout of the western hognose snake enables it to dig for its preferred prey: frogs, toads, lizards, and small eggs.

snakes, mice, reptile eggs, birds and their eggs, and frogs and toads. Captive diet should consist of appropriately sized pre-killed rodents, chicks, and the occasional feeder anole or house gecko.

Longevity: The western hognose may live for better than a decade in captivity when housed and maintained under ideal conditions.

Habitat and Terrarium: Open plains and loose, sandy, and rocky soil. Provide deep, loose substrate to accommodate this snake's burrowing habits. Sand mixed with bark or coconut husk and recycled newspaper bedding are great substrates. Plentiful hides and ground cover are also necessary, as this species is fond of terrestrial hideaways. A strictly terrestrial species, the western hognose snake should be housed in broad, wide environs that afford plenty of lateral room to slither about. Keep a large dish of water at your snake's disposal at all times.

Temperatures and Humidity: Provide daily temperature range from 75° to 85°F (24° to 29.4°C) at the hottest spot with nightly dips to the low 70s F (21.1° to 22.8°C). Relative humidity should not dip below 45 percent and may spike as high as the mid 60s . As is true of all desert species, the western hognose is prone to respiratory infections if housed in excessively humid environs.

Lighting: Enough for viewing is adequate. No specialized lighting is necessary.

Reproduction: Mates in early spring after hibernation. Females deposit clutches

of up to two dozen eggs. Young are 6 to 8 inches (15.2 to 20.3 cm) long and emerge in as little as seven to eight weeks. Sexually mature at two years of age.

Pet Suitability: 1

A western hognose snake is a great choice for a young enthusiast or beginning hobbyist, as they are mild mannered, hardy, and typically feed well in captivity. Most juveniles available for purchase are captive bred and seldom demand an exorbitant price. More experienced snake keepers might want to house one of this snake's cousins, the eastern or southern hognose. Care for those animals is as described here but with a more humid, forest-like terrarium and a diet of common toads.

The Rat Snakes

A subgroup within the family Colubridae, there are several genera of rat snakes. Most commonly, the rat snakes include *Bogertophis*, *Elaphe*, *Pantherophis*, and *Senticolis*. In recent years, taxonomists have reclassified many species within the *Elaphe* genus as *Pantherophis* (and a few other genera as well for some of the Asian species), and those species names have changed accordingly. So while a book written in the late 1990s might call a corn snake by the Latin name *Elaphe guttata guttata*, a more modern text may refer to this species as *Pantherophis guttatus guttatus*. Don't let the name change fool you, however, as these two names both refer to the same animal; certainly care and husbandry practices are also unchanged.

Regardless of nomenclature, the rat snakes comprise some 50-odd species hailing from North America, Europe, and Asia. Despite the fact that they hail from the far-flung corners of the globe, all share some basic characteristics. All are devout mousers, all are accomplished climbers (by utilizing their rigid belly scales, these snakes can slowly but surely climb straight up the rough bark of a tree or brick wall), and all defend themselves by hissing loudly and raising their fore portions into a classic "S" shape with the mouth agape. If the attacker is not thwarted by this intimidating presentation, the rat snake will lunge forward and strike repeatedly. In the captive environment, however, with most species (the Texas rat snake [*Pantherophis obsoletus lindheimeri*] notwithstanding), this

Fanged but not Deadly

The Latin genus name *Heterodon* literally means "different tooth" and refers to the elongate, hollow teeth situated in the back of this snake's mouth. These "fangs" are capable of injecting a mild venom into prey items. More a sedative than a venom, the chemical substance does not kill prey items; it merely drugs or sedates struggling prey, thereby aiding the snake in swallowing its meal. The hognose snake is not a constrictor, nor is it lethally venomous, so this sort of semi-venom helps these snakes, which typically swallow their prey alive, to effectively feed. These "fangs" and their "venom" pose absolutely no threat to humans.

Good Snakekeeping

Most of the rat snakes are skilled climbers and will hunt prey in tree branches and barn rafters. This is a corn snake in its natural habitat.

defensive behavior is quickly abandoned.

The rat snakes are popular in the pet trade for a great many reasons: manageable size for most species, low maintenance demands, willingness to feed on rodents in the home terrarium, and their crisp, clean markings and brilliant colors. Rat snakes present the hobbyist with some of the truest blacks, deepest reds, most vibrant yellows or oranges, and foggiest grays to appear in the snake world. The purchase price of most rat snakes is affordable. Perhaps Ray Staszko, in his *Rat Snakes: A Hobbyist's Guide to Elaphe and Kin*, said it best: "Of all the snakes, rat snakes are probably the easiest and most suitable for keeping as pets."

What's up With Rat Snakes?

Many hobbyists are confused by the changes that have occurred in the taxonomy and naming of the rat snakes. If you want to dig further into the subject, start with these papers:

- Burbrink, Frank T. 2001. Systematics of the Eastern Ratsnake Complex (*Elaphe obsoleta*). *Herpetological Monographs*. 15: 1–53.
- Burbrink, Frank T., Robin Lawson, and Joseph B. Slowinski. 2000. Mitochondrial DNA Phylogeography of the Polytypic North American Rat Snake (*Elaphe obsoleta*): a Critique of the Subspecies Concept. *Evolution*. 54 (6): 2107–2108.
- Crother B.I., Boundy J., Campbell J.A., De Quieroz K., Frost D., Green D.M., Highton R., Iverson J.B., McDiarmid R.W., Meylan P.A., Reeder T.W., Seidel M.E., Sites Jr. J.W., Tilley S.G., Wake D.B. 2003. Scientific and Standard English Names of Amphibians and Reptiles of North America North of Mexico: Update. *Herpetological Review*. 34: 196–203.
- Utiger U, Helfenberger N, Schatti B, Schmidt C, Ruf M, Ziswiler V. 2002. Molecular systematics and phylogeny of Old and New World ratsnakes, *Elaphe* Auct., and related genera (Reptilia, Squamata, Colubridae). *Russian Journal of Herpetology* 9(2):105–124.

AMERICAN RAT SNAKE
PANTHEROPHIS OBSOLETUS SSP. SAY *IN* JAMES, 1823

Range: Extensive throughout eastern and central United States. Northern and urban ranges are broken.

Size: To 8 feet (2.4 m). Average adult lengths do not exceed 5 to 6 feet (1.5 to 1.8 m). Unlike the boas and pythons, these snakes, even at such lengths, are lithe and lightweight.

Subspecies and Similar Species: Four major subspecies occur in this species. The black rat snake (*P. o. obsoletus*) is the largest of the subspecies, and owing to its marginally maligned disposition, is not as frequently owned in the home terrarium. However, several color morphs of this subspecies exist, including the beautiful white-sided or licorice morph. The second subspecies, the yellow rat snake (*P. o. quadrivittata*), is a more southerly variant that has four lateral stripes lining the body on a dull yellow background. The Everglades rat snake (*P. o. rossalleni*) is easily one of the most gorgeous of the North American rat snakes. The vibrantly orange to red Everglades rat snake is one of the most sought-after rat snakes in the pet industry for its

Good Snakekeeping

Normal black rat snakes (left) are not very popular pets; however, breeders produce the licorice morph (right) in fairly large numbers.

fiery coloration. The gray rat snake (*P. o. spiloides*) wears a whitish, tree bark-colored coat with darker saddles. The notoriously ill-tempered Texas rat snake (*P. o. lindheimeri*) is mottled tan (to a bright orange) with darker saddles. Recent taxonomic work has concluded that these subspecies names do not reflect the real relationships of the snakes, although these are used commonly by hobbyists.

Description: Although they appear diverse as adults, the black, yellow, everglades, and gray rat snakes are, at their most basic level, similar. So similar are these snakes, in fact, that as hatchlings they can be hard to tell apart. Base coloration in youth is tan to grayish or sandy with darker rectangular or "H"-shaped saddles occurring at regular intervals along the midline of the back. Smaller blotches and squares occur along the lateral surfaces, and stripes occur through the eyes and corner of the jaw. Reddish or pinkish to white flecks are often visible in the interstitial spaces between the body scales. Adults, however, vary considerably. Black rat snakes are grayish to jet or uniformly black dorsally with creamy to rosy-colored belly. Yellows, at maturation, will develop four roughly continuous brown to black lines running the length of the body and base coloration of sandy yellow to yellowish orange. Everglades rat snakes have darker lateral lines and a much rosier, orange-red base coloration. Unlike all of the other subspecies, the gray rat snakes maintain their gray, stony appearance throughout adulthood. This multitone gray coloration has earned this snake its alternate common name, "oak snake." Dorsal scales of all subspecies are moderately keeled.

Physically, these snakes are lithe, powerful climbers and wide-eyed, alert, diurnal mousers and active hunters. Devoutly arboreal, they frequent barn lofts, treetops, attics, and old stone outcroppings. With belly scales that are quite rigid, they are accomplished climbers and can easily scale straight up the side of a tree. Black rat snakes, also known as pilot black snakes, regularly gather in winter dens with copperheads (*Agkistrodon* spp.) and rattlesnakes (*Crotalus* spp. and *Sistrurus* spp.). Although few hobbyists do so, these snakes are social and may be housed communally.

Captive Diet: Wild diet includes all manner of small mammals, including bats, mice, rats, moles, voles, and birds and their eggs. Some Western species will also take lizards. The captive diet may consist of pre-killed rodents, chicks, and quail eggs.

Longevity: May exceed 15 years, depending on exact species. Black rat snakes are, reputedly, the longest lived of all the *obsoletus* group.

Habitat and Terrarium: All species and subspecies of American rat snakes thrive in both naturalistic habitats as well as more spartan or sparsely outfitted enclosures. Any number of different substrates will work for rat snakes: bark, aspen, paper, recycled newspaper, leaf litter, sand and soil mixtures, etc. Large environs will allow your snake room to slither, and tall environs will grant it plenty of climbing space. Vegetative cover is a definite plus, while numerous

Gray rat snakes range from southernmost Illinois to Florida and Mississippi.

The Everglades rat snake is the most vibrantly colored subspecies of the American rat snake. It has a small natural range in southern Florida.

hides will also be used. Climbing logs, branches, and wooden slabs, coupled with acrylic or artificial vines, are also climbed upon and enjoyed by both juvenile and adult specimens.

All rat snakes are consummate escape artists and must be kept in extremely secure habitats. Holes in the lid, gaps, cracks, and other such openings will provide avenues for escape, as will lightweight or nonlocking lids, which the rat snake can easily push open. Lids that lock into place are best—weighted lids or those piled high with heavy objects are a disaster waiting to happen.

Temperatures and Humidity: All subspecies of *obsoletus* will thrive with ambient daily temperatures in the low 80s F (26.7° to 28.3°C), basking spots to the upper 80s F (30.6° to 31.7°C), and cooler retreats in the mid-70s F (23.3° to 24.4°C) Nightly dips to the low 70s F (21.1° to 22.8°C) are recommended. Black rat snakes, which naturally occur as far north as the Great Lakes region and southern Canada, can tolerate cooler temperatures than can Everglades rat snakes. Maintain relative humidity of about 60 percent.

Lighting: Because they are not often prolific baskers (many rat snakes become almost entirely nocturnal during the heat of the summer months), these snakes do not require any specialized UV lighting. That being said, I have also seen a marked color enhancement in specimens that have been exposed to two to four hours of full-spectrum UV lighting daily. Taking your rat snake outside (when and wherever possible) for short periods and exposing it to true sunlight may also increase the depth of color.

Reproduction: Breeding occurs throughout the spring (and late winter in extreme southern regions), with large clutches of eggs being deposited two to three months later. Females reach sexual maturity at roughly 24 to 30 months and may lay clutches of more than 30 eggs. Eggs hatch in roughly 60 to 80 days, with young measuring 10 inches (25.4 cm) at hatching. Extensive crossbreeding occurs where ranges of American rat snakes overlap.

Pet Suitability: 2

Even though these snakes may be somewhat more temperamental or flighty as pets, they are long lived and beautiful. The American rat snakes are also infinitely hardy, disease and illness resistant, and typically handle tolerant. Although not as perfect as the corn snake, these rat snake species do make excellent captives.

BAIRD'S RAT SNAKE
PANTHEROPHIS BAIRDI (YARROW, 1880)

Range: American Southwest, central to west Texas, south into eastern Mexico.

Size: Smaller than the closely related *obsoletus* group, the Baird's rat snake seldom exceeds 4 to 4.5 feet (1.2 to 1.4 m), although some adults may reach 60 inches (1.5 m).

Subspecies and Similar Species: None. Baird's rat snake was once considered a subspecies of *P. obsoletus*.

Description: With a basal coloration of pearl to gray or sometimes brownish, the Baird's rat snake is unique among rat snakes in that it has a secondary basal coloration underlying the first; the anterior edge of each scale is rusty orange to a blazing sunset coloration. Interstitial skin and belly scales are likewise orange. Making for an unusual appearance, this color scheme of flame on pearl is highlighted by faint dorsolateral lines running the length of the body, which, like the yellow and Everglades rat snakes, may be more or less pronounced, depending on the individual specimen in question. Remnant saddles or blotches may be visible in juvenile or hybridized (Baird's rat snake x Texas rat snake) specimens. When they are visible, the saddles on a Baird's rat snake are much more numerous than most other members of the *obsoletus* group. The head is small and the rostral and frontal scales are slightly reinforced, which aids the snake in nosing in tight crevices for its favorite prey: lizards.

Captive Diet: Wild specimens take mice, fledgling birds, eggs, lizards, and some reptile eggs. Captive fare should consist of pre-killed mice and quail chicks. Wild-caught specimens may refuse mammalian prey and may only take lizards. Wean

The Baird's rat snake is usually easy to care for, although hatchlings sometimes insist on lizards for food.

such specimens to mice by scenting the mice on lizards. (See Chapter 4.)

Longevity: 15 years.

Habitat and Terrarium: Arid and dry. These rat snakes, like all desert-dwelling serpents, are prone to skin and respiratory infections when housed in excessively damp or humid environs. In a naturalistic habitat, employ a sandy substrate and small water dishes. They are nocturnal by nature, so caves and deep hides are also relished. They thrive in spartan enclosures as long as ventilation is sufficient to maintain a low humidity level. Large terrariums with plenty of rocks work well because these snakes are devout roamers and will need plenty of room to slither about. Climbing branches or vertical rocks will also be utilized by a curious Baird's rat snake.

Temperatures and Humidity: Relative humidity below 50 percent with daily ambient temperatures in the mid 80s F (29° to 30°C) with a cooler retreat and a hot spot reaching near 90°F (32.2°C). Nightly drops to the mid-70s F (23.3° to 24.4°C).

Lighting: No special lighting is required.

Reproduction: Springtime copulation. The eggs hatch in 80 days. This species may hybridize with the Texas rat snake (*P. o. lindheimeri*) in the wild.

Pet Suitability: 1

Although it has never attained a following as large as that of the corn snake, the Baird's rat snake is one of my favorite species. Quietly attractive and relatively mild mannered, the Baird's rat snake is best purchased as a juvenile. Wild-caught adult specimens do not tame to handling the same way a juvenile will. To me, the pearly, rosy coloration of the Baird's rat snake is half the reason for owning one; in all the serpentine world, it is simply a uniquely gorgeous snake.

CORN SNAKE
PANTHEROPHIS GUTTATUS GUTTATUS (LINNAEUS, 1766)

Range: Extensive throughout the eastern and central United States: New Jersey to Florida west to Louisiana and Tennessee.

Size: To 6 feet (1.8 m). Most adults do not exceed 4 to 5 feet (1.2 to 1.5 m) in length, however. Wild specimens typically grow larger than those reared in captivity.

Subspecies and Similar Species: Only two subspecies of corn snakes appear in the pet trade with any regularity. A third subspecies exists, but many scientists now treat all three as full species. The Great Plains rat snake (*P. g. emoryi*) is a Midwestern variant of corn snake and wears a subdued coat of grayish tan with brown to slate-colored saddles. Although the Great Plains rat snake makes an excellent and handle-friendly captive, its somewhat drab coloration has kept it from attaining the wild popularity of its eastern cousin. The Slowinski's corn snake (*P. g. slowinskii*), first described in 2002, is a drab brown to grayish serpent native to Louisiana and Texas.

Description: An accomplished climber, the corn snake is frequently encountered in treetops, attics, and the exposed rafters of old barns and haylofts. The corn snake wears a highly variable coat. Specimens from the Carolinas are particularly desirable because their base coloration is bright orange to red with crimson to blood-colored saddles down the midline of the back (the so-called "Okeetee" variant). South Georgia specimens also bear vibrant, flaming coloration. Mountainous populations, conversely, wear much more subdued coats of brownish to silvery gray with rust to maroon-colored saddles. Dorsal markings include rectangles of yellow to rust. The ventral surface is white and black checkered. Literally hundreds of color and pattern variations—some found in the wild and some the product of selective breeding—are seen in corn snakes. Albino (amelanistic), anerythristic (lacking all red colors), snow, blizzard, bloodred, striped, albino striped, and motley are just a sample of the most popular morphs in the hobby.

Captive Diet: Rodents. Wild corn snakes are highly accomplished hunters that dine on a variety of fare: rats, mice, chipmunks, moles, lizards, birds, bird eggs,

Like ball pythons, corn snakes are bred in a dazzling number of different morphs. Shown here (clockwise from top left) are a particularly nice normal corn (often called an Okeetee), an albino Miami phase, a butter, and a snow.

and even bats. Pre-killed mice, supplemented with the occasional chick or brown chicken egg, will suffice in the home terrarium.

Longevity: 15 to 20 years is not uncommon.

Habitat and Terrarium: Woodland. Outfit the corn snake terrarium with ample hides (hollow logs, clay pot halves, etc.) and foliage; live plants will work for smaller specimens, while artificial plants are best for larger, stronger snakes. Climbing branches are absolutely essential to the long-term happiness and physiological well-being of your corn snake. Corn snakes, like all rat snakes, are some of the most accomplished escape artists in the snake world, so a secure, tight-fitting lid is definitely in order. A naturalistic substrate of virtually any type suitable for a woodland or jungle habitat will work well for a corn snake enclosure, as will more spartan elements, such as recycled newspaper bedding or paper towels.

Temperatures and Humidity: Maintain ambient temperatures in a range from the upper 70s to low 80s F (25° to 28.3°C); many hobbyists keep corn snakes at warmer room temperatures with a hot spot of about 90°F (32.2°C) at one end of the enclosure. Nightly dips into the mid- to upper 60s F (17.8° to 20.6°C) are recommended. Wild corn snakes are primarily nocturnal, but basking lamps (which may or may not be utilized by your snake) will accommodate viewing and add additional warmth. Make sure that your snake has one or more cooler retreats, however, into which it can escape such heat. Maintain relative humidity of about 60 percent. Keep a large water dish at your corn snake's disposal.

While the Great Plains rat snake is not as colorful as most corn snakes, it makes an equally good pet.

Red and Rosy Rat Snakes

Corn snakes are sometimes called red rat snakes. The rosy rat snake was once considered a subspecies of the corn snake (*P. g. rosacea*), but it is now considered a local color variety. It lives in the Florida Keys. Rosy rat snakes have less black pigments in their pattern, resulting in brighter reds and oranges than normally seen in other corns.

Lighting: No specialized UV is necessary, although daily exposure to a full-spectrum UV bulb may enhance the coloration of this species.

Reproduction: Breeding occurs in early spring, with females depositing up to 36 eggs two months after copulation. Young emerge in 60 to 90 days, depending somewhat on incubation temperature. It is well known among snake-keeping enthusiasts that the corn snake is, by far, the easiest species to breed, incubate, and hatch in captivity. Anyone wishing to step up to the challenge of breeding snakes should begin with the corn snake.

Pet Suitability: 1

The corn snake has long been a favorite among snake keepers. Thus, I rank this animal a perfect 1 and grant it the distinction of being the Absolute Best Pet Snake in the World. With a benign disposition, strikingly lovely coloration, hardy constitution, and long life, this snake is a best bet for any beginning hobbyist. Corn snakes also breed so readily in captivity that I'd recommend anyone to begin his breeding project with this species.

MANDARIN RAT SNAKE
ELAPHE MANDARINA (CANTOR, 1842)

Range: Southern China, Vietnam, Burma, and surrounding montane areas.

Size: Although they are known to exceed 5 feet (1.5 m), few adult specimens ever grow over 3.5 feet (1.1 m) long.

Subspecies and Similar Species: None described, although some subspecies are theorized to exist.

Description: In their *Rat Snakes: A Hobbyist's Guide to Elaphe and Kin*, Stazko and Walls say of the Mandarin rat snake: "This snake is one of the most spectacular additions to the hobby in recent decades." Anyone who has seen the Mandarin rat snake cannot help but agree; this is simply an amazingly attractive animal. Wearing a base color of slate gray to bluish gray, the Mandarin's dorsal surface is marked with two-toned diamond-shaped saddles with lemon-yellow centers and black outer edges. Each saddle is also thinly outlined in yellow. Reddish to maroon flecks adorn the center of many dorsolateral scales, and the head is banded in alternating black and yellow chevrons. The overall effect of these colors and patterns is nothing short of

Unfortunately, the Mandarin rat snake is one of the most beautiful of the rat snakes and one of the most difficult to keep and breed.

breathtaking. The body is lithe and muscular, belying this species' propensity for climbing through the treetops.

Captive Diet: Pre-killed mice. Wild specimens thrive on birds, bird eggs, and small rodents.

Longevity: May exceed 20 years. This species has been available in the herp hobby for only a couple of decades, so much information is still being gathered about its longevity, habits, etc.

Habitat and Terrarium: Hailing from the high-altitude forests of southern China, this is a montane species that thrives under conditions of relatively low humidity, cool temperatures, and lots of hides (one humidified hide box is recommended), climbing branches, and vegetative cover. A naturally arboreal species, the Mandarin rat snake thrives in vertically oriented enclosures. Numerous intersecting climbing branches should provide both nooks and niches for it to rest or lurk arboreally. Lofty vegetative clumps (either living bromeliads or artificial foliage) can be glued or wired into place to provide a forest-canopy effect. Keep a large water dish at your snake's disposal at all times. Establish its habitat away from areas of human traffic or loud human activity because this snake tends to be high strung.

Temperatures and Humidity: Mandarin rat snakes like things cool; daily highs should not rise above the mid 70s F (23.3° to 24.4°C) with a basking spot at one end of the terrarium reaching the upper 70s F (25° to 26.1°C). Levels of relative humidity should be low. Occasional light mistings of the terrarium with lukewarm water may be conducted early in the morning, although this species does better with an overall dry terrarium habitat. Superior air circulation is also paramount to the long-term survival of this species.

Lighting: No specialized lighting is necessary, although full-spectrum bulbs will bring out the true beauty of your snake.

Reproduction: Mates in spring, young emerge after 80 days of incubation. Young may be difficult to feed for the first time.

Pet Suitability: 3

The Mandarin rat snake is a slightly nervous and flighty captive and is not a beginner's pet by any stretch of the imagination. An expensive and somewhat delicate animal, this snake is best left to advanced hobbyists. Anyone wishing to purchase a Mandarin rat snake is advised to pay the extra money upfront and purchase from an established breeder of these snakes; the breeder's insight and experience can go a long way in helping you have a successful and enjoyable relationship with your Mandarin rat snake. Although they are available, imported Mandarin rat snakes are often laden with internal parasites and may refuse food in the captive environment.

RED BAMBOO RAT SNAKE
ELAPHE PORPHYRACEA (CANTOR, 1839)

Range: Extensive throughout southeastern Asia, including parts of Indonesia.

Size: 3 to 4 feet (0.9 to 1.2 m) long at adulthood.

Subspecies and Similar Species: Several subspecies exist, and several are known in the herp hobby: *E. p. pulchra, E. p. coxi, E. p. laticinctus, E. p. vaillanti. E. p. coxi* is especially coveted because it is orangey-red with two glossy black stripes—a truly stunning rat snake. The others are beautiful as well.

Other species of Asian rat snakes (or trinket snakes) may be kept in accordance with the parameters set down for the red bamboo rat snake. Such animals include the green trinket snake (*Elaphe prasina*) and the red-headed rat snake (*E. moellendorffi*). As of the time of this writing, none of these snakes is common but their following is growing.

Description: Known in some locations as the black-banded trinket snake, the red mountain racer, and red bamboo racer, the red bamboo rat snake wears a

The red bamboo rat snake is a rare and expensive snake in American collections. The striped subspecies, *E. p. coxi* (left), is especially prized. The subspecies of the animal on the right is not known but possibly is *E. p. nigrofasciata*.

base coloration of rust to cherry red with darker red to brownish bands, edged in black and spaced at wide, regular intervals, down the length of the body. Three dark lines exist atop the head. This snake is unmarked otherwise. The lower jaw and belly are cream colored. Intensity of the colors varies by subspecies. *E. p. vaillanti* is brownish, while *E. p. laticinctus* is especially orange. As mentioned earlier, *E. p. coxi* is a striped variety. A diurnal hunter of rodents and small reptiles, the smooth-scaled red bamboo rat snake is equally at home in low bushes and foliage as it is on the ground.

Captive Diet: Small rodents. May take nontoxic frogs and lizards as well.

Longevity: May exceed 10 to 15 years.

Habitat and Terrarium: A montane species, the red bamboo rat snake prefers a cooler environment than do its North American counterparts. Width, length, and height are equally critical dimensions in housing this snake because it needs both room to slither and plenty of climbs. Naturalistic environs meet with higher levels of success than do spartan enclosures. Substrate of commercially manufactured "jungle-mix" works well. Large stones are recommended in the terrarium, as are copious clusters of living or artificial vegetation and numerous climbing branches. Light terrarium mistings in the early morning or late evening are recommended.

Temperatures and Humidity: Native to montane forests, these snakes thrive under cool, humid conditions. Maintain daily high temperatures in the low 70s

Breeders produce a small number of red-headed rat snakes every year, and they remain expensive. Their care is similar to the Mandarin and twin-spotted rat snakes.

F (21.1° to 22.8°C) up to 83°F (28.3°C) at the warmest spot in the cage. Keep relative humidity at 70 percent or so. Air circulation is paramount. A humidified hide box is recommended.

Lighting: No specialized UV lighting is necessary, although full-spectrum exposure is recommended.

Reproduction: Egg layers. Captive reproduction is little known, but increasingly, commercial breeders are producing this species for the high-end herp market.

Pet Suitability: 3

Of all of the montane species to appear in the pet trade, the red bamboo rat snake is perhaps the easiest to maintain.

STRIPE-TAILED RAT SNAKE/BEAUTY SNAKE
ELAPHE TAENIURA COPE, 1860

Range: Extensive throughout southeastern Asia: Borneo, Sumatra, Vietnam, Burma, the Philippines, and surrounding areas.

Size: Specimens exceeding 5 feet (1.5 m) are not uncommon, and some will grow to about 7 feet (2.1 m).

Subspecies and Similar Species: Numerous subspecies are poorly defined. Current subspeciation includes *E. t. taeniura, E. t. mocquardi, E. t. friesei, E. t. grabowskyi, E. t. ridleyi,* and *E. t. schmakeri*. The most commonly available subspecies in the American pet trade are *E. t. taeniura,* the Chinese beauty snake; *E. t. friesei,* the Taiwan beauty snake; *E. t. ridleyi,* the cave-dwelling rat snake or cave-dwelling beauty snake; and *E. t. mocquardi* (often seen under the old name *E. t. vaillanti*). Another species altogether, the radiated rat snake (*E. radiata*) may

Stripe-tailed rat snakes vary considerably in temperament. Some are quite docile and others are just the opposite.

Bogertophis and *Senticolis*: the Other Rat Snakes

Although many rat snakes make excellent pets for even beginning hobbyists, they have a few cousins that I have not discussed here. Members of the genera *Senticolis* and *Bogertophis*, the green and Trans-Pecos rat snakes respectively, tend to be expensive and fragile in captivity. These desert-dwelling reptiles are gorgeous and mild mannered, but they often fare poorly in captivity. These are animals that need specific and exacting humidity, lighting, and heating if they are to survive in captivity. Even when all of these minutiae are met, there is still no guarantee that these snakes will *thrive* in captivity. Many advanced hobbyists report encountering serious husbandry problems in nondesert states.

Nature sometimes makes her animals better suited to life in the wild than to life in captivity. The rat snakes of the *Senticolis* and *Bogertophis* genera are such animals. Enjoying pictures, films, etc., of these snakes is simply the closest that general hobbyists will ever come to such snakes. Doing otherwise is cruel and unfeeling for the snakes and financially and emotionally short sighted for the hobbyist.

be kept under identical conditions to the stripe-tailed rat snake.

Description: Hailing from the "trinket snake" group of Asian rat snakes (and sometimes called the striped trinket snake), the stripe-tailed rat snake is a gorgeous and still poorly understood animal. Dorsal patterning varies widely among subspecies; base color can be tan to coppery or yellow to white to greenish blue or even a ghostly translucent white in some *E. t. ridleyi*. Lateral surfaces may be vastly different in color from the mid-dorsal color. Longitudinal striping occurs on the neck and forequarters of some specimens, yet these stripes may break into individual "H"-shaped saddles in other specimens. White or gray interstitial markings are pronounced. The ventral surfaces are uniformly cream colored. The head is unmarked except for a singular dark stripe coming from the back of the eyes and down the neck—usually present even in the very pale snakes. Taking its name from the lower half of its body, this snake's aft quarters and tail are heavily striped in a mixture of basal coloration and black, gunmetal, or dark brown. In the wild, these snakes sometimes thrive deep in caves, which is unusual for any type of snake. They are widely harvested throughout their range for food, medicinal, and leather markets.

Captive Diet: Pre-killed mice, rats (for large adults), and chicks. Some young specimens also take lizards or nontoxic frogs.

Longevity: Exceeds 15 years.

Habitat and Terrarium: The stripe-tailed rat snakes—of all subspecies—do best when housed in very large terrariums. These snakes need room to slither, climb, and move about. They are powerfully arboreal. Adults are largely diurnal, while younger specimens are devoutly nocturnal. Provide a tall but wide and long habitat. These snakes do best when housed under naturalistic (jungle- or forest-type) conditions. Plenty of sturdy climbing branches, cover, and hides are mandatory. A large pool of clean water is also recommended.

Temperatures and Humidity: Hailing from diverse habitats in southern and eastern Asia, these snakes like it warm: daily highs in the low 80s F (26.7° to 28.3°C) with a hot spot of near 90°F (32.2°C) and nightly drops to 70° to 75°F (21.1° to 24°C) are recommended. Adults may bask. Undertank heating pads may be useful in areas where substrate is very thin (beneath a hide, for example), while in-tank heating apparatuses are also recommended. Maintain high levels of relative humidity, but do not deny your snake good air circulation or a dry area within its environment.

Lighting: Some hobbyists, myself included, recommend full-spectrum lighting. Others report that no specialized lighting is necessary. I suggest using a full-spectrum bulb for not less than three hours daily.

The care of the radiated rat snake is the same as that of the stripe-tailed rat snake. However, radiated rat snakes are often very aggressive animals.

Reproduction: Mating occurs in early spring with 10 to 18 eggs being deposited in leaf litter or other rotting vegetation. Young emerge in 70 to 90 days. Young feed well on pinkie mice.

Pet Suitability: 3

Imported adult specimens tend to be particularly aggressive but tame with patience and gentle handling. Newly imported specimens must be treated for internal parasites. Captive-bred juveniles take to life in the home terrarium much better. Rat snake aficionados should have no problems with the stripe-tailed rat snake, while newcomers to the hobby should look for a more congenial and possibly smaller species. Pet suitability for the closely related radiated rat snake (*E. radiata*) is, for all intents and purposes, exactly as described for the stripe-tailed rat snake, although it has a worse reputation for aggression.

TWIN-SPOTTED RAT SNAKE
ELAPHE BIMACULATA (SCHMIDT, 1925)

Range: Southeastern China.

Size: Small; seldom attains 3.5 feet (1.1 m).

Subspecies and Similar Species: None.

Description: A quietly attractive little rat snake, the twin-spot is highly variable in appearance. The dullest specimens are gray to brownish with a dual row of poorly defined reddish spots going down either side of the midline of the back. More vibrantly colored specimens, however, wear a base of lemon yellow and display maroon to rust-colored spots and triangular markings and longitudinal lines on the head and nape of the neck. Such vibrantly colored specimens have recently been the subject of captive breeding projects.

Captive Diet: Pre-killed rodents. This species tends to prefer small meals.

Longevity: May exceed 15 years.

Habitat and Terrarium: As described for the Mandarin rat snake.

Temperatures and Humidity: Like many Asian rat snakes, the twin-spotted rat snake likes cooler temperatures. The cool end of its tank should be around 68° to 70°F (20° to 21.1°C) with a basking spot to the mid-70s F (23.3° to 25°C). Dry conditions should prevail, although a permanent source of water should be at this species' disposal at all times.

Lighting: No specialized lighting is necessary.

Reproduction: Aside from the corn snake, the twin-spotted rat snake is one of the easiest snakes to breed in captivity. After emerging from a brief brumation period, this snake will copulate. Females will deposit a small clutch of oblong eggs within a couple of months. The incubation period is very short; eggs may hatch in less than a month's time. Young readily accept pre-killed pinkie mice. Young reach sexual maturity around two years.

Pet Suitability: 1

Twin-spotted rat snakes are hardy in the terrarium but not very common.

Usually quite docile, hardy, and long lived, the twin-spotted rat snake makes an excellent captive and a great starter snake for either young enthusiasts or newcomers to the herpetological hobby. Inexpensive, these snakes can be a great introductory animal to the world of the rat snakes.

The Kingsnakes and Milk Snakes

In the spring of my 12th year, I and my neighbor, who was a year older than I was, went for a walk down our road. On the first hill down from my house, I spotted a long black and yellow ribbon slowly gliding across the road. My heart leapt into my throat, and I raced down the hill and grasped my first real pet snake: a 5-foot-long (1.5-m) eastern chain kingsnake (*Lampropeltis getula getula*). At my approach, the snake barely moved, and even when I picked him up, old Kingy (as I affectionately named him) neither musked nor offered to bite. It was love at first sight.

Docile, hardy, and infinitely beautiful, the kingsnakes and their close cousins, the milk snakes, are a group unique to the New World. The kingsnakes are indigenous to North America only, and the milk snakes thrive in North,

Many of the milk snakes and kingsnakes are banded in a combination of red, yellow, and black, mimicking the venomous coral snakes. This is a Pueblan milk snake.

Central, and parts of South America. Forming a diverse group, the king and milk snakes thrive in virtually every habitat and biome within their range, from the dark, rocky shores of Rhode Island to the sand and palmetto thickets of central Florida and from the alkali flats of southern California to the steamy jungles of Honduras. These snakes are equipped for survival.

Kingsnakes are notorious cannibals; a larger one will always fight with, kill, and devour even its own siblings or offspring. Kingsnakes (especially *L. getula*) are also known for their partial immunity to venom. Species from the family Crotalidae (the rattlesnakes) and members of the genus *Agkistrodon* (the copperheads and cottonmouths) have little to no chance of killing a kingsnake through envenomation. Because the kingsnakes have evolved to prey on these snakes, they have developed this immunity. Other than venomous snakes, kingsnakes and milk snakes feed on almost any type of vertebrate within their natural range, save fish. Most species feed primarily on lizards, snakes, and small mammals, but they will take birds and frogs on occasion.

And talk about gorgeous! When it comes to beauty, the kingsnakes and milk snakes have it all: crimson reds, lush oranges, banana yellows, midnight blacks, slate grays, and all mixtures of these colors. They wear bars, chains, speckles, flecks, diamonds, saddles, and all manner of other cryptic markings. These snakes are very handle friendly (more so than most rat snakes), and most eat well in captivity. They are disease resistant and grow to impressive but manageable proportions. A kingsnake is a best bet for the hobbyist who truly wants a pet snake—that is, a snake that you can interact with, one that you can safely use to teach your children or your students the intrigue that these legless wonders represent. I don't believe that you can ever get more "bang for your buck" out of a snake in the pet market than you can with a kingsnake or a milk snake.

Lastly, *Lampropeltis* are long-lived snakes; with a life expectancy exceeding 25 years, the eastern chain kingsnake is easily one of the most long-lived colubrid snakes in the world.

New View of the Common Kingsnake

As this book was going to press, a complete analysis of the common kingsnake (*L. getula* ssp.) was published that concludes that this species should be divided into five species: *L. getula*, *L. californiae*, *L. holbrooki*, *L. nigra*, and *L. splendida*. No subspecies are recognized. It remains to be seen if this conclusion will stand, but hobbyists should at least recognize the likelihood that that the common kingsnake is more than one species. For complete details see the paper by Pyron and Burbrink in the References section.

CALIFORNIA KINGSNAKE
LAMPROPELTIS GETULA CALIFORNIAE
(BLAINVILLE, 1835)

Range: This kingsnakes range extensively throughout the American West, from Oregon south to Baja, east to Utah and Arizona.

Size: To 5 feet (1.5 m), although 3 feet (91.4 cm) is more common.

Subspecies and Similar Species: The desert or Sonoran kingsnake (*L. g. splendida*) of central Texas, Arizona, and northern Mexico is a handsome snake that makes an excellent pet. It has evenly speckled sides and a black back with occasional thin yellow bands crossing it. The Mexican black kingsnake (*L. g. nigrita*) occurs in extreme southern Arizona and adjacent and coastal Mexico (not including the Baja Peninsula). Although it may start life with some white or yellow speckles, most adults are solid glossy black snakes—unless they have been intergrading with other kingsnake subspecies.

The California kingsnake is the most popular kingsnake in the hobby. It is a very variable snake. Brown and yellow individuals are called "coastal phase."

Description: Highly variable in its patterning, the California kingsnake may appear in banded, ringed, striped, dashed (or broken-striped), or blotched form. Intergrading with subspecies is common where ranges overlap or as selective breeders supplying the pet trade desire. Colors range from chocolate brown to black mingled with yellow-sandy to ivory or alabaster white. Wild albino or amelanistic specimens exist in some locales and are now bred in large numbers. A diurnal animal during the cooler months of the year, the California kingsnake becomes almost entirely nocturnal during the heat of summer, when it may be seen easing across blacktop highways in the hours after sunset.

A wide range of color morphs exists in the California kingsnake and to a lesser extent in the desert king. These include the albino, striped, and high-yellow morphs. This species is also prone to extreme color and pattern variation: striped phases, banded phases, semi-speckled phases, and all-black phases (the so-called *L. g. "conjuncta"* form) exist at certain localities within the California kingsnake's range. Some of the unique phases command considerably more money than do some of the more common or less striking specimens.

Captive Diet: Wild specimens take all manner of rodent and reptile life, although a captive can be successfully maintained on a diet of pre-killed mice, chicks, and the occasional feeder lizard.

Longevity: 15 years or more is not unheard of.

Habitat and Terrarium: The California kingsnake occurs in many habitats within its range, but it can be safely treated as a desert animal as long as it is not kept overly hot or overly dry. Sandy substrate and sturdy, well-anchored rocks will make for a happy California kingsnake. Of course, this snake also fares well in spartan or minimalist enclosures and thrives on newsprint or recycled newspaper bedding. Snug-fitting hides are paramount. Climbing branches are sometimes enjoyed, as the California kingsnake is one of the more arboreal members of the family and will climb on occasion. Juveniles seem especially prone to short excursions off the ground.

Temperatures and Humidity: Low to moderate relative humidity. Maintain temperatures in the low 80s F (26.7° to 28.3°C) with cooler retreats and a hot spot reaching 88° to 90°F (31.1° to 32.2°C). Heating apparatuses (such as logs or heated caves) may be enjoyed by your snake. In locations were your substrate is thin, an undertank heating pad may be employed for further warmth. Nighttime temperatures can safely drop to the low 70s F (21.1° to 22.8°C).

Lighting: Even though it is secretive, this snake seems to benefit from exposure to full-spectrum lighting. Night-cycle bulbs can be a great source of heat at nighttime and will not interfere with the snake's nocturnal movements or habits. It basks intermittently.

Reproduction: Eggs are deposited in late spring in abandoned mammal burrows. Young emerge in three months or less depending on incubation

Black and white California kingsnakes (left) are called "desert phase." These may be striped or banded. Albino California kingsnakes (right) are just one of the many morphs found in this subspecies.

High-yellow California kingsnakes are usually called banana kings by hobbyists.

temperature. Most kingsnakes seen in local pet shops are some morph of captive-bred California kingsnake. Hatchlings typically fare well and make a great starter snake. This snake may hybridize with other subspecies where their ranges overlap.

Pet Suitability: 1

The California kingsnake has long been recognized as a great starter snake, although it is not always as gentle as some other members of the *Lampropeltis* genus. With gentle handling, however, this species quickly becomes more or less tame.

CALIFORNIA MOUNTAIN KINGSNAKE
LAMPROPELTIS ZONATA (LOCKINGTON, 1876)

Range: Broken distribution throughout California, Baja, and Oregon. Isolated population exists in extreme southern Washington.

Size: Small; adults of any subspecies seldom exceed 3 to 3.5 feet (0.9 to 1.1 m).

Subspecies and Similar Species: Several subspecies exist, not all of which popularly occur in the pet trade. Many private breeders specialize in the mountain kingsnakes, and they offer their hatchlings for sale annually. These varieties include the San Pedro (*L. z. agalma*), the Sierra Nevada (*L. z.*

multicincta), the San Diego (*L. z. pulchra*), and the stunningly beautiful St. Helena (*L. z. zonata*), which is both rare and expensive in the pet trade.

The similarly patterned Sonoran mountain kingsnake (*Lampropeltis pyromelana* ssp.) is another gorgeous example of these so-called tricolor kingsnakes. The Sonoran can be kept just like the California mountain kingsnake and tends to be more available and less expensive.

Description: Appearance is similar to that of the western and desert-dwelling milk snakes: alternating bands of black and white or black and yellow ring the body. Black bands are often imperfectly split by splashes or wedges of red. The mountain kingsnakes have many more bands on their bodies than do the milk snakes. As is true of the milk snakes and the gray-banded kingsnakes, no two sibling mountain kingsnakes may look alike; phenotypic variation can be profound between sibling snakes.

It is hard to imagine a snake species more retiring and shy than the milk snakes, but the mountain kingsnakes can be. Not always handle friendly at first, these snakes (especially wild-caught individuals) may thrash, twist, and wriggle to escape your grasp; projectile defecation and musking are also common defense mechanisms. Gentle handling will quickly settle their nerves in most

The California mountain kingsnakes remain rare in the hobby, although they are being captive bred. This is a Sierra Nevada mountain kingsnake in its habitat.

Smart Snakes

Some studies have shown that the mountain kingsnakes are inordinately intelligent snakes, capable of figuring out simple latches and countersinking lids. Locking lids are recommended to ensure that these consummate escape artists do not pull a vanishing act!

cases, however. Captive-bred animals seldom resist human touch.

Captive Diet: Pre-killed rodents of appropriate size and feeder lizards may compose the dietary staples, while quail eggs may also be taken as a treat. Wild specimens actively seek out ground-nesting birds.

Longevity: 15 years or more.

Habitat and Terrarium: Arid. Habitat and housing conditions are as described for the milk snakes.

Temperatures and Humidity: Dry uplands and rocks coupled with humid hideaways work well. Many hobbyists weekly plunge a long-necked funnel into the sandy substrate at one corner of the terrarium, pour 1/2 cup of water into the funnel, and allow it to slowly seep into the deepest layers of the substrate. This allows moisture to rise from the depths of the substrate (as it would in nature) while keeping the air and rockwork at the top of the terrarium arid. The mountain kingsnakes—both California and Sonoran—like cooler conditions than do most other kingsnakes. The temperature range should be in the low 70s F (21.1° to 22.8°C) with a hot spot that gets about 85°F (29.4°C). Nighttime temperatures can safely drop to 65°F (18.3°C).

Lighting: No specialized lighting necessary. Some hobbyists do, however, employ full-spectrum lighting as well as night-cycle lighting to observe the movements of their mountain kingsnakes.

Reproduction: Egg layers. Newly hatched young may feed exclusively on small lizards. Feeder geckos or anoles may be required. Clutch sizes are typically small, ranging from a half-dozen to a dozen. Depending on the subspecies in question, the emerging neonates can also be somewhat diminutive at hatching. Gestation is roughly two months from conception to deposition, while incubation may exceed three months.

Pet Suitability: 3

The mountain kingsnakes are delicate enough that I would not recommend that they be purchased as a first snake, but they are hardy enough that the dedicated colubrids enthusiast could enjoy the challenges and aesthetic rewards they present. As is true of the milk snakes, the wide variety of mountain kingsnakes necessitates that the keeper interested in trying his hand at these gorgeous little serpents learns all that he can about the exact subspecies he will be acquiring. This is because a specimen from southern California, for example,

The Sonoran mountain kingsnake occurs in several subspecies. This is the most common in the hobby, the Arizona mountain kingsnake (*L. p. pyromelana*).

will require slightly different husbandry parameters than will a subspecies native to north-central Oregon. Likewise, juvenile mountain kingsnakes can be *very* picky in their diet. Always buy a specimen that you know is eating, and if possible, has been weaned onto pinkie mice since hatching.

EASTERN CHAIN KINGSNAKE
LAMPROPELTIS GETULA GETULA (LINNAEUS, 1766)

Range: Extensive throughout eastern seaboard of the US.

Size: Most experts agree that 6 feet (1.8 m) is the adult maximum, although I have owned two specimens that measured 7 feet 9 inches (2.4 m) and 8 feet 2 inches (2.5 m) long, respectively.

Subspecies and Similar Species: The black kingsnake (*L. g. niger*) of northern

257

Alabama to Illinois and West Virginia is a solid black snake that may or may not bear faint speckling along its lower lateral surfaces. The speckled kingsnake (*L. g. holbrooki*) is a handsome subspecies found in Iowa to Louisiana and eastern Texas. And the Outer Banks kingsnake (*L. g. sticticeps*, which some authorities do not consider a valid subspecies) is a uniquely chained-and-speckled animal found off the islands and banks near Cape Hatteras.

Description: The largest of all of the kingsnakes, this animal wears a base coloration of raven black to chocolate brown and is adorned with yellowish to ivory or white rings or intersecting arcs forming a more or less chain-link pattern dorsally. Lateral surfaces have alternating black and white blocks, and the belly is checkered in the same color scheme. All black specimens are known, and intergrading with other subspecies (where their ranges overlap) is also known to occur. Females tend to have thinner rings dorsally and more black ventrally, while males have thicker rings or chains dorsally and a greater amount of white or yellow ventrally.

Captive Diet: In the wild, these snakes will consume virtually any living thing that they can subdue, kill, and swallow. Captive diet should include pre-killed

Eastern kingsnake consuming a venomous water moccasin. Kingsnakes are partially immune to the venom of the snakes upon which they prey.

mice, chicks, and feeder lizards.

Longevity: 20 years is not uncommon, and 25 years is possible.

Habitat and Terrarium: Kingsnakes are almost fully terrestrial animals with a penchant for seeking out the burrows of other animals. Employ long, wide tanks with plenty of ground cover and hides. Substrate is of little importance as long as it is loose enough for the snake to easily slide under. I have found that in the naturalistic terrarium, a base of mulch topped by leaf litter works well. Some hobbyists use pine straw, but I find that this dries the kingsnake's scales out too much. Leave a large bowl of clean water at your snake's disposal at all times.

One per Cage

Most the king and milk snakes will eat other snakes, including members of their own species. Never house any of the *Lampropeltis* together, except for breeding attempts.

Temperatures and Humidity: Upper 70s to low 80s F (25° to 28.3°C) is best; as with the corn snake, many hobbyists keep *L. getula* at room temperature with a hot spot of 88° to 90°F (31.1° to 32.2°C). Keep relative humidity moderate because these snakes hail from temperate forests. A moist underground retreat is also highly recommended, as kingsnakes seem to dehydrate more easily than some other colubrid species. Beware of blister disease and nose rubbing, however.

Lighting: No specialized lighting necessary.

Reproduction: Mating occurs in early spring, shortly after emerging from brumation. Females will deposit up to two dozen oblong eggs in rotting forest mulch or in leaf litter. Young, which are 7 to 9 inches (17.8 to 22.9 cm) long, hatch in roughly two months. Eastern kingsnakes will cannibalize one another when they meet in the wild outside the mating season. Likewise, newly hatched young must be separated within a few days of hatching, as it will not be long before they begin consuming one another.

Pet Suitability: 1

Maybe I'm biased in the matter, but I believe that the eastern chain kingsnake ranks a perfect 1 on the pet suitability scale. Long lived, hardy, and very handle friendly, these snakes are universally adored.

FLORIDA KINGSNAKE
LAMPROPELTIS GETULA FLORIDANA BLANCHARD, 1919

Range: Central and southern Florida.

Size: To nearly 6 feet (1.8 m), although most seldom exceed 4 to 4.5 feet (1.2 to 1.4 m).

Subspecies and Similar Species: Although no longer considered a valid subspecies, the handsome Brook's kingsnake (formerly *L. g. brooksi*) is speckled and crossbanded with reddish bars. Many taxonomists consider this snake merely a color variant of the Florida kingsnake found in extreme southern Florida. Breeders still maintain the name *brooksi* on their stock to indicate lineage. Beautiful color morphs of this snake are available.

The blotched or Apalachicola kingsnake (*L g. meansi* [formerly *L. g. goini*]) of north-central Florida has long been the topic of taxonomic debate, and is a beautiful animal. The blotched kingsnake was popular in the pet trade in the mid-1990s and can still be purchased at a reasonable price.

Description: An oddly attractive species, the Florida kingsnake wears a mixture of patterns, seemingly wearing the chain-link pattern of the eastern kingsnake and the heavily speckled pattern of the speckled kingsnake. Each dorsal scale has several colors: The center of each scale bears a yellowish to whitish spot, with the outer edge ringed or tipped in black. Although this coloration may sound garish, it provides the snake with superior camouflage when lying amid the sandy and pine straw flats of central Florida. Although not as large as the eastern kingsnake, the Florida kingsnake is a sturdy, powerfully built constrictor.

Captive Diet: Pre-killed mice, chicks, and feeder lizards. Younger specimens may have to be weaned from lizards to mice.

The Florida kingsnake is the most yellow of the common kingsnake subspecies.

The blotched kingsnake is one of the most popular of the kingsnake subspecies due to its interesting color and pattern.

Longevity: 15 to 20 years.

Habitat and Terrarium: As described for the eastern chain kingsnake: sandy or loose mulch substrate with plenty of leaf litter and other ground cover. Like most other kingsnakes, this species also does well in spartan enclosures with recycled newspaper bedding. Numerous hides are a must, as is a large water dish. Because kingsnakes have a habit of tipping their water dish, I recommend using a broad-based, heavily constructed dish, such as those designed for large dogs. These are much less easily tipped and spilled by a snake that is nosing about under the substrate.

Temperatures and Humidity: Maintain daily temperatures of 78° to 83°F (25.6° to 28.3°C). Because most kingsnakes are semi-subterranean in their habits, an undertank heating pad is a good source of additional warmth. Maintain a moderately high relative humidity, but good ventilation is also paramount because members of the *Lampropeltis* genus are prone to respiratory infection and pneumonia.

Lighting: No specialized lighting is necessary.

Reproduction: Mating occurs in early spring. Up to 18 eggs deposited in abandoned mammal burrows. Young hatch in 12 weeks and feed primarily on lizards and small snakes.

Pet Suitability: 1

This snake, like most kingsnakes, is a mild-mannered, handsome animal that eats well in captivity and seldom presents the hobbyist with any serious problems. Longevity, beauty, and reasonable price make this species a desirable pet.

GRAY-BANDED KINGSNAKE
LAMPROPELTIS ALTERNA (GARMAN, 1884)

Range: Trans-Pecos, Texas south through Durango Mountains, Mexico.

Size: To 3 feet (91.4 cm).

Subspecies and Similar Species: Once considered a subspecies of the variable kingsnake (*L. mexicana*), the gray-band is now considered a full species. However, all of the kingsnakes in the *mexicana* complex—*alterna, mexicana,* "*greeri*," "*thayeri*," and possibly *ruthveni*—are closely related and not well understood. Currently, taxonomists treat *L. alterna, L. mexicana,* and *L. ruthveni* (the Queretaro or Ruthven's kingsnake) as separate species, with none having any subspecies. Hobbyists and breeders use the various subspecific names to describe the appearance and lineage of their snakes.

Description: An absolutely gorgeous snake, the gray-banded kingsnake has long been held as the Holy Grail of North American colubrids and once commanded a high price. Fortunately, through the concerted breeding efforts of private hobbyists, these snakes are now widely available and much more reasonably priced. Coloration is highly variable. The base color may be slate to silvery; particularly striking specimens may wear a base of whitish, gunmetal, or even bluish. Black-bordered dorsal saddles of reddish to orange or maroon adorn the midline of the back in some specimens, while they form rings that wrap the dorsal and lateral surfaces of others. The black rings edging these saddles, like the saddles themselves, are of alternating thicknesses. The reddish bands are absent or reduced on many specimens. It has been said that the color and pattern of each and every gray-banded kingsnake are as unique as a fingerprint, and it is no rare thing when no two siblings hatching from the same clutch look anything like one another or like either parent. The scales are smooth, and the head is triangular with the jaws slightly wider than the neck. This snake is secretive and retiring in its habits. It may refuse to feed during daylight hours.

Captive Diet: Wild gray-banded kingsnakes thrive almost exclusively on lizards, frogs, and small snakes, although captive specimens may be weaned onto rodents. Ornery feeders may, however, never take fare other than feeder lizards. Anoles and house geckos work well for this species.

Gray-banded kingsnakes are now captive bred in good numbers. Hatchlings can still be picky and insist on eating lizards.

Longevity: May exceed ten years. This snake is not known for its excessive longevity.

Habitat and Terrarium: Hailing from arid areas as well as humid montane slopes, these snakes do best when housed in a desert-type environment but with more forest-like humidity levels. Extensive rock work (Mexican lava rock is favored by these snakes and works well as a hide) and numerous hideaways are a must, as is superior air circulation. Sandy or stony substrate works well. It is important to note that gray-bands do not thrive in spartan enclosures as well as other kingsnakes do. I personally recommend establishing a naturalistic habitat for this species instead of a minimalist enclosure.

Temperatures and Humidity: These snakes like moderate temperatures: Something in the range of 75° to 82°F (24 to 27.8°C) is best, with an undertank heating pad to supply additional heat. Nightly drops to as low as 65°F (18.3°C) are fine because this species' natural habitat is subject to pronounced temperature drops at night. Maintain moderate relative humidity; 50 to 60 percent is good, although depending on the climate in which you live, modifications or adjustments may be necessary. The gray-banded kingsnake, unlike many desert snakes, is tolerant of a wide range of relative humidity.

The variable kingsnake is closely related to the gray-banded kingsnake and requires the same care.

Lighting: Almost fully nocturnal. No specialized lighting is necessary. Some experts have reported success with partial exposure to full-spectrum bulbs, however, and some specimens will bask in the early morning.

Reproduction: Eggs deposited in early summer, with 9- to 10-inch-long (22.9- to 25.4-cm) hatchlings emerging in just over two months' time. Clutches range in size from three to four eggs to more than a dozen. Hatchlings may refuse to eat anything except lizards for some time.

Pet Suitability: 3

Infinitely beautiful yet sometimes fragile of constitution and sometimes picky at the dinner table, these snakes can present numerous challenges in the home terrarium. Anyone skilled with both desert snakes and the milk snakes, however, should have no problems with this coveted species. I do not recommend this snake as a beginner's choice or a starter snake.

MILK SNAKE
LAMPROPELTIS TRIANGULUM
(LACÈPÉDE, 1788)

Range: Extensive; one of the most widely distributed snake species on the planet. The range is discontinuous but extends from Quebec, Canada, south to Venezuela, and covers more than 3,500 miles (5,632 km) of latitudinal terrain.

Size: Most subspecies are 3 to 4 feet (0.9 to 1.2 m) long at best; a few do reach 5 feet (1.5 m). The black milk snake (*L. t. gaigeae*) is the largest subspecies and may reach 7 feet (2.1 m).

Subspecies and Similar Species: Numerous. There are 25 subspecies known, with others suspected. Many of these occur in the pet trade frequently, and many others can be ordered from specialty breeders, retailers, and importers. Some of the most popular are the Honduran milk snake (*L. t. hondurensis*), the Sinaloan milk snake (*L. t. sinaloae*), the Mexican milk snake (*L. t. annulata*), the Nelson's milk snake (*L. t. nelsoni*), the Pueblan milk snake (*L. t. campbelli*) and the red milk snake (*L. t. syspila*), just to name a few. One subspecies is called the scarlet kingsnake (*L. t. elapsoides*), even though it is technically a milk snake. For more information on the many subspecies and varieties of milk snake, I highly recommend reading Ronald Markel's *Kingsnakes and Milksnakes*.

Description: One of the most varied and diverse species of snakes in existence, the milk snake ranges in color from a tan to gray base with brownish to maroon saddles, to a crimson base with orange bands

The Two Gray-Bands

In the past, taxonomists recognized two subspecies in gray-banded kingsnakes, *L. alterna alterna* and *L. a. blairi*, usually called Blair's kingsnake. Now we know that these are just two pattern variations within one species, and many gray-bands are intermediate between the two forms. Hobbyists sometimes use the older names for descriptive purposes. The "alterna"-phase snakes have a greater number of saddle markings, but the saddles mostly lack the red coloration. "Blair's"-phase have fewer saddles, and these saddles are red to orange. Breeders tend to produce more "Blair's" phase because they tend to be prettier and more popular with hobbyists.

edged in black, to red, yellow, and black rings speckled in black flecks. As its common name suggests, the black milk snake turns solid black as it grows. Most, however, are a variant of the tricolor combination. A natural mimicry of the deadly coral snakes (family Elapidae), the milk snakes wear some color variant of a red base with whitish to yellow and black rings. As a result, would-be predators see the harmless milk snake's garish colors and read them as a warning to stay away. Small in stature and extremely secretive, the milk snakes are demure burrowers that spend the lion's share of their time underground or in piles of forest debris searching for rodent or reptilian prey. When encountered in the wild, these snakes attempt to escape and may even lunge, but they seldom actually bite.

The milk snake occurs in 25 known subspecies that vary considerably in color and pattern. Four are shown here to represent the range of that variability: (clockwise from top left) eastern milk snake, pale milk snake, Honduran milk snake, and Sinaloan milk snake.

Albinism occurs in several of the milk snake subspecies. One of the most commonly available albino milk snakes is the albino Nelson's milk snake.

Captive Diet: Varies between subspecies, but all may be reared on either pre-killed rodents, chicks, or lizards. Some varieties are more picky than others, and I highly recommend making sure that you can get a continual (or frozen) supply of feeder lizards before you purchase a milk snake unless you are certain it is feeding on rodents. The scarlet kingsnake is notorious for refusing all food except lizards.

Longevity: Varies. Most can be expected to exceed 10 to 15 years in captivity. The record life span is 18 years.

Habitat and Terrarium: Will vary based on the exact subspecies you are housing. Most can be kept in a similar fashion to California kingsnakes. House temperate species atop a mixture of leaf litter and mulch. Supply large, flat stones, hollow logs, and low, sturdy climbing branches. Desert-dwelling species should be housed on sand and stone substrates with rocky outcroppings and hides. The substrate should be loose enough to accommodate burrowing for all subspecies. Mexican bowl rock (aka Mexican lava rock) is an excellent addition to the desert milk snake terrarium. Tank dimensions in both cases should stress length and breadth over height.

Temperatures and Humidity: Will vary based on the exact subspecies. Moderate to high levels of humidity are appropriate for New England and other northern or coastal North American subspecies or South American jungle subspecies, while desert subspecies should have accordingly lower humidity levels. Likewise,

The Mexican milksnake ranges into central Texas, and captive-bred individuals are available regularly.

temperatures will vary accordingly. A good general temperature gradient will range from 75° to 85°F (24° to 29.4°C) at the hottest spot with a humidity level of 50 to 65 percent.

Lighting: Owing to the nocturnal and secretive nature of the milk snakes, specialized lighting is not necessary.

Reproduction: Egg layers. Milk snakes have moderately sized broods. Young hatch in 11 to 12 weeks and may take tiny lizards as their first meal. Young may have to be weaned onto rodents. If purchasing a newly hatched milk snake, make sure that it is taking rodent prey.

Pet Suitability: 2

Pet suitability varies based on the exact subspecies in question, but as a general rule, the milk snakes are a very congenial, handleable group of snakes. Although they are not quite my top choice for a beginning serpent, the milk snakes are an excellent choice for the hobbyist who has some experience dealing with terrestrial colubrids. Again, owing to the excessively wide variety of milk snakes, I highly recommend that you educate yourself to the utmost on the exact subspecies you wish to purchase because the general guidelines provided here may need modifications for the long-term success of your endeavor.

PRAIRIE KINGSNAKE
LAMPROPELTIS CALLIGASTER CALLIGASTER
(HARLAN, 1827)

Range: Louisiana, eastern Texas, Oklahoma, north to Iowa and east to Indiana and central Kentucky.

Size: A modestly sized species, adults seldom exceed 3.5 feet (1.1 m) in length.

Subspecies and Similar Species: The mole kingsnake (*L. c. rhombomaculata*) is an eastern and Gulf Coast variant that is known locally as the brown kingsnake. Although not often encountered in the pet trade, the mole kingsnake makes an excellent, albeit reclusive, pet.

Description: Wears a base coat of tan to gray or light brown with reddish, gray, or darker brown saddles. The saddles are occasionally "H"-shaped, leading many people to confuse this snake with the Great Plains rat snake (*Pantherophis guttatus emoryi*). The scales are smooth. Nocturnal hunters, these secretive snakes spend their days beneath piles of debris, under logs, or in abandoned mammal burrows. They are also known to frequent barnyards and old farmsteads.

Although they are uncommon in the pet trade, prairie kingsnakes make good pets.

Individualism in Snakes

While it is well known that dogs, cats, and even pet birds can have widely variable dispositions, most of us don't tend to think of snakes as being individuals or possessing discernable personalities. The truth of the matter is, however, that the personalities of individual snakes of the same species can be wildly different from one another; each snake within a species has its own unique personality. I once owned two eastern kingsnakes. One was a large male, and the other was a moderately sized female. Both hatched from the same clutch of eggs, both had been raised under similar conditions, and both had been reared on the same dietary regimen. When I took the male out of his tank, he would slither about my arms and shoulders, flicker an inquisitive tongue along my skin, and after a bit, quietly coil about my arm or wrist to soak up my body heat.

If a potential snake hobbyist based his decision to keep an eastern kingsnake based solely on this animal, then my female eastern kingsnake would have come as a shock to him. When I took the female out of her tank, she would twitch and jerk nervously under my grasp, musk on me, sometimes even empty her cloacal contents on me, and on the rare occasion that I had not put her back in her tank by this point, would even bite me repeatedly! Truly, the disposition or personalities of these two snakes were as different as night and day. It is just as important, therefore, that you learn as much as you can about an individual snake before making a purchase. Just as some species are unsuited to you as a keeper, certain individuals within the same species may also be unfit to be the type of pet you desire.

Within the captive environment, these snakes enjoy piles of old boards, wooden deadfalls, slabs of bark, and other such surface litter under which they may securely hide.

Captive Diet: Wild specimens take all manner of small rodent, reptilian, and some amphibian prey. This species has been known to eat insects on occasion in nature, although there is no need to feed them in captivity. Captive diet should be varied: pre-killed mice, chicks, nontoxic frogs (leopard frogs and bullfrogs), feeder lizards, and small quail.

Longevity: May exceed 15 years. Record longevity is 18.5 years.

Habitat and Terrarium: Does well in both naturalistic environs as well as spartan enclosures. Loose substrate is a must because this species is perhaps the most avid burrower of all of the kingsnakes. A horizontally oriented enclosure is advisable. Lengths of half-buried PVC work well as hides, as do slabs of cork bark. These snakes thrive in moderately sized enclosures— anything long enough that an adult specimen can stretch completely out in is recommended.

Temperatures and Humidity: Maintain temperatures in the upper 70s to low 80s F (26.7° to 28.3°C). A light morning misting to the environment every few days is advisable, and air circulation is critical because this animal is prone to respiratory infections. Keep water at your snake's disposal at all times, but make sure that it is not soaking itself excessively. A sign that your prairie kingsnake is too hot is that it will spend copious amounts of time submerged in the water dish.

Lighting: No special lighting necessary.

Reproduction: Egg laying. Young hatch in three months and feed on small lizards, small snakes, and reptile eggs.

Pet Suitability: 1

A nice pet snake. Although it is quite shy, even for a kingsnake, this animal is quite docile and tolerant of human touch. This is a great starter snake for children or younger hobbyists. Remember that these snakes are secretive, and secure hides are absolutely paramount in the captive environment.

SPECIES REFERENCE CHART

The following chart is designed to be a quick reference guide to understanding the basic parameters of all the snake species included in this book. Use the key below to better understand the chart. While a great many subspecies are described in detail within each species entry, only the main entries are considered in this chart. Likewise, while the main entry for each species are organized by family, the snakes in this chart are, for convenience sake, arranged alphabetically by common name.

The size column gives the snake's length in feet and meters. The letters listed in the Diet column are in order of that species' preference. For example, if R is listed before B, that species will eat both rodents and birds, but primarily takes rodents. The Pet Suitability column follows the same system as that in the main text.

Key

Diet	Habitat	Accepts Handling?
A: Amphibians	D: Desert	Y: Yes
B: Birds	J: Jungle	M: Maybe/Varies
F: Fish	S: Savanna/Grassland	N: No/Seldom
I: Insects	Sw: Swamp/Wetland	
L: Lizards	W: Woodland/Forest	
R: Rodents		

Species	Size (feet/meters)	Diet	Life Span (years)	Habitat	Accepts Handling?	Pet Suitability
African Rock Python (*Python sebae*)	12-22/3.7-6.7	R	20	S	N	5
American Rat Snake (*Pantherophis obsoletus* ssp.)	5-6/1.5-1.8	R, B	15	W	M	2
Baird's Rat Snake (*Pantherophis bairdi*)	4-5/1.2-1.5	R, B, L	15	D, S	Y	1
Ball Python (*Python regius*)	3-5/0.9-1.5	R	20	S	Y	1
Blood Python (*Python brongersmai*)	4-6/1.2-1.8	R	20	J, S	M	3
Burmese Python (*Python molurus bivattatus*)	15-20/4.6-6.1	R	20	J, Sw	M	4
California Kingsnake (*Lampropeltis getula californiae*)	3-4/0.9-1.2	R, L	15	D, S	Y	1
California Mountain Kingsnake (*Lampropeltis zonata*)	3/0.9	R, L, B	15	D, S	M	3

Species	Size (feet/meters)	Diet	Life Span (years)	Habitat	Accepts Handling?	Pet Suitability
Chinese Garter Snake (*Elaphe rufodorsata*)	2-3/0.6-0/9	F, A	8-10	W, Sw	Y	3
Common Garter Snake (*Thamnophis sirtalis*)	3/0.9	F, A, I, R	10	W, Sw	M	1
Corn Snake (*Pantherophis guttatus guttatus*)	4-5/1.2-1.5	R, B	15-20	W	Y	1
Diamond Python (*Morelia spilota*)	8/2.4	R, B	15	J, S	Y	2
Dumeril's Boa (*Acrantophis dumerili*)	6-8/1.8-2.4	R, B	15-20	J, S	Y	1
Eastern Kingsnake (*Lampropeltis getula getula*)	6/1.8	R, L, B	20	W	Y	1
Emerald Tree Boa (*Corallus caninus*)	6-8/1.8-2.4	R, B	20	J	N	5
Florida Kingsnake (*Lampropeltis getula floridana*)	4-6/1.2-1.8	R, L, B	15-20	W	Y	1
Garden Boa (*Corallus hortulanus*)	6-7/1.8-2.1	R, B, L, A	15	J, W	N	4
Gray-Banded Kingsnake (*Lampropeltis alterna*)	3/0.9	L, R	10	D, S	Y	3
Kenyan Sand Boa (*Eryx colubrinus loveridgei*)	2/0.6	R, L, I	10	D	Y	1
Long-Nosed Snake (*Rhinochelius lecontei*)	2-3/0.6-0.9	L, A, R	10	D, S	Y	2
Malagasy Giant Hognose Snake (*Leioheterodon madagascariensis*)	4-6/1.2-1.8	L, A, R	10-15	J, W	Y	3
Mandarin Rat Snake (*Elaphe mandarina*)	3-4/0.9-1.2	B, R	20	W	Y	3
Milk Snake (*Lampropeltis triangulum*)	3-4/0.9-1.2	R, L, B	10-15	D, W, S, J	Y	2

Species	Size (feet/meters)	Diet	Life Span (years)	Habitat	Accepts Handling?	Pet Suitability
Pacific Island Boa (*Candoia carinata*)	3/0.9	R, A, L, B	10	J, W	M	2
Pine Snake / Bullsnake (*Pituophis* spp.)	7 -8/2.1-2.4	R, B	25	W, S, D	M	2
Prairie Kingsnake (*Lampropeltis calligaster*)	3/0.9	R, L	15	W, S	Y	1
Rainbow Boa (*Epicrates cenchria*)	5-6/1.5-1.8	R, B, L	15	J, Sw	M	4
Red-Bellied Water Snake (*Nerodia erythrogaster*)	3-5/0.9-1.5	F, A	10	Sw	N	4
Red-Tailed Boa (*Boa constrictor*)	8-10/2.4-3	R, B	20	J, S	Y	3
Reticulated Python (*Python reticulatus*)	18-22/5.5-6.7	R	20	J	N	5
Rosy Boa (*Lichanura trivirgata*)	2-3/0.6-0.9	R, L	15	D	Y	1
Rough Green Snake (*Opheodrys aestivus*)	3/0.9	I, L	10	W	Y	1
Stripe-Tailed Rat Snake (*Elaphe taeniura*)	5-6/1.5-1.8	R, B, L	15	J, W	M	3
Twin-Spotted Rat Snake (*Elaphe bimaculata*)	2-3/0.6-0.9	R	15	W	Y	1
Western Hognose Snake (*Heterodon nasicus nasicus*)	3/0.9	R, A, L	10-15	D, S	Y	1

Resources

CLUBS AND SOCIETIES

American Society of Ichthyologists and
Herpetologists (ASIH)
Grice Marine Laboratory
Florida International University
Biological Sciences
11200 SW 8th St.
Miami, FL 33199
Phone: (303) 348-1235
E-mail: asih@fiu.edu
www.asih.org

Amphibian, Reptile, and Insect Association
23 Windmill Rd.
Irthlingsborough
Wellingborough NN9 5RJ
United Kingdom

Society for the Study of Amphibians and
Reptiles (SSAR)
The Claremont Colleges
925 N. Mills Ave.
Claremont, CA 91711
Phone: (909) 607-8014
E-mail: mpreest@jsd.claremont.edu
www.ssarherps.org

RESCUE AND ADOPTION SERVICES

Petfinder.com
www.petfinder.com

Directory of Herp Rescue Agencies
www.anapsid.org/societies/

New England Amphibian and Reptile Rescue
www.reptilerescue.net/

VETERINARY RESOURCES

Association of Reptile and Amphibian
Veterinarians
810 East 10th
PO Box 1897
Lawrence, KS 66044
Phone: (800) 627-0326
Fax: (785) 843-6153
www.arav.org

WEB SITES

Center for North American Herpetology
www.naherpetology.org

HerpDigest
www.herpdigest.org

Herp Network
www.herpnetwork.com

Herpo.com
Listing of herpetological societies
www.herpo.com/societies.html

Kingsnake.com
www.kingsnake.com

Kingsnake.com (UK)
www.kingsnake.co.uk

Melissa Kaplan's Herp Care Collection
www.anapsid.org
Reptile Forums
www.reptileforums.com

The Reptile Rooms
www.reptilerooms.com

SPECIES-SPECIFIC SITES

The Boa Kingdom (Amazon tree boa site)
www.amazontreeboa.org/treeboa.html

Good Snakekeeping

Corn Snake Pictures and Facts
//fohn.net/corn-snake-pictures-facts/

Cornsnakes.com
www.cornsnakes.com/forums

Dealing With Ball Python Feeding Problems
http://www.anapsid.org/ballfeed.html

The Emerald Tree Boa Organization
www.emeraldtreeboa.org/

Garter Snake Home Page
www.gartersnake.co.uk/

Gartersnake.info
www.gartersnake.info/

The Green Tree Python Page
www.kingsnake.com/viridis/

Martin Schmidt's *Lampropeltis* page
www.pitt.edu/~mcs2/herp/Lampropeltis.html

Pituophis.org
www.pituophis.org/

The *Pituophis* Page
www.kingsnake.com/pituophis/

Pyromelana.com
www.pyromelana.com

Ratsnake Foundation
www.ratsnakefoundation.org/#

The Ratsnakes of North America
www.kingsnake.com/ratsnake/

RedTailBoaFAQ
www.redtailboafaq.com

RedTailBoas Ultimate Reptile Community
www.redtailboas.com/forum

Rosyboa.com
www.rosyboa.com/

The Sand Boa Page
www.kingsnake.com/sandboa/sandboa.html

A Troubleshooting Guide to Ball Pythons
www.kingsnake.com/ballpythonguide

References

Broadley D.G. 1999. The southern African python, *Python natalensis*. A. Smith 1840 is a valid species. *African Herp News* 29: 31-32.

Burbrink, Frank T. 2001. Systematics of the eastern ratsnake complex (*Elaphe obsoleta*). *Herpetological Monographs* 15: 1–53.

Burbrink, Frank T., Robin Lawson, and Joseph B. Slowinski. 2000. Mitochondrial DNA phylogeography of the polytypic North American rat snake (*Elaphe obsoleta*): a critique of the subspecies concept. *Evolution* 54 (6): 2107–2108.

Crother B.I., J. Boundy, J.A. Campbell, K. De Quieroz, D. Frost, D.M. Green, R. Highton, J.B. Iverson, R.W. McDiarmid, P.A. Meylan, T.W. Reeder, M.E. Seidel, J.W. Sites Jr., S.G. Tilley, and D.B. Wake. 2003. Scientific and standard English names of amphibians and reptiles of North America north of Mexico: Update. *Herpetological Review* 34: 196–203.

de Vosjoli, Philippe. 1997. *The Lizard Keeper's Handbook*. Mission Viejo, CA: Advanced Vivarium Systems Press.

Henderson, R.W. 1997. A taxonomic review of the *Corallus hortulanus* complex of neotropical tree boas. *Caribbean Journal of Science.* 33 (3-4): 198-221.

Keogh, J.S., D.G. Barker, and R Shine. 2001. Heavily exploited but poorly known: systematics and biogeography of commercially harvested pythons (*Python curtus* group) in Southeast Asia. *Biological Journal of the Linnean Society* 73:113-129.

McDiarmid, Roy W.; T'Shaka Touré, and Jay M. Savage. 1996. The proper name of the neotropical tree boa often referred to as *Corallus enydris* (Serpentes: Boidae). *Journal of Herpetology* 30 (30): pgs. 320–326.

Pauwels, O.S.G. et al. 2000. Herpetological investigations in Phang-Nga Province, southern Peninsular Thailand, with a list of reptile species and notes on their biology. *Dumerilia* 4 (2): 123-154.

Pyron, R. Alexander and Frank T. Burbrink. 2009. Systematics of the common kingsnake (*Lampropeltis getula*; Serpentes: Colubridae) and the burden of heritage in taxonomy. *Zootaxa* 2241: 22-32.

Ross, Richard A. and Gerald Marzec. 1990. *The Reproductive Husbandry of Boas and Pythons*. Stanford, CA: Institute for Herpetological Research.

Stafford P.J. and R.J. Henderson 1996. *Kaleidoscopic Tree Boas: The Genus Corallus of Tropical America*. Malabar, FL: Krieger Publishing Company.

Staszko, Ray and Jerry G. Walls. 1994. *Rat Snakes: A Hobbyist's Guide to Elaphe and Kin.* Neptune City, NJ: T.F.H. Publications, Inc.

Utiger U., N. Helfenberger, B. Schatti, C. Schmidt, M. Ruf, and V. Ziswiler. 2002. Molecular systematics and phylogeny of Old and New World ratsnakes, *Elaphe* Auct., and related genera (Reptilia, Squamata, Colubridae). *Russian Journal of Herpetology* 9(2):105–124.

Index

Index

Species Illustrated by Page

Dedication

For Sally Sauer.
For your faith in believing I *could* do it, and your generosity in ensuring that I *did*.

And for Ashley Straut.
For whom I, like mighty Odin, would gladly give my left eye.

Thanks.

About the Author

A former state ranger and interpretive herpetologist for the Georgia Department of Natural Resources, Dr. Phil Purser has been keeping, breeding, and writing about snakes for nearly 30 years. While much of his field research has centered on population biology of the North American kingsnakes, rat snakes, and rattlesnakes, he has also worked extensively with pythons and boas; particularly the rosy boas, sand boas, and other ground boas. *Good Snakekeeping* is Phil's ninth book in the field of herp husbandry.

Photo Credits